Applied C++

The C++ In-Depth Series

Bjarne Stroustrup, Editor

"I have made this letter longer than usual, because I lack the time to make it short."
—BLAISE PASCAL

The advent of the ISO/ANSI C++ standard marked the beginning of a new era for C++ programmers. The standard offers many new facilities and opportunities, but how can a real-world programmer find the time to discover the key nuggets of wisdom within this mass of information? **The C++ In-Depth Series** minimizes learning time and confusion by giving programmers concise, focused guides to specific topics.

Each book in this series presents a single topic, at a technical level appropriate to that topic. The Series' practical approach is designed to lift professionals to their next level of programming skills. Written by experts in the field, these short, in-depth monographs can be read and referenced without the distraction of unrelated material. The books are cross-referenced within the Series, and also reference *The C++ Programming Language* by Bjarne Stroustrup.

As you develop your skills in C++, it becomes increasingly important to separate essential information from hype and glitz, and to find the in-depth content you need in order to grow. The C++ In-Depth Series provides the tools, concepts, techniques, and new approaches to C++ that will give you a critical edge.

Titles in the Series

Accelerated C++: Practical Programming by Example, Andrew Koenig and Barbara E. Moo

Applied C++: Practical Techniques for Building Better Software, Philip Romanik and Amy Muntz

The Boost Graph Library: User Guide and Reference Manual, Jeremy G. Siek, Lie-Quan Lee, and Andrew Lumsdaine

C++ In-Depth Box Set, Bjarne Stroustrup, Andrei Alexandrescu, Andrew Koenig, Barbara E. Moo, Stanley B. Lippman, and Herb Sutter

C++ Network Programming, Volume 1: Mastering Complexity Using ACE and Patterns, Douglas C. Schmidt and Stephen D. Huston

C++ Network Programming, Volume 2: Systematic Reuse with ACE and Frameworks, Douglas C. Schmidt and Stephen D. Huston

Essential C++, Stanley B. Lippman

Exceptional C++: 47 Engineering Puzzles, Programming Problems, and Solutions, Herb Sutter

Modern C++ Design: Generic Programming and Design Patterns Applied, Andrei Alexandrescu

More Exceptional C++: 40 New Engineering Puzzles, Programming Problems, and Solutions, Herb Sutter

Applied C++

Practical Techniques for
Building Better Software

Philip Romanik
Amy Muntz

✦ Addison-Wesley

Boston • San Francisco • New York • Toronto • Montreal
London • Munich • Paris • Madrid
Capetown • Sydney • Tokyo • Singapore • Mexico City

Many of the designations used by manufacturers and sellers to distinguish their products are claimed as trademarks. Where those designations appear in this book, and Addison-Wesley was aware of a trademark claim, the designations have been printed with initial capital letters or in all capitals.

Intel Integrated Performance Primitives and Intel C++ Compiler are trademarks or registered trademarks of Intel Corporation or its subsidiaries in the United States and other countries.

The authors and publisher have taken care in the preparation of this book, but make no expressed or implied warranty of any kind and assume no responsibility for errors or omissions. No liability is assumed for incidental or consequential damages in connection with or arising out of the use of the information or programs contained herein.

The publisher offers discounts on this book when ordered in quantity for special sales. For more information, please contact:

> U.S. Corporate and Government Sales
> (800) 382-3419
> corpsales@pearsontechgroup.com

For sales outside of the U.S., please contact:
International Sales
(317) 581-3793
international@pearsontechgroup.com

Visit Addison-Wesley on the Web: www.aw.professional.com

Library of Congress Cataloging-in-Publication Data

Romanik, Philip.
     Applied C++ : practical techniques for building better software / Philip Romanik, Amy Muntz.
          p. cm.
     Includes biographical references and index.
     ISBN 0-321-10894-9 (alk. paper)
     1. C++ (Computer program language) 2. Computer software—Development. I. Muntz,
Amy. II. Title.

     QA76.73.C153R66 2003
     005.13'3—dc21

                                                                          2003040449

ISBN 0-321-10894-9
Text printed on recycled paper
1 2 3 4 5 6 7 8 9 10—CRS—0706050403
First printing, April 2003

Contents

Preface

This book is about applying C++ to solve the problems inherent in building commercial software. Those of you who have worked on engineering teams building complex software will know exactly what we mean by calling it commercial software.

Commercial software is delivered to customers (internal or external) who will rely on the interface you provide. It may be in an embedded system, or it may be a software library or application for standard platforms. No matter where it ultimately runs, the software must be released at a particular time with all of the features it needs to be successful in the market. It is software that is built by one group of engineers and potentially extended and maintained by other engineers. The engineers who take over maintaining the software may not have been part of the original team, and they might have to add features or try to fix problems while visiting customer sites.

Getting a group of engineers to build a complex piece of software and deliver it on time with full functionality is one of software engineering's biggest challenges. An even bigger challenge is building that same software in such a way that it can be handed off to others to extend and maintain. The C++ techniques and practical tips we have compiled into this book have been used repeatedly to accomplish just this. In many cases, we draw a distinction between the ideal solution and the practical one. We try to provide discussions of the trade-offs so that you can make informed decisions, and we tell you what our criteria are when selecting one method over another. We leave it to you to determine what works best in your application. Our goal is to share practical techniques that we have found made our commercial software efforts much more successful than they otherwise would have been. We hope you will find them useful.

For those of you who prefer to learn by looking at the code, you will find plenty of examples. We illustrate all of the techniques by using a concrete example that runs throughout the book. Because it was our experiences with imaging software that prompted us to write this book, our example comes from the image processing domain, but the C++ techniques are applicable to any domain.

We start with a simple, although inadequate, application that generates thumbnail images. We use this application in our prototyping phases to experiment with different C++ design and implementation techniques. The application is simple to understand and the results of applying various C++ techniques are immediately obvious, making it a nice candidate for prototyping.

This simple thumbnail image generator has many of the same inherent problems that our final image framework will have to address. The application is:

- Memory intensive. Working with images requires efficient use of memory, because images can get quite large and unwieldy. Managing memory becomes critical to the overall performance of the application.

- Performance intensive. While generating thumbnails is a straightforward image processing technique, others that we introduce later in the book (such as edge sharpening and noise reduction) require thoughtful designs to make them usable. It's great to have cool image functions to manipulate your digital images, but they are useless if they take a really long time to run.

Upon completion, you will have an image processing framework for manipulating your digital images and a practical toolkit of C++ utilities. The framework will provide efficient image storage and memory usage, routines for manipulating your digital images (like edge sharpening, image resizing, noise reduction, edge detection, image subtraction, and more), interfaces to third-party software, and many performance optimizations. It will be a useful piece of software that has practical design and implementation features, so that you could even use it as the basis of a commercial software product.

The complete source code for the thumbnail generator application, the prototypes, and the final image framework can be found on the included CD-ROM. Any updates to the software can be found at the web site: **http://www.appliedcpp.com**.

Intended Audience

We expect you to be familiar with C++ so that when we apply various constructs from the language, you have seen or used them before. We also assume that you have built applications either for personal or commercial use and are familiar with what the Standard Template Library (STL) can provide. We hope to engage you in detailed discussions of the advantages and disadvantages of certain C++ constructs. Finally, we hope you really like to look at actual code examples, because the book is filled with them.

We do not attempt to provide a reference for the C++ language, but we do provide primers and reviews of those topics that have exacting syntax or are not used as frequently. For the basics of the C++ language, we refer you to *The C++ Programming Language, Special Edition* [Stroustrup00] For in-depth discussions on certain C++ constructs, such as reference counting, we refer you to *Effective C++, Second Edition* [Meyers98]. For information on the Standard Template Library, we refer you to *Effective STL* [Meyers01]. For information on using C++ templates, we refer you to *C++ Templates* [Vandevoorde03].

As for our chosen domain of digital imaging, we don't expect you to have any experience with writing software that manipulates images. We provide some basic information about imaging that you can review; if you are familiar with imaging, you can skip that section. Whenever we talk about a particular operation that we apply to an image, we take the time to give a simple explanation, as well as some before and after pictures, before proceeding to the code example. If you want an in-depth, mathematical discussion of image processing operations, we refer you to *Digital Image Processing* [Pratt01].

How to Use This Book

The book is intended to be read sequentially, since there is a concrete example introduced in Chapter 2 and used to evolve the final design of the image framework that is presented in Chapter 5. Throughout the book, we highlight the C++ techniques we are exploring in heading titles and in summary boxes that appear on the first page of each chapter.

The book is organized as follows:

Chapter 1, Introduction, provides an overview of what we set out to accomplish by writing this book, and reveals our background and biases as they apply to the C++ techniques we recommend. We also provide an optional background section on digital imaging. If you have experience working with imaging applications, you may want to skip the final section of this chapter.

Chapter 2, A Test Application, introduces our simple, inadequate application, used as a test bed for prototyping C++ techniques. We deliberately create this strikingly simple application because it effectively demonstrates the trade-offs of various design and implementation decisions.

Chapter 3, Design Techniques, begins our discussion of C++ design. We use lots of code examples to demonstrate design strategies, and we provide a primer on templates since they are used so heavily within the book. Finally, we prototype various aspects of the design and build general utilities needed to support the design.

Chapter 4, Design Considerations, explores guidelines and additional strategies you may want to use in your designs. We offer a practical set of coding guidelines, reusability strategies, and a simple but effective debugging strategy.

Chapter 5, System Considerations, explores system-level design issues, like multi-threaded and multi-process designs, exception handling (including a framework we provide for handling exceptions), compile time and run-time issues, template specialization, and internationalization concerns.

Chapter 6, Implementation Considerations, applies the C++ techniques we have explored to the final design and implementation of all pieces in the image framework. In addition, this chapter introduces global image processing functions, like edge sharpening and noise reduction, and provides both a visual overview of these techniques and the C++ implementations. We also provide a high-level interface to libraries and other third-party software. Specifically, we introduce you to the Intel Integrated Performance Primitives (IPP) library and show you how to use IPP for high-speed imaging applications.

Chapter 7, Testing and Performance, provides a reasonable strategy for integrating unit tests into your software development cycle, including a full unit test framework and a discussion of how you can extend it to meet your particular needs. We also focus on performance, giving specific techniques that you can use to immediately improve the run-time performance of your application.

Chapter 8, Advanced Topics, explores those issues that we felt warranted more detailed discussion, such as copy on write, caching, **explicit** keyword usage, **const**, and pass by reference. We also include a section on extending the image framework, to serve as a guide for taking the existing framework and adding your own processing functions. We've highlighted some routines that work particularly well for enhancing your digital photographs.

Appendix A, Useful Online Resources, provides links to those software tools and resources that we thought might be helpful.

Appendix B, CD-ROM Information, outlines the contents of the CD-ROM included with this book. There is a great deal of code presented in this book. All of the source code for our test application, prototypes, and image framework is included on the disc. In addition, we provide all of the unit tests, unit test framework, and makefiles necessary to run the software on a variety of platforms. We also include some useful third-party software: the freeware DebugView utility by SysInternals for Microsoft Windows, the evaluation version of the Intel Integrated Performance Primitives (IPP) library for Microsoft Windows and Linux, the evaluation version of the Intel C++ Compiler for Microsoft Windows, the source code to build the JPEG file delegate, and the source code to build the TIFF file delegate.

Conventions We Use

The conventions we use in this book are as follows:

boldface	Indicates code.
italics	Highlights a new term.
❖	Is a navigational aide that highlights a topic being discussed.
―――――――――	Encloses an object's declaration as it appears in the corresponding header file.

Indicates a coding practice that is not recommended. The indicated code may be syntactically correct, but it may be inefficient, unsafe, or problematic in other ways, as discussed in the corresponding text.

 Introduces one of our tips. Tips can be either things to do or things not to do; they are highlighted to draw your attention to important information.

`//comments` Indicates a comment in the code. In the interest of brevity, the code comments that we include in the book do not include the full comments that are present in the source code. The CD-ROM contains the complete source code, which is fully commented.

Acknowledgments

This book would not have been possible without the tremendous encouragement, support, and help we received from many people. We thank you all for your time and patience.

We would especially like to thank Donald D. Anderson, Louis F. Iorio, and David Lanznar, all of whom spent enormous amounts of personal time reviewing and re-reviewing the entire manuscript. Your insightful comments and technical expertise have made this a better text. We would especially like to note Don's invaluable contributions and expertise in the area of run-time issues.

We are also deeply appreciative of the comprehensive and thorough technical reviews and suggestions provided by Mary Dageforde, Steve Vinoski, and Jan Christiaan van Winkel. Your careful attention to details and persistent comments pushed us to improve both the code and the manuscript.

The following people also made technical contributions on various subjects throughout the text: Neil Jacobson, Benson Margulies, Neil Levine, Thomas Emerson, David Parmenter, Evan Morton, and John Field. Thank you!

We feel lucky to have worked with such an incredible team at Addison-Wesley, whose professionalism and dedication to exacting standards encouraged us to undertake and complete this manuscript: Debbie Lafferty, Peter Gordon, Mike Hendrikson, Bernard Gaffney, John Fuller, Tyrrell Albaugh, Chanda Leary-Coutu, Melanie Buck, Curt Johnson, and Beth Byers.

Finally, we thank Team Checkpoint for inspiring us.

Philip Romanik, 2003
Amy Muntz, 2003

1

Introduction

Everyone who uses C++, or any programming language, brings along their biases and experiences to their software development efforts. In this book, we will apply C++ to solve problems in our chosen problem space of digital imaging. What better way to apply C++ constructs and see the immediate effects than by manipulating digital images, perhaps from your own digital camera.

We begin with a simple, inadequate application that generates thumbnail images from digital pictures. Through prototyping, we test a variety of C++ techniques and design ideas on the thumbnail application. We then use what we learn by applying the appropriate C++ techniques to build a robust image framework, as shown in Figure 1.1.

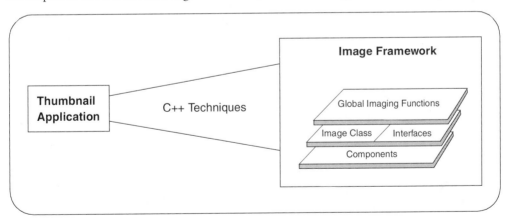

Figure 1.1: Development Road Map

Along the way, we explore such issues as: What's the best way to design this application, using inheritance or templates? Should we do everything at static initialization time or use a Singleton object? Does explicit template instantiation give us any syntactic or functional advantages? Does reference counting using rep objects and handles add to the design? How do we partition functionality between global functions and objects? What kind of framework makes sense for handling exceptions? Does template specialization help us? How can I make my routines run faster? We don't just discuss these issues; we write lots of code to test our assumptions and to examine the trade-offs in choosing a particular application.

Our background is in developing commercial software, that is, software with the following characteristics: built by many, expandable, maintainable, understandable, and stable. The C++ design and implementation techniques that we explore are evaluated in terms of all of these characteristics:

- **Built by many**: Software that is built by a team inherently means that no single person has firsthand knowledge of all of the code. It also means that good communication among the team members is critically important to the software's success. Communication has to start at the beginning; everyone on the team must share an understanding of what exactly is being built, for whom, and when it is needed. By understanding the customers and their requirements, you can always go back and ask yourself, "Is this feature I'm adding really necessary?" Understanding both the business and product requirements can help you avoid the dreaded feature creep or increasing scope that often delays products. Communication has to continue throughout the process: conveying interface designs so that integration among components runs smoothly; accurately and completely documenting your code; and conveying new member functions and their purpose to the Software Quality Assurance (SQA) and Documentation groups.

- **Expandable**: You must be able to add new features quickly and extend existing features in commercial software. These requests often seem to come when an influential customer finds that they need just one more thing to solve their problem. Even worse is when a limitation is discovered only after the product is released. Whether or not code can be easily expanded to accommodate these requests is often a function of the design. While it may be as easy as adding a new member function, significant new features require that the design be extended. Put simply, you have to think ahead when designing and writing code. Just implementing to a specification, with no thought to future expansion or maintainability, makes future changes much more difficult. A further complication is that most software won't allow features to be deprecated once the product is in use. You can't simply remove a class that was ill conceived, as it is certain that if you do so, you'll find a whole host of customers using it. Backward compatibility is often a key design constraint.

- **Maintainable**: No matter how many unit tests are written, automated tests are run, or functional tests are executed, it is inevitable that bugs will be found after the product has been released. For commercial software, the goal of all of the rigorous testing and preparation is to ensure that any post-release bugs have minor consequences to the product. What becomes crucial is that these bugs be easily and quickly corrected for the next release. It is also likely that the person who implemented a particular component won't be the person responsible for fixing the bug, either because enough time has passed that he has been assigned to a different project, or there are designated engineers responsible for support and maintenance. Given these constraints, maintainability must be designed into the software. There has to be an emphasis on solid design practices and clarity in coding styles, so that the software can be efficiently maintained without further complicating it.

- **Understandable**: Commercial software often includes visible software interfaces. If you are building an embedded system library, it needs to be understandable to the application engineers within your company. If you are building a software library, the interface you present must be easily understood by your customers so that they can use it to build their own applications. This doesn't just mean that naming conventions must make sense, but more importantly that your design and your use of language elements, like templates, are clear and appropriate.

- **Stable**: Commercial software must be stable; that is, it must be able to run for extended periods of time without crashing, leaking memory, or having unexplained anomalies.

Our biases are probably most evident in our approach to building software. We start each product development cycle knowing that we will be successful. We reduce the risk by getting things running as soon as possible. We start with the infrastructure and move on to the actual code. By doing so, we ensure the success of the product in a number of ways:

- We establish a code base or mainline and make sure it builds nightly from the very first day.

- We establish a simple unit test framework and make sure it runs every night using the nightly build system.

- We get very simplistic prototypes up and running quickly, so that we can apply different C++ techniques and methods to achieve the appropriate design and final implementation.

- We never break the main code base; it is always running so that other engineers and support groups, such as SQA and Documentation, always have a working base.

- We never meet as a team for more than thirty minutes. If you can't say what you need to in that amount of time, you need to rethink the purpose of the meeting or meet with a smaller, more focused group.

So what do you get when you finish this book, aside from a better understanding of when to apply specific C++ techniques and the trade-offs in doing so? You get the complete source code for both the thumbnail application and the image framework. The image framework offers efficient storage and manipulation of images, routines for processing images (such as sharpening edges, reducing noise, and subtracting images), and interfaces to third-party image processing and file format libraries. You can use the image framework to create your own robust application, either by using the framework directly, interfacing to some third-party image processing libraries, or by expanding the image processing routines we provide to create your own library.

We also include all of the unit tests and the unit test harness that we designed to run those tests. And, should you want to internationalize your software to use double-byte languages, such as Chinese or Japanese, we've included a simple resource manager to help you.

We provide a list of useful libraries and software tools in Appendix A.

1.1 Imaging Basics

This section provides a brief overview of some of the concepts we use when referring to image processing. If you are familiar with digital images and their properties, you can skip this section and proceed to Chapter 2.

An *image processing* application is any program that takes an image as input, performs some manipulation of that image, and produces a resulting image that may or may not be different from the original image.

An image has a specific meaning in image processing. The final image framework will handle many types of images, such as 8-bit and 32-bit grayscale and color images. However, as an introduction to image properties, we'll start with 8-bit grayscale images.

You can think of a *grayscale image* as a picture taken with black and white film. An 8-bit grayscale image is made up of *pixels* (picture elements, also referred to as *pels*) in varying levels of gray with no color content. A pixel contains the image information for a single point in the image, and has a discrete value between 0 (black) and 255 (white). Values between 0 and 255 are varying levels of gray.

We specify the *image size* by its width (x-axis) and height (y-axis) in pixels, with the *image origin* **(0,0)** being in the top left corner. By convention, the image origin is the top left corner because this makes it easier to map the coordinates of a pixel to a physical memory location where that pixel is stored. Typically, increasing pixel locations (left to right) is in the same direction as memory. These properties are illustrated in Figure 1.2.

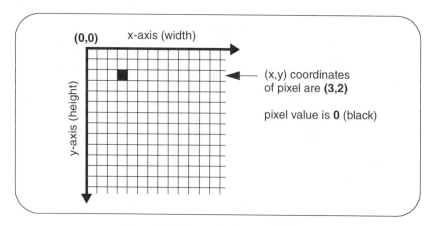

Figure 1.2: Grayscale Image Properties

While most of us choose to take color pictures with our digital cameras, grayscale images are important for a number of applications. Industrial applications, such as machine vision, x-rays, and medical imaging rely on grayscale imaging to provide information. In the case of machine vision, inspections for dimensional measurements like width, height, and circumference are often taken from grayscale images. This is because grayscale images can be processed three times faster than color images, which means greater throughput on production lines. Grayscale images are also the standard for mass detection and analysis in x-ray technology.

In our initial prototype, we represent a grayscale image as a two-dimensional array of pixels. We represent each pixel as an 8-bit unsigned quantity (`unsigned char`).

Other sophisticated image processing applications require color images. Color may be required for accurate analysis, for example in applications where sorting occurs based on color (such as in pharmaceutical applications that use color to represent different types of pills). In addition, color pictures are the most frequently captured images with digital cameras.

1.1.1 RGB Images

While they can be represented in many ways, in our prototype a *color image* is a 24-bit image where each pixel element consists of 8 bits of Red, 8 bits of Green, and 8 bits of Blue, each with a value between 0 and 255 (where 0 means no color and 255 means pure color). This is called *RGB* (Red-Green-Blue) color space. Combining the light of these three primary colors can produce all the colors detectable by humans. It is intuitive to use the RGB color space to process color images, because the algorithms that work on grayscale images extend easily to color images simply by tripling the processing.

As we mentioned, there are many other ways to represent an RGB value, and some are based on human perception. In these color models, more bits are reserved for the green channel, with fewer bits for the red and blue channels because our eyes have greater sensitivity to green than to either red or blue. If your application produces images that are viewed by people, this is an important issue. For applications employing machine analysis of images, this is not as important.

Usually, the representation is a compromise between storage requirements and required resolution. For example, a 16-bit RGB image requires only two-thirds the storage of a 24-bit RGB image. Since you cannot allocate the same number of bits for red, green, and blue in a 16-bit color space, it is typical to allocate the additional bit to the green channel. This is referred to as the *5:6:5 color model*, because 5 bits are allocated to the red channel, 6 bits to green, and 5 bits to blue.

1.1.2 HSI Images

An alternative color space is *HSI* (short for Hue-Saturation-Intensity). This color space mimics how the human eye perceives color. The *hue* of a color is its location within the visible portion of the electromagnetic spectrum of radiation. For example, the color may be aqua, teal, or green. You can think of hue as an angle on a *color wheel*, where all the colors are mapped on the wheel. Figure 1.3 shows a color wheel where red is at zero degrees, which is a common representation. Note that the arrows are provided to show angle; their length is not significant.

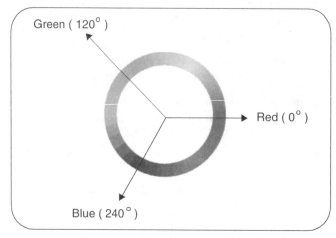

Figure 1.3: Hue on a Color Wheel

The *saturation* of the color is determined by how much the color is mixed with gray and white. A fully saturated color contains no gray or white, only the color. As gray and white are mixed into the color, it becomes less saturated. For example, the color of a lemon is a fully saturated yellow, and the color of a banana is a less saturated yellow.

The *intensity* of a color (also called *luminance* in some graphics programs) is the brightness of the color.

While it may be easier to describe colors using the HSI color space, it is not as fast for our purposes. As with grayscale images, the size of a color image is its width and height in pixels. Similarly, its x,y origin **(0,0)** is the top left corner. The properties of color images that we use in our prototype are shown in Figure 1.4.

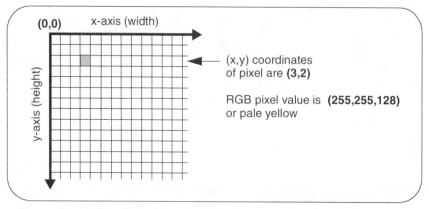

Figure 1.4: Color Image Properties Using RGB Color Space

1.2 Summary

In this chapter, we presented an overview of the commercial software characteristices that shape the techniques presented in this book. We also introduced the image framework application that we evolve throughout the book, as a test bed for various C++ constructs and design techniques. Finally, we concluded with a basic introduction to images and image processing terminology. We believe that this is all you will need to understand the examples in the book and to subsequently, if desired, apply image processing techniques to your own digital images using the framework provided here.

In Chapter 2, we will begin our journey by creating a simple test application that generates thumbnail images, as a reference for future C++ experimentation.

2

A Test Application

Our test application is a simple image processing application that accepts full-resolution grayscale images and produces thumbnails of those images. This is a deliberately simple, inadequate application that we use as a test bed for the C++ techniques we explore in later chapters. Our goal is to use prototypes to evolve our design of a robust, commercial-quality image framework by applying C++ techniques effectively.

A *thumbnail image* is a much smaller version of an image, which still contains enough image content to look like the original. Web sites, for example, often make use of thumbnail images because they are smaller and faster to transmit. By convention, clicking on a thumbnail image often displays the original, full-resolution image.

With limited details about what this test application should do, the list of design objectives is small. The application will

- Accept a grayscale image as input.
- Compute a thumbnail image with a user-specified scale factor (such as 1/2, 1/3, or 1/4 of the size of the original).

It is fairly easy to design and implement a C++ class to solve this problem. Our initial design is very simple, using only these design objectives and good programming practices as a guide. Later, we will expand the design as more requirements are added.

We use this iterative process to show how a design that initially appears to meet the objectives may not be the optimum solution. Techniques and tips introduced later in this book will be used to ensure a solid expandable design that will ultimately meet the goals of a comprehensive image framework.

2.1   Image Class Design

Both the original grayscale image and the generated thumbnail image share some common properties. For example, both are two-dimensional images that can be stored in a file or manipulated in memory. The only differences are the size and contents of the images. For example, a thumbnail image produced by our class could also be used as the input image. For this design, an image class has the following properties:

- It is a two-dimensional array of grayscale pixels. In our example, a pixel can be expressed as an 8-bit unsigned quantity (i.e., **unsigned char**). The size of the image is specified by its width and height.

- It allows random read/write access to the pixels in the image. Every pixel in an image has coordinates (**x,y**) to describe its location. We specify the image origin (**0,0**) as the top left corner of the image, and (**width-1**, **height-1**) represents the pixel in the bottom right corner of the image.

- It uses a simple memory allocation scheme for image data. Memory for an image whose x-dimension is **width** and y-dimension is **height** is allocated by:

      unsigned char* pixels = new unsigned char [width * height];

  The address of any pixel (**x,y**) in the image is:

      unsigned char* address = pixels + y*width + x;

- It throws a C++ exception, **rangeError**, if any attempts are made to reference pixels not within the image.

Our initial design for the image class is this simple. On the surface, it appears to meet the design objectives. The image class definition is shown in Section 2.3.1 on page 12.

2.2   Thumbnail Class

In our design, the image class is a container for image pixels and nothing else. Since the purpose of this application is to create thumbnail images, a thumbnail class is needed to handle file I/O and the thumbnail algorithm. The thumbnail class has the following properties:

- Reads the input image from a file.

- Computes the thumbnail image given the input file and the reduction factor to use (i.e., how small a thumbnail image to create).

- Throws a C++ exception, **invalid**, if any errors are encountered. If the image class throws a **rangeError** error, this exception is caught and the **invalid** exception is thrown instead.

- Writes the thumbnail image to a file.

The complete definition of the thumbnail class is shown in Section 2.3.2 on page 16.

2.2.1 Thumbnail Algorithm

Each pixel in the thumbnail image is found by averaging a number of pixels in the input image. The pixel value in the thumbnail image, `T(x0,y0)`, is computed as shown in Figure 2.1, where **factor** is the desired reduction value.

$$
T[x0,y0] = \frac{\displaystyle\sum_{x=0}^{factor-1}\ \sum_{y=0}^{factor-1} P[(x0*factor)+x, (y0*factor)+y]}{factor * factor}
$$

Figure 2.1: Computing the Thumbnail Pixel Value

A picture helps clarify this equation. Each pixel in the original image **P** is reduced, by averaging pixel values in image **P**, to a corresponding point in the thumbnail image **T** using the equation from Figure 2.1. In Figure 2.2, we show how a group of pixels in the original image is reduced to the group of pixels shown in the thumbnail image.

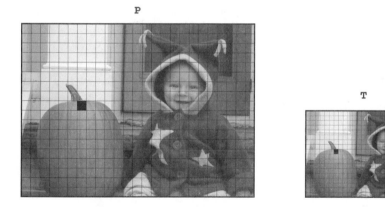

Figure 2.2: Pictorial Representation of Thumbnail Computation

To further simplify our application, we ignore the condition created by integer arithmetic where the division by the reduction factor results in a fraction. For example, if the original image is **640x480** pixels in size, and the desired reduction factor is **6**, the thumbnail image will be **(640/6)x(480/6)** pixels in size or **106.67x80**. To avoid the fractional result, we ignore the last 4 pixels in each line, effectively making the thumbnail image **(636/6)x(480/6)** pixels in size or **106x80**.

2.3 Implementation

This section shows the implementation of both the image class and the thumbnail classes. For brevity in the book, we have omitted many of the comments in the code snippets. We have chosen instead to explain our design choices in a narrative fashion. The full implementation, including complete comments, can be found on the CD-ROM.

2.3.1 Image Class

We define our image class in **image.h** as follows:

```
class apImage
{
public:
  apImage  ();
  apImage  (int width, int height);
  ~apImage ();

  apImage              (const apImage& src);
  apImage& operator= (const apImage& src);

  void swap (apImage& src);

  void          setPixel (int x, int y, unsigned char pixel);
  unsigned char getPixel (int x, int y) const;

  bool isValid () const { return pixels_ != 0;}
  // Tests if the image data exists, and presumably valid.

  int width ()  const { return width_;}    // Image width
  int height () const { return height_;}   // Image height

  class rangeError {};    // Exception class
private:
  void init    ();
  void cleanup ();
  // Initialize or cleanup the allocated image data

  int width_;              // Image width
  int height_;             // Image height
```

The implementation for the **apImage** class is straightforward. We'll start with memory allocation and deallocation.

❖ MEMORY ALLOCATION AND DEALLOCATION

Instead of duplicating code every time the image data is allocated or deleted, we define **init()** and **cleanup()** functions.

The **init()** function uses the **new** operator to allocate memory for storing image data of size **width** x **height**.

The orthogonal function is **cleanup()**, which deletes any memory allocated to the **apImage** class, as shown here.

```
void apImage::cleanup ()
{
  // Put the object back into its original, null state.
  delete [] pixels_;

  width_  = 0;
  height_ = 0;
  pixels_ = 0;
}

void apImage::init ()
{
  // All memory allocation passes through this function.
  if (width_ > 0 && height_ > 0)
    pixels_ = new unsigned char [width_ * height_];
}
```

Create orthogonal functions whenever possible. For example, if your class has an `open()` function, you should also have a `close()` function.

❖ CONSTRUCTORS AND DESTRUCTORS

By using **init()** and **cleanup()**, our constructors and destructors become very simple.

```
apImage::apImage () : width_ (0), height_ (0), pixels_ (0)
{}
apImage::apImage (int width, int height)
: width_ (width), height_ (height), pixels_ (0)
{
  init ();
}
apImage::~apImage ()
{
  cleanup ();
}
```

Constructors should initialize all data members to a default state.

The default constructor for **apImage** creates a *null image*, which is an image with no memory allocation and zero width and height. Null images are very useful objects, and are necessary because some image processing operations can legitimately be null. For example, image processing routines often operate on a particular set of pixels present in multiple images. If there is no overlap in pixels among the images, then a null image is returned. A null image is also returned if an error occurs during an image processing operation. The **isValid()** member function tests whether an image is null as shown here.

```
apImage input;
...
apImage output = input.arbitraryAlgorithm (args);
if (!output.isValid()) {
  // Error processing. arbitraryAlgorithm failed.
}
```

❖ ASSIGNMENT OPERATOR AND COPY CONSTRUCTOR

We define an assignment operator and copy constructor, because the one that the compiler automatically generates performs a member-wise copy of the class data, which incorrectly copies the image data pointer `pixels_`. So, we use the standard C library `memcpy()` function to duplicate the image data:

```
apImage::apImage (const apImage& src)
: width_ (0), height_ (0), pixels_ (0)
{
  if (src.isValid()) {
    width_  = src.width ();
    height_ = src.height ();
    init ();
    memcpy (pixels_, src.pixels_, width_ * height_);
  }
}

apImage& apImage::operator= (const apImage& src)
{
  if (&src != this) {
    // Delete any existing data and recreate the source image
    cleanup ();
    width_  = src.width ();
    height_ = src.height ();
    init ();

    memcpy (pixels_, src.pixels_, width_ * height_);
  }

  return *this;
}
```

Use the version of `memcpy()` or `std::copy()` supplied on your system. It will be difficult to write a faster version.

As shown, our copy constructor and assignment operator use much of the same code. One way to eliminate this duplication is to use Sutter's technique for writing safe assignment operators. See [Sutter00]. In a nutshell, his technique requires that you define the assignment operator by calling the copy constructor. In addition, his technique requires that you define a `swap()` function, which switches the data of two `apImage` objects as shown here.

```
template<class T> void swap (T& a, T& b)
{
  T copy(a);
  a = b;
  b = copy;
}

void apImage::swap (apImage& src)
{
  ::swap (width_,  src.width_);
  ::swap (height_, src.height_);
  ::swap (pixels_, src.pixels_);
}

apImage& apImage::operator= (const apImage& src)
{
  apImage temp (src);
  swap (temp);

  return *this;
}
```

The **swap<>** template function simply exchanges the data of two objects of the same type. It allows us to implement a **swap()** method for the **apImage** class that exchanges all of the data in the object with another **apImage** object. The assignment operator uses the copy constructor to create a copy of **src**, which is then exchanged with the existing data members of the object. When the assignment operator returns, the temporary **apImage** object is automatically destroyed. This behavior is especially useful because it guarantees that if any exceptions are thrown, the object will not be left in a partially constructed state.

❖ READING AND WRITING IMAGE PIXELS

Our **apImage** class is complete once we define the functions that read and write image pixels. Both will throw **rangeError** if the coordinates do not specify a pixel within the image, or if the image is null.

```
void apImage::setPixel (int x, int y, unsigned char pixel)
{
  if (x < 0 || y < 0 ||
      x >= width_ || y >= height_ ||
      !isValid())
    throw rangeError ();
  unsigned char* p = pixels_ + y*width_ + x;
  *p = pixel;
}

unsigned char apImage::getPixel (int x, int y) const
{
  if (x < 0 || y < 0 ||
      x >= width_ || y >= height_ ||
      !isValid())
    throw rangeError ();
  // Image data is stored a row at a time.
  unsigned char* p = pixels_ + y*width_ + x;
  return *p;
}
```

2.3.2 Thumbnail Class

Now we are ready to define the thumbnail image class, **apThumbNail**, which computes the thumbnail image from an input image. As with **apImage**, we initially keep the definition in **apThumbnail.h** as simple as possible, as shown here.

```
class apThumbNail
{
public:
  apThumbNail ();
  ~apThumbNail ();
  // The default copy constructor and assignment operator are ok

  void createThumbNail (const char* inputFile,
                        const char* outputFile, int factor);
  class invalid {};    // Exception class

private:
  void readImage  (const char* inputFile);
  void writeImage (const char* outputFile) const;
  unsigned char averagePixels (int x0, int y0, int factor);

  apImage image_;          // input image
  apImage thumbnail_;      // thumbnail image
};
```

In this class, we considered whether a copy/assignment operator is necessary, but decided it is not. Because it is a common oversight to not define a copy/assignment operator, we explicitly include a comment to let others know that this is a deliberate choice.

 If the default copy constructor and assignment operator are acceptable, add a comment stating this to your class declaration.

❖ CONSTRUCTOR AND DESTRUCTOR

Let's discuss the implementation of the thumbnail class, starting with the constructor and destructor.

```
apThumbNail::apThumbNail ()
{}
apThumbNail::~apThumbNail ()
{}
```

Although they are both empty, they do serve a purpose. A common mistake during development is to add a new data member to an object and forget to initialize it in the constructor. Defining a constructor makes it more likely that you will remember to initialize new data members.

In addition, you may wonder why these trivial functions are not placed in the header file as an inline definition. Keeping these definitions in the source file is appropriate, because the constructor and destructor are apt to be modified frequently during development and maintenance. We have also found that on some platforms, especially embedded, cross-compiled platforms, inlined constructors cause the memory footprint of an application to increase, because the compiler adds additional housekeeping code. This isn't a problem if the object is referenced only a few times in the code, but, if used frequently, it can dramatically increase the memory footprint.

 Except in very trivial objects, never define a constructor or destructor in the header file. These functions are apt to change frequently and inlining these definitions can increase the memory footprint on some platforms.

❖ READING AND WRITING IMAGES

Let's skip ahead to the implementation of the **readImage()** and **writeImage()** functions. These functions are designed to read an image from a file and convert it into an **apImage** class, or to write an **apImage** to a file, respectively. There are numerous file formats designed to store image data, and we deal with them later. For now, we simulate these functions to quickly verify that the design is working properly, before getting bogged down in the details of supporting numerous file formats. **readImage()** creates an **apImage** and populates it with image pixels, and **writeImage()** simply displays the **apImage**. **readImage()** also demonstrates how we catch the **rangeError** thrown by **apImage** and rethrow it as an **invalid** error.

```
void apThumbNail::readImage  (const char* /*inputFile*/)
{
  // Create a synthetic 64x64 image
  image_ = apImage (64, 64);
  try {
    for (int y=0; y<image_.height(); y++)
      for (int x=0; x<image_.width(); x++)
        image_.setPixel (x, y, (unsigned char)(y % 255));
  }
  catch (apImage::rangeError) {
    throw invalid ();
  }
}

void apThumbNail::writeImage  (const char* /*outputFile*/) const
{
  // Save formatting state of stream
  std::ios_base::fmtflags flags = std::cout.flags (std::cout.hex);
  int width = std::cout.width (2);

  for (int y=0; y< thumbnail_.height(); y++) {
    for (int x=0; x< thumbnail_.width(); x++)
      std::cout << (int) thumbnail_.getPixel (x, y) << " ";
    std::cout << std::endl;
  }
  std::cout.flags (flags);
  std::cout.width (width);
}
```

❖   CREATING THUMBNAIL IMAGES

With that out of the way, we can look at the function that actually does the work. `createThumbNail()` takes the name of an input file, the name of the output thumbnail file to create, and how much reduction is desired. Once the input image is read and the thumbnail image is allocated, the function loops through each pixel in the thumbnail image and computes its value:

```
void apThumbNail::createThumbNail (const char* inputFile,
                                   const char* outputFile,
                                   int factor)
{
  // Validate the arguments
  if (inputFile == 0 || outputFile == 0 ||
      factor <= 1)
    throw invalid ();

  // Read the source image
  readImage (inputFile);
  if (!image_.isValid())
    throw invalid ();

  // Create our internal thumbnail image
  thumbnail_ = apImage (image_.width()  / factor,
                        image_.height() / factor);

  // Turn any rangeErrors from apImage into our invalid error
  unsigned char pixel;
  try {
    for (int y=0; y<thumbnail_.height(); y++) {
      for (int x=0; x<thumbnail_.width(); x++) {
        // Convert to image_ coordinates to find the average
        pixel = averagePixels (x*factor, y*factor, factor);
        thumbnail_.setPixel (x, y, pixel);
      }
    }
  }
  catch (apImage::rangeError) {
    throw invalid ();
  }

  writeImage (outputFile);
}
```

`createThumbNail()` calls `averagePixels()` to compute the average of pixels in the input image needed to compute a single pixel in the thumbnail image. To be precise, the pixels in a small **factor** x **factor** subset of **image_** are summed and averaged as shown:

```
unsigned char apThumbNail::averagePixels (int x0, int y0,
                                          int factor)
{
  int sum = 0;

  // Average factor x factor pixels in the input image
  try {
    for (int y=0; y<factor; y++) {
      for (int x=0; x<factor; x++)
        sum += image_.getPixel (x+x0, y+y0);
    }
```

```
      }
      catch (apImage::rangeError) {
        throw invalid ();
      }

      // This cast (an int to an unsigned char) is very safe
      return static_cast<unsigned char>(sum / (factor * factor));
    }
```

Although `apThumbNail` is a simple class, it can also be confusing, because it contains two images with different coordinate systems. In our example, the input image has dimensions `width` x `height`, while the thumbnail image has dimensions `width/factor` x `height/factor`. Coding mistakes can be made when these coordinate systems are accidentally swapped or blended together. Even though the `getPixel()` and `setPixel()` methods in `apImage` will throw an error if the coordinates are out of bounds, these problems will not be found until a unit test is written (or worse, if there is no unit test, until the integration and test stage of the project).

 Functions should not mix or blend coordinate systems, because this greatly increases the chances of introducing bugs.

To decrease the likelihood of bugs, the coordinates used in `averagePixels()` are all in terms of the input image, `image_`. Likewise, the coordinates used in `createThumbNail()` are mostly in terms of the thumbnail image.

The following line creates the thumbnail image, given the dimensions of the input image, and is written to be self-documenting:

```
    thumbnail_ = apImage (image_.width()  / factor,
                          image_.height() / factor);
```

The line that computes the average isn't as obvious, so we add a comment:

```
    // Convert to image_ coordinates to find the average
    pixel = averagePixels (x*factor, y*factor, factor);
```

2.4 Summary

In this chapter, we created a test application that takes an image and generates a thumbnail image, which is an image of reduced size. We designed and implemented an image class for the original input image, and a thumbnail class that computes the thumbnail image. In doing so, we employed a very simple memory management scheme for manipulating images, which was useful in highlighting the deficiencies that we may want to correct in the final image framework. We also used this simple application to explore assignment operators and how to write safe ones using Sutter's technique. See [Sutter00].

In Chapter 3, we construct a more robust memory management object that can effectively fulfill our defined requirements for a real image framework. We also review reference counting and provide a primer on templates, including some of the exacting syntactic requirements. We use this memory management object as we prototype various aspects of the image framework, with each prototype employing different C++ constructs and techniques to arrive at the final design for the image framework. Although we concretely apply these techniques to an image framework to explore their advantages and disadvantages, these techniques can be applied to other types of software.

3

Design Techniques

In this chapter, we lay the groundwork for extending our digital imaging framework. We begin by designing a memory allocation object, and then continue with a templates primer that provides a road map to subtleties of templates and their use. Finally, we apply C++ constructs to specific aspects of the design by creating detailed prototypes, and discussing the advantages and disadvantages of each technique.

3.1 Memory Allocation

In our test application's image class described in Section 2.3.1 on page 12, we use the operators **new** and **delete** to allocate and free storage for our image pixels in **apImage::init()** and **apImage::cleanup()**. Our test application employs this simple memory management scheme to demonstrate that it can be trivial to come up with a working solution. This simple mechanism, however, is very inefficient and breaks down quickly as you try to extend it. Managing memory is critical for a fully functional image framework. Therefore, before we delve into adding functionality, we will design an object that performs and manages memory allocation.

3.1.1 Why a Memory Allocation Object Is Needed

Images require a great deal of memory storage to hold the pixel data. It is very inefficient to copy these images, in terms of both memory storage and time, as the images are manipulated and processed. You can easily run out of memory if there are a large number of images. In addition, the heap could become fragmented if there isn't a large enough block of memory left after all of the allocations.

You really have to think about the purpose of an image before duplicating it. Duplication of image data should only happen when there is a good reason to retain a copy of the image (for example, you want to keep the original image and the filtered image result).

▶ **EXAMPLE** ──

A simple example illustrates the inefficiencies that can occur when manipulating images. Try adding two images together as follows:

```
apImage a (...);
apImage b (...);
apImage c = a + b;
```

The code allocates memory to store image **a**, allocates memory to store image **b**, allocates more memory to store the temporary image **(a+b)**, and finally allocates memory for the resulting image **c**. This simple example is bogged down with many memory allocations, and the time required for copying all the pixel data is excessive.

── ◀

We use this example as a simple way of showing how much memory and time a seemingly trivial operation can require. Note that some compilers can eliminate the temporary **(a+b)** storage allocation by employing a technique called return value optimization [Meyers96].

3.1.2 Memory Allocation Object Requirements

Instead of designing an object that works only for images, we create a generic object that is useful for any application requiring allocation and management of heap memory. We had to overcome the desire to produce the perfect object, because we do not have an unlimited budget or time. Commercial software is fluid; it is more important that we design it such that it can be adapted, modified, and extended in the future. The design we are presenting here is actually the third iteration.

Here's the list of requirements for our generic memory allocation object:

■ Allocates memory off the heap, while also allowing custom memory allocators to be defined for allocating memory from other places, such as private memory heaps.

■ Uses reference counting to share and automatically delete memory when it is no longer needed.

■ Employs locking and unlocking as a way of managing objects in multithreaded applications (not shown here, but included in the software on the CD.-ROM For more information, see section *apLock* on page 128).

■ Has very low overhead. For example, no memory initialization is done after allocation. This is left to the user to do, if needed.

■ Uses templates so that the unit of allocation is arbitrary.

■ Supports simple arrays, **[]**, as well as direct access to memory.

■ Throws Standard Template Library (STL) exceptions when invalid attempts are made to access memory.

■ Aligns the beginning of memory to a specified boundary. The need for this isn't obvious until you consider that certain image processing algorithms can take advantage of how the data is arranged in memory. Some compilers, such as Microsoft Visual C++, can control the alignment when memory is allocated. We include this feature in a platform-independent way.

Before we move forward with our own memory allocation object, it is wise to see if any standard solutions exist.

Before designing your own solution, look to see if there is an existing solution that you can adapt or use directly.

The STL is always a good resource for solutions. You can imagine where **std::vector**, **std::list**, or even **std::string** could be used to manage memory. Each has its advantages, but none of these template classes offer reference counting. And even if reference counting were not an issue, there are performance issues to worry about. Each of these template objects provides fast random access to our pixel data, but they are also optimized for insertion and deletion of data, which is something we do not need.

Why Reference Counting Is Essential

Our solution is to create a generic object that uses *reference counting* to share and automatically delete memory when finished. Reference counting allows different objects to share the same information. Figure 3.3 shows three objects sharing image data from the same block of memory.

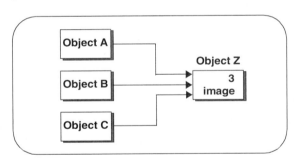

Figure 3.3: Objects Sharing Memory

In Figure 3.3, the object containing the image data, **Object Z**, also contains the reference count, **3**, which indicates how many objects are sharing the data. **Objects A**, **B**, and **C** all share the same image data.

Consider the following:

```
apImage image2 = image1
```

If reference counting is used in this example, **image2** will share the same storage as **image1**. If **image1** and **image2** point to identical memory, a little bookkeeping is necessary to make sure this shared storage is valid while either image is in scope. That's where reference counting comes in.

Here's how it works in a nutshell. A memory allocation object allocates storage for an image. When subsequent images need to share that storage, the memory allocation object increments a variable, called a reference count, to keep track of the images sharing the storage; then it returns a pointer to the memory allocation object. When one of those images is deleted, the reference count is decremented. When the reference count decrements to zero, the memory used for storage is deleted. Let's look at an example using our memory allocation object, **apAlloc<>**.

```
apAlloc<int> array1 (100);
int i;
for (i=0; i<100; i++)
  array1[i] = i;
apAlloc<int> array2 = array1;
for (i=0; i<100; i++)
  array1[i] = i*2;
```

Once the **apAlloc<>** object is constructed, it is used much like any pointer. In this example, we create and populate an object **array1** with data. After assigning this object to **array2**, the code modifies the contents of **array1**. **array2** now contains the same contents as **array1**. Reference counting is not a new invention, and there are many in-depth discussions on the subject. See [Meyers96] and [Stroustrup00].

3.1.3 A Primer on Templates

The memory allocator objects use templates. The syntax can be confusing and tedious if you aren't used to it. Compilers are very finicky when it comes to handling templates, so the syntax becomes extremely important. Therefore, we provide a quick review of template syntax using a cookbook format. For a more detailed discussion, see [Stroustrup00] or [Vandevoorde03].

Converting a Class to Templates

Consider this simple image class that we want to convert to a template class:

```
class apImageTest
{
public:
  apImageTest (int width, int height, char* pixels);
  char* getPixel (int x, int y);
  void setPixel (int x, int y, char* pixel);
private:
  char* pixels_;
  int width_, height_;
};
```

The conversion is as easy as substituting a type name **T** for references to **char** as shown:

```
template<class T> class apImageTest
{
public:
```

```
    apImageTest (int width, int height, T* pixels);
    T* getPixel (int x, int y);
    void setPixel (int x, int y, T* pixel);
  private:
    T* pixels_;
    int width_, height_;
  };
```

To use this object, you would replace references of **apImageTest** with **apImageTest<char>**.

 Be careful of datatypes when converting a function to a template function. When using common types, like **int**, and converting it to **T**, there may be places where **int** is still desired, such as in loop counters.

Type Argument Names

Any placeholder name can be used to represent the template arguments. We use a single letter (usually **T**), but you can use more descriptive names if you want. Consider the following:

```
    template<class Pixel> class apImageTest;
```

Pixel is much more descriptive than **T** and may make your code more readable. There is no requirement to capitalize the first letter of the name, but we recommend doing so to avoid confusing argument names and variables. If you write a lot of template classes you will probably find that single-letter names are easier to use. Our final **apImage<>** class will have two arguments, **T** and **S,** that mean nothing out of context; however, when you are looking at the code, the parameters quickly take on meaning.

class Versus typename

The word **class** is used to define an argument name, but this argument does not have to be a class. In our **apImageTest** example shown earlier, we wrote **apImageTest<char>**, which expands the first line of the class declaration to:

```
    template<class char> class apImageTest;
```

Although **char** is not a class, the compiler does not literally assume that the argument name **T** must be a class. You are also free to use the name **typename** instead of **class** when referring to templates. These are all valid examples of the same definition:

```
    template<class T> class apImageTest;
    template<typename T> class apImageTest;
    template<class Pixel> class apImageTest;
    template<typename Pixel> class apImageTest;
```

Is there ever a case where **class** is not valid? Yes, because there can be parsing ambiguities when dependent types are used. See [Meyers01]. Late-model compilers that have kept current with the C++ Standard, such as gcc v3.1, will generate warning messages if `typename` is missing from these situations. For example, using gcc v3.1, the following line of code:

```
apImage<T1>::row_iterator i1 = src1.row_begin();
```

produces a warning:

```
warning: 'typename apImage<T1>::row_iterator' is implicitly a
typename
warning: implicit typename is deprecated, please see the
documentation for details
```

The compiler determines that `row_iterator` is a type rather than an instance of a variable or object, but warns of the ambiguity. To eliminate this warning, you must explicitly add `typename`, as shown:

```
typename apImage<T1>::row_iterator i1 = src1.row_begin();
```

Another case where `typename` is an issue is in template specialization, because the use of `typename` is forbidden. [Vandevoorde03] points out that the C++ standardization committee is considering relaxing some of the `typename` rules. For example, you might think that the previous example could be converted as follows:

```
typename apImage<apRGB>::row_iterator i1 = src1.row_begin();
```

where `apRGB` is the specialization. However, this generates an error:

```
In function '...': using 'typename' outside of template
```

To resolve the error, you must remove `typename`, as shown:

```
apImage<apRGB>::row_iterator i1 = src1.row_begin();
```

There is a growing movement to use `typename` instead of `class` because of the confusion some new programmers encounter when using templates. If you do not have a clear preference, we recommend that you use `typename`. The most important thing is that you are consistent in your choice.

Default Template Arguments

You can supply default template arguments much like you can with any function argument. These default arguments can even contain other template arguments, making them extremely powerful. For example, our `apAlloc<>` class that we design in Section 3.1.5 on page 31 is defined as:

```
template<class T, class A = apAllocator_<T> >
class apAlloc
```

As we will see in that section, anyone who does not mind memory being allocated on the heap can ignore the second argument, and the `apAllocator_<>` object will be used to allocate memory. Most clients can think of `apAlloc<>` as having only a single parameter, and be blissfully ignorant of the details.

The syntax we used by adding a space between the two '>' characters is significant. Defining the line as:

✗ `template<class T, class A = apAllocator_<T>>`

will produce an error or warning. The error message that the compiler produces in this case is extremely cryptic, and can take many iterations to locate and fix. Basically, the compiler is interpreting `>>` as `operator>>`. It is best to avoid this potential trap by adding a space between the two > characters.

Inline Versus Non-Inline Template Definitions

❖ INLINE DEFINITION

Many template developers put the implementation inside the class definition to save a lot of typing. For example, we could have given the `getPixel()` function in our `apImageTest<>` object an inline definition in the header file this way:

```
template<class T> class apImageTest
{
public:
  ...
  T* getPixel (int x, int y)
  { return pixels_[y*width_ + x];} // No error detection
  ...
};
```

❖ NON-INLINE DEFINITION

We can also define `getPixel()` after the class definition (non-inline) in the header file:

```
template <class T>
T* apImageTest<T>::getPixel (int x, int y)
{ return pixels_[y*width_ + x];}
```

Now you know why many developers specify the implementation inside the definition — it is much less typing. For more complex definitions, however, you may want to define the implementation after the definition for clarity, or even in a separate file. If the template file is large and included everywhere, putting the implementation in a separate file can speed compilation. The choice is yours.

The copy constructor makes a particularly interesting example of complex syntax:

```
template<class T>
apImageTest<T>::apImageTest (const apImageTest& src)
{...}
```

It is hard to get the syntax correct on an example like this one. The error messages generated by compilers in this case are not particularly helpful, so we recommend that you refer to a C++ reference book. See [Stroustrup00] or [Vandevoorde03].

Template Specialization

Templates define the behavior for all types (type **T** in our examples). But what happens if the definition for a generic type is slow and inefficient? Specialization is a method where additional member function definitions can be defined for specific types. Consider an image class, **apImage<T>**. The parameter **T** can be anything, including some seldom used types like **double** or even **std::string**. But what if 90 percent of the images in your application are of a specific type, such as **unsigned char**? An inefficient algorithm is fine for a generic parameter, but we would certainly like the opportunity to tell the compiler what to do if the type is **unsigned char**.

To define a specialization, you first need the generic definition. It is good to write this first anyway to flesh out what each member function does. If you choose to write only the specialization, you should define the generic version to throw an error so that you will know if you ever call it unintentionally.

Once the generic version is defined, the specialization for **unsigned char** can be defined as shown:

```
template<> class apImageTest<unsigned char>
{
public:
  apImageTest (int width, int height, unsigned char* pixels);
  unsigned char* getPixel (int x, int y);
  void setPixel (int x, int y, unsigned char* pixel);
private:
  unsigned char* pixels_;
  int width_, height_;
};
```

We can now proceed with defining each specialized member function. Is it possible to define a specialization for just a single member function? The answer is yes. Consider a very generic implementation for our **apImageTest<>** constructor:

```
template<class T>
apImageTest<T>::apImageTest (int width, int height, T* pixels)
: width_ (width), height_ (height), pixels_ (0)
{
  pixels_ = new T [width_ * height_];
  T* p = pixels_;
  for (int y=0; y<height; y++) {
    for (int x=0; x<width; x++)
      *p++ = *pixels++;  // use assignment to copy pixels
  }
}
```

This definition is careful to use assignment to copy each pixel from the given array to the one controlled by the class. Now, let us define a specialization when **T** is an **unsigned char**:

```
apImageTest<unsigned char>::apImageTest
  (int width, int height, unsigned char* pixels)
  : width_ (width), height_ (height), pixels_ (0)
{
  pixels_ = new unsigned char [width_ * height_];
  memcpy (pixels_, pixels, width_ * height_);
}
```

We can safely use **memcpy()** to initialize our pixel data. You can see that the syntax for specialization is different if you are defining the complete specialization, or just a single-member function.

Function Templates

C++ allows the use of templates to extend beyond objects to also include simple function definitions. Finally we have the ability to get rid of most macros. For example, we can replace the macro **min()**:

```
#ifndef min
#define min(a,b) (((a) < (b)) ? (a) : (b))
#endif
```

with a function template **min()**:

```
template<class T> const T& min (const T& a, const T& b)
{ return (a<b) ? a : b;}
```

❖ FUNCTION TEMPLATE SPECIALIZATION

We can even define function template specializations:

```
template<> const char& min<char> (const char& a, const char& b)
{ return (a<b) ? a : b;}
```

In this example, the specialization is unnecessary, but it does show the special syntax you will need to use for specialization.

Function templates can also have multiple template parameters, but don't be surprised if the compiler sometimes selects a function you don't expect. Here is an example of a function that we used in an early iteration of our image framework:

```
template<class T1, class T2, class T3>
void add2 (const T1& s1, const T2& s2, T3& d1)
{ d1 = s1 + s2;}
```

We needed such a function inside our image processing functions to control the behavior in overflow and underflow conditions. Specialized versions of this function test for overflow and clamp the output value at the maximum value for that data type, while other versions test for underflow and clamp the output value at the minimum value. The generic definition shown above just adds two source values and produces an output.

You must be careful with these mixed-type function templates. It is entirely possible that the compiler will not be able to determine which version to call. We could not use the above definition of **add2<>** with recent C++ compilers, such as Microsoft Visual Studio, because our numerous overrides make it ambiguous, according to the latest C++ standard, as to which version of **add2<>** to call. So, our solution is to define non-template versions for all our expected data types, such as:

```
void add2 (int s1, int s2, int& d1);
```

If you plan on using mixed-type function templates, you should definitely create prototypes and compile and run them with the compilers you expect to use. There are still many older compilers that will compile the code correctly, but the code does not comply with the latest C++ standards. As compilers gain this compliance, you will need to implement solutions that conform to these standards.

Explicit Template Instantiation

C++ allows you to explicitly instantiate one or more template arguments. We can rewrite our **add2()** example to return the result, rather than pass it as a reference, as follows:

```
template<class R, class T1, class T2>
R add2 (const T1& s1, const T2& s2)
{ return static_cast<R> (s1 + s2);}
```

There is no way for the compiler to decide what the return type is without the type being specified explicitly. Whenever you use this form of **add2()**, you must explicitly specify the destination type for the compiler, as follows:

```
add2<double>(1.1, 2.2);
add2<int>(1.1, 2.2);
```

We will use explicit template instantiation later in the book to specify the data type for intermediate image processing calculations. For more information on explicit instantiation or other template issues, see [Vandevoorde03].

3.1.4 Notations Used in Class Diagrams

Table 3.1 shows a simple set of notations we use throughout the book to make the relationships clear in class diagrams. See [Lakos96].

Table 3.1: Notations Used in Class Diagrams

Notation	Meaning
X	**X** is a class
A ↑ B	**B** is a kind of **A** (inheritance)
A ——● B	**B**'s implementation uses **A**

3.1.5 Memory Allocator Object's Class Hierarchy

The class hierarchy for the memory allocator object is shown in Figure 3.4.

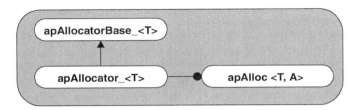

Figure 3.4: Memory Allocator Object Class Diagram

It consists of a base class, a derived class, and then the object class, which uses the derived class as one of its arguments. All three classes use templates. Note that we have appended an underscore character, _, to some class names to indicate that they are internal classes used in the API, but never called directly by its clients.

apAllocatorBase_<> is a base class that manages memory and contains all of the required functionality, except for the actual allocation and deallocation of memory. Its constructor basically initializes the object variables.

apAllocator_<> is derived from **apAllocatorBase_<>**. **apAllocator_<>** manages the allocation and deallocation of memory from the heap. You can use **apAllocator_<>** as a model for deriving the classes from **apAllocatorBase_<>** that use other allocation schemes.

apAlloc<> is a simple interface that the application uses to manage memory. **apAlloc<>** uses an **apAllocator_<>** object as one of its parameters to determine how to manage memory. By default, **apAlloc<>** allocates memory off the heap, because this is what our **apAllocator_<>** object does. However, if the application requires a different memory management scheme, a new derived allocator object can be easily created and passed to **apAlloc<>**.

apAllocatorBase_<> Class

The **apAllocatorBase_<>** base class contains the raw pointers and methods to access memory. It provides both access to the raw storage pointer, and access to the reference count pointing to shared storage, while also defining a reference counting mechanism. **apAllocatorBase_<>** takes a single template parameter that specifies the unit of memory to be allocated. The full base class definition is shown here.

```
template<class T> class apAllocatorBase_
{
public:
    apAllocatorBase_ (unsigned int n, unsigned int align)
    : pRaw_ (0), pData_ (0), ref_ (0), size_ (n), align_ (align)
    {}
```

```
    // Derived classes alloc memory; store details in base class

    virtual ~apAllocatorBase_ () {}
    // Derived classes will deallocate memory

    operator          T* ()          { return pData_;}
    operator const T* () const { return pData_;}
    // Conversion to pointer of allocated memory type

    unsigned int size  () const { return size_;}   // Number of elements
    unsigned int ref   () const { return ref_;}    // Number of references
    unsigned int align () const { return align_;}  // Alignment

    void addRef () { ref_++; }
    void subRef ()
    {
      --ref_;
      if (ref_ == 0) delete this;
    }
    // Increment or decrement the reference count
protected:
    virtual void allocate   () = 0;
    virtual void deallocate () = 0;
    // Used to allocate/deallocate memory.

    T* alignPointer (void* raw);
    // Align the specified pointer to match our alignment

    apAllocatorBase_               (const apAllocatorBase_& src);
    apAllocatorBase_& operator= (const apAllocatorBase_& src);
    // No copy or assignment allowed.

    char*         pRaw_;   // Raw allocated pointer
    T*            pData_;  // Aligned pointer to our memory
    unsigned int size_;   // Number of elements allocated
    unsigned int ref_;    // Reference count
    unsigned int align_;  // Memory alignment (modulus)
};
```

❖ ALLOCATION AND DEALLOCATION

You'll notice that the constructor in **apAllocatorBase_** doesn't do anything other than initialize the object variables. We would have liked to have had the base class handle allocation and deallocation too, but doing so would have locked derived classes into heap allocation. This isn't obvious, until you consider how objects are constructed, as we will see in the next example.

▶ **EXAMPLE**

Suppose we designed the base class and included allocate and deallocate functions as shown:

✗

```
template<class T> class apAllocatorBase_
    {
public:
    apAllocatorBase_ (unsigned int n) : size_ (n) { allocate ();}
    virtual ~apAllocatorBase_ ()                  { deallocate();}

    virtual void allocate () { pData_ = new T [size_];}
    virtual void deallocate () { delete [] pData_;}
    };
```

It appears that we could derive an object, **apAllocatorCustom**<>, from **apAllocatorBase_**<> and override the **allocate()** and **deallocate()** methods. There is nothing to stop you from doing this, but you won't get the desired results. The reason is that when the **apAllocatorBase_**<> constructor runs, it obtains its definition for **allocate()** and **deallocate()** from the base class, because the derived versions are not available until the object is fully constructed.

Watch out for bugs introduced in the constructor of base and other parent classes. Make sure an object is fully constructed before calling any virtual function.

We found it cleaner to define a base class, **apAllocatorBase_**<>, and later derive the object **apAllocator_**<> from it. The derived object handles the actual allocation and deallocation. This makes creating custom memory management schemes very simple. **apAlloc**<> simply takes an **apAllocator_**<> object of the appropriate type and uses that memory management scheme.

We made **apAllocatorBase_**<> an abstract class by doing the following:

```
virtual void allocate   () = 0;
virtual void deallocate () = 0;
```

apAllocatorBase_<> never calls these functions directly, but by adding them we provide an obvious clue as to what functions need to be implemented in the derived class.

❖ CONVERSION OPERATORS

Let's take a look at the non-obvious accessor functions in **apAllocatorBase_**<>:

```
operator       T* ()       { return pData_;}
operator const T* () const { return pData_;}
```

We define two different types of **T*** conversion operators, one that is **const** and one that isn't. This is a hint to the compiler on how to convert from **apAlloc**<> to a **T*** without having to explicitly specify it. See Section 8.2.2 on page 283.

It isn't always the right choice to define these conversion operators. We chose to use **operator T*** because **apAlloc**<> is fairly simple and is little more than a wrapper around a memory pointer. By simple, we mean that there is little confusion if the compiler were to use **operator T*** to convert the object reference to a pointer.

▶ **EXAMPLE**

For more complex objects, we could have used a **data()** method for accessing memory, which would look like:

```
T* data     () { return pData_;}
```

This means that we would have to explicitly ask for a memory pointer by using the **data()** method as follows:

```
apAllocatorBase_ a (...);
T* p1 = a;    // Requires operator T* to be defined.
T* p2 = a.data();
```

Note that the STL **string** class also chooses not to define conversion operators, but rather uses the **c_str()** and **data()** methods for directly accessing the memory. The STL purposely does not include implicit conversion operators to prevent the misuse of raw string pointers.

❖ REFERENCE COUNTING

Next we'll look at the functions that manage our reference count.

```
void addRef () { ref_++;}
void subRef () { if (--ref_ == 0) delete this;}
```

These methods are defined in the base class for convenience but are only used in the derived class. Whenever an **apAllocatorBase_<>** object is constructed or copied, **addRef()** is called to increment our reference count variable. Likewise, whenever an object is deleted or otherwise detached from the object, **subRef()** is called. When the reference count becomes zero, the object is deleted. Note that later we will modify the definitions for **addRef()** and **subRef()** to handle multi-threaded synchronization issues.

❖ MEMORY ALIGNMENT

Memory alignment is important because some applications might want more control over the pointer returned after memory is allocated. Most applications prefer to leave memory alignment to the compiler, letting it return whatever address it wants. We provide memory alignment capability in **apAllocatorBase_<>** so that derived classes can allocate memory on a specific boundary. On some platforms, this technique can be used to optimize performance. This is especially useful for imaging applications, because image processing algorithms can be optimized for particular memory alignments.

When a derived class allocates memory, it stores a pointer to that memory in **pRaw_**, which is defined as a **char***. Once the memory is aligned, the **char*** is cast to type **T*** and stored in **pData_**, which serves as a pointer to the aligned memory.

alignPointer() is defined in **apAllocatorBase_<>** to force a pointer to have a certain alignment. The implementation presented here is acceptable for single-threaded applications and is sufficient for our current needs. Later it will be extended to handle multi-threaded applications. Here is the final version of this implementation:

```
T* alignPointer (void* raw)
{
  T* p = reinterpret_cast<T*>(
    (reinterpret_cast<uintptr_t>(raw) + align_ - 1)
    & ~(align_ - 1));
  return p;
}
```

Here is how we arrived at this implementation: in order to perform the alignment arithmetic, we need to change the data type to some type of numeric value. The following statement accomplishes this by casting our **raw** pointer to a **uintptr_t** (a type large enough to hold a pointer):

```
reinterpret_cast<uintptr_t>(raw)
```

By subsequently casting the **raw** pointer to an **uintptr_t**, we're able to do the actual alignment arithmetic, as follows:

```
(reinterpret_cast<uintptr_t>(raw) + align_ - 1) & ~(align_ - 1);
```

Basically, we want to round up the address, if necessary, so that the address is of the desired alignment. The only way to guarantee a certain alignment is to allocate more bytes than necessary (in our case, we must allocate **(align_-1)** additional bytes). **alignPointer()** works for any alignment that is a power of two.

For example, if **align_** has the value of 4 (4-byte alignment), then the code would operate as follows:

```
(reinterpret_cast<uintptr_t>(raw) + 3) & ~3);
```

It now becomes clear that we are trying to round the address up to the next multiple of 4. If the address is already aligned on this boundary, this operation does not change the memory address; it merely wastes 3 bytes of memory. The only thing left is to cast this pointer back to the desired type. We use **reinterpret_cast<>** to accomplish this, since we must force a cast between pointer and integer data types.

Conversely, this example uses old C-style casting:

✗
```
T* p = (T*)(((uintptr_t)(raw + align_ - 1)) & ~(align_ - 1));
```

This is still legal, but it doesn't make it obvious what our casts are doing. Note that for systems that do not define the symbol **uintptr_t**, you can usually define your own as:

```
typedef int uintptr_t;
```

 Stop using C-style casting and start using the C++ casting operators. reinterpret_cast<> and static_cast<> allow you to perform arbitrary casting and the casting operators make your intent clear. It is also easier to search for using an editor.

❖ COPY CONSTRUCTOR AND ASSIGNMENT

The only thing we haven't discussed from **apAllocatorBase_<>** is the copy constructor and assignment operator:

```
apAllocatorBase_            (const apAllocatorBase_& src);
apAllocatorBase_& operator= (const apAllocatorBase_& src);
// No copy or assignment is allowed.
```

We include a copy constructor and assignment operator, but don't provide an implementation for them. This causes the compiler to generate an error if either of these functions is ever called. This is intentional. These functions are not necessary, and worse, will cause our reference counting to break if the default versions were to run. Once an **apAllocatorBase_<>** object or derived object is created, we only reference them using pointers.

apAllocator_<> Class

The **apAllocator_<>** class, which is derived from **apAllocatorBase_<>**, handles heap-based allocation and deallocation. Its definition is shown here

```
template<class T> class apAllocator_ : public apAllocatorBase_<T>
{
public:
    explicit apAllocator_ (unsigned int n, unsigned int align = 0)
    : apAllocatorBase_<T> (n, align)
    {
        allocate ();
        addRef ();
    }

  virtual ~apAllocator_ () { deallocate();}

private:
    virtual void allocate () ;
  // Allocate our memory for size_ elements of type T with the
  // alignment specified by align_. 0 and 1 specify no alignment,
  // 2 = word alignment, 4 = 4-byte alignment, ... This must
  // be a power of 2.

  virtual void deallocate ();

  apAllocator_              (const apAllocator_& src);
  apAllocator_& operator= (const apAllocator_& src);
  // No copy or assignment is allowed.
};
```

Constructor and Destructor

The **apAllocator_<>** constructor handles memory allocation, memory alignment, and setting the initial reference count value. The destructor deletes the memory when the object is destroyed.

The implementation of the constructor is:

```
public:
    explicit apAllocator_ (unsigned int n, unsigned int align = 0)
    : apAllocatorBase_<T> (n, align)
    {
      allocate ();
      addRef ();
    }

  virtual ~apAllocator_ () { deallocate();}

    ...
```

```
private:
    apAllocator_               (const apAllocator_& src);
    apAllocator_& operator= (const apAllocator_& src);
    // No copy or assignment is allowed.
```

❖ MEMORY ALIGNMENT

The **apAllocator_<>** constructor takes two arguments, a size parameter and an alignment parameter.

Although the alignment parameter is an **unsigned int**, it can only take certain values. A value of 0 or 1 indicates alignment on a byte boundary; in other words, no special alignment is needed. A value of 2 means that memory must be aligned on a word (i.e., 2-byte) boundary. A value of 4 means that memory must be aligned on a 4-byte boundary.

▶ **EXAMPLE**

Suppose we use operator **new** to allocate memory and we receive a memory pointer, **0x87654325**. This hexidecimal value indicates where storage was allocated for us in memory. For most applications, this address is fine for our needs. The compiler makes sure that the address is appropriate for the type of object we are allocating. Different alignment values will alter this memory address, as shown in Table 3.2.

Table 3.2: Effect of Alignment on Memory Address

Alignment	Memory Address
0 or 1	0x87654325
2	0x87654326
4	0x87654328
8	0x87654328

❖ REFERENCE COUNTING

The constructor also calls **addRef()** directly. This means that the client code does not have to explicitly touch the reference count when an **apAllocator_<>** object is created. The reference count is set to 1 when the object is constructed.

What would happen if the client does call **addRef()**? This would break the reference counting scheme because the reference count would be 2 instead of 1. When the object is no longer used and the final instance of **apAllocator_<>** calls **subRef()**, the reference count would be decremented to 1 instead of to 0. We would end up with an object in heap memory that would never be freed.

Similarly, if we decided to leave out the call to **addRef()** in the constructor and force the client to call it explicitly, it could also lead to problems. If the client forgets to call **addRef()**, the reference count stays at zero. Our strategy is to make it very clear through the comments embedded in the code about what is responsible for updating the reference count.

❖ EXPLICIT KEYWORD USAGE

We use the **explicit** keyword in the constructor. This keyword prevents the compiler from using the constructor to perform an implicit conversion from type **unsigned int** to type **apAllocator_<>**. The **explicit** keyword can only be used with constructors that take a single argument, and our constructor has two arguments. Or does it? Since most users do not care about memory alignment, the second constructor argument has a default value of 0 for alignment (i.e., perform no alignment). So, this constructor can look as if it has only a single argument (i.e., **apAllocator_<char> alloc (5);**).

> Use the **explicit** keyword to eliminate the chance that single-argument constructors will be misused by the compiler for implicit conversions.

Allocation

The constructor calls the **allocate()** function to perform the actual memory allocation. The full implementation of this function is as follows:

```
protected:
  virtual void allocate ()
  {
    if (size_ == 0) {
      // Eliminate possibility of null pointers by allocating 1 item.
      pData_ = new T [1];
      pRaw_  = 0;
      return;
    }

    if (align_ < 2) {
      // Let the compiler worry about any alignment
      pData_ = new T [size_];
      pRaw_  = 0;
    }
    else {
      // Allocate additional bytes to guarantee alignment.
      // Then align and cast to our desired data type.
      pRaw_  = new char [sizeof(T) * size_ + (align_ - 1)];
      pData_ = alignPointer (pRaw_);
    }
  }
```

Our **allocate()** function has three cases it considers.

■ The first is what to do when an allocation of zero bytes is requested. This is a very common programming concern, because we cannot allow the user to obtain a null pointer (or worse, an uninitialized pointer). We can eliminate all of this checking by simply allocating a single element of type **T**. By doing this, our definition for **operator T*** in the base class never has to check the pointer first. And, because, our **size()** method will return zero in this case, the client code can safely get a valid pointer that it presumably will never use.

■ The next case that **allocate()** considers is when no memory alignment is desired. Since this is a common case, we bypass our alignment code and let the compiler decide how to allocate memory:

```
pData_ = new T [size_];
```

Our function uses two pointers, **pData_** and **pRaw_**, to manage our heap allocation. **pData_** is a **T*** pointer, which references the aligned memory. **pRaw_** contains the pointer returned after calling **operator new**. Since we do not perform any alignment, we don't use the **pRaw_** pointer in this case, so we set this variable to **0**.

■ Our final case in **allocate()** is when a specific kind of memory alignment is desired; for example, as it does when managing images using third-party imaging libraries. Many libraries require memory alignment to avoid the performance hit of copying images. We use the **pRaw_** pointer (defined as a **char***) for the allocation, and then align and coerce the pointer to be compatible with **pData_**:

```
pRaw_  = new char [sizeof(T) * size_ + (align_ - 1)];
pData_ = alignPointer (pRaw_);
```

Our base class provides a function, **alignPointer()**, to handle the alignment and conversion to type **T***. We saw how this function can alter the memory address by up to **(align_-1)** bytes during alignment. For this reason, we must allocate an additional **(align_-1)** bytes when we make the allocation, to make sure we never access memory outside of our allocation.

Deallocation

Our **deallocate()** function must cope with the **pRaw_** and **pData_** pointers. Whenever we bypass performing our own memory alignment, the **pRaw_** variable will always be null. This is all our function needs to know to delete the appropriate pointer. The **deallocate()** definition is as follows:

```
virtual void deallocate ()
{
  // Decide which pointer we delete
  if (pRaw_)
    delete [] pRaw_;
  else
    delete [] pData_;
  pRaw_  = 0;
  pData_ = 0;
}
```

At the end of the **deallocate()** function, we set both the **pRaw_** and **pData_** variables to their initial state (**0**). Some developers will skip this step, because **deallocate()** is only called by the destructor, so in an attempt to be clever, a possible bug is introduced. Sometime in the future, the **deallocate()** function may also be used in other places, such as during an assignment operation. In this case, the values of **pRaw_** and **pData_** will appear to point to valid memory.

 Whenever memory is deallocated in any function other than the destructor, remember to set all memory pointers to 0.

---

apAlloc<> Class

apAlloc<> is our memory allocation object. This is the object that applications will use directly to allocate and manage memory. The definition is shown here.

```
template<class T, class A = apAllocator_<T> >
class apAlloc
{
public:
  static apAlloc& gNull ();
  // We return this object for any null allocations
  // It actually allocates 1 byte to make all the member
  // functions valid.

  apAlloc ();
  // Null allocation. Returns pointer to gNull() memory

  explicit apAlloc (unsigned int size, unsigned int align=0);
  ~apAlloc ();
  // Allocate the specified bytes, with the correct alignment.
  // 0 and 1 specify no alignment. 2 = word alignment,
  // 4 = 4-byte alignment. Must be a power of 2.

  apAlloc           (const apAlloc& src);
  apAlloc& operator= (const apAlloc& src);
  // We need our own copy constructor and assignment operator.

  unsigned int  size   () const { return pMem_->size ();}
  unsigned int  ref    () const { return pMem_->ref ();}
  bool          isNull () const { return (pMem_ == gNull().pMem_);}

  const T* data () const { return *pMem_;}
  T*       data ()       { return *pMem_;}
  // Access to the beginning of our memory region. Use sparingly

  const T& operator[] (unsigned int index) const;
  T&       operator[] (unsigned int index);
  // Access a specific element. Throws the STL range_error if
  // index is invalid.

  virtual A* clone ();
  // Duplicate the memory in the underlying apAllocator.

  void duplicate ();
  // Breaks any reference counting and forces this object to
  // have its own copy.

protected:
    A*   pMem_;   // Pointer to our allocated memory

  static apAlloc* sNull_; // Our null object
};
```

The syntax may look a little imposing because **apAlloc<>** has two template parameters:
```
template<class T, class A> class apAlloc
```

 The keywords **class** and **typename** are synonymous for
template parameters. Use whichever keyword you are more
comfortable with, but be consistent.

Parameter **T** specifies the unit of allocation. If we had only a single parameter, the meaning
of it would be identical to the meaning for other STL types. For example,

```
vector<int> v;
apAlloc<int> a;
```

describe instances of a template whose unit of storage is an **int**.

Parameter **A** specifies how and where memory is allocated. It refers to another template
object whose job is to allocate and delete memory, manage reference counting, and
allow access to the underlying data. If we have an application that requires memory
to be allocated differently, say a private memory heap, we would derive a specific
apAllocator_<> object to do just that.

In our case, the second parameter, **A**, uses the default implementation **apAllocator_<>** to
allocate memory from the heap. This allows us to write such statements as:

```
apAlloc<int> a1;          // Null allocation
apAlloc<int> a2 (100);    // 100 elements
apAlloc<int> a3 (100, 4); // 100 elements, 4-byte align
```

The null allocation, an allocation with no specified size, is of special interest because of how
we implement it. We saw that the **apAllocator_<>** object supported null allocations by
allocating one element. It is possible that many (even hundreds) of null **apAlloc<>** objects
may be in existence. This wastes heap memory and causes heap fragmentation.

Our solution is to only ever have a single null object for each **apAlloc<>** instance. We do
this in a manner similar to constructing a Singleton object. Singleton objects are typically
used to create only a single instance of a given class. See [Gamma95] for a comprehensive
description of the Singleton design pattern. We use a pointer, **sNull_**, and a **gNull()**
method to accomplish this:

```
template<class T, class A>
apAlloc<T,A>* apAlloc<T, A>::sNull_ = 0;
```

This statement creates our **sNull_** pointer and sets it to null.

❖ GNULL() METHOD

The only way to access this pointer is through the **gNull()** method, whose implementation
is shown here.

```
template<class T, class A>
apAlloc<T,A>& apAlloc<T, A>::gNull ()
```

```
{
  if (!sNull_)
    sNull_ = new apAlloc (0);
  return *sNull_;
}
```

The first time **gNull()** is called, **sNull_** is zero, so the single instance is allocated by calling **apAlloc()**. For this and subsequent calls, **gNull()** returns a reference to this object. A null **apAlloc<>** object is created by passing zero to the **apAlloc<>** constructor. This is a special case. When zero is passed to the **apAllocator_<>** object to do the allocation, a single element is actually created so that we never have to worry about null pointers. In this case, all null allocations refer to the same object. Note that this behavior differs from the C++ standard, which specifies that each null object is unique.

gNull() can be used directly, but its main use is to support the null constructor.

```
template<class T, class A>
apAlloc<T, A>::apAlloc () : pMem_ (0)
{
  pMem_ = gNull().pMem_;
  pMem_->addRef ();
}
```

apAlloc<> contains a pointer to our allocator object, **pMem_**. The constructor copies the pointer and tells the **pMem_** object to increase its reference count. The result is that any code that constructs a null **apAlloc<>** object will actually point to the same **gNull()** object. So, why didn't we just write the constructor as:

```
*this = gNull();
```

This statement assigns our object to use the same memory as that used by **gNull()**. We will discuss the copy constructor and assignment operator in a moment. The problem is that we are inside our constructor and the assignment assumes that the object is already constructed. On the surface it may look like a valid thing to do, but the assignment operator needs to access the object pointed to by **pMem_**, and this pointer is null.

Assignment Operator and Copy Constructor

The assignment operator and copy constructor are similar, so we will only look at the assignment operator here:

```
template<class T, class A>
apAlloc<T, A>& apAlloc<T, A>::operator= (const apAlloc& src)
{
  // Make sure we don't copy ourself!
  if (pMem_ == src.pMem_) return *this;

  // Remove reference from existing object. addRef() and subRef()
  // do not throw so we don't have to worry about catching an error
  pMem_->subRef ();   // Remove reference from existing object
  pMem_ = src.pMem_;
  pMem_->addRef ();   // Add reference to our new object

  return *this;
}
```

First, we must detach from whatever memory allocation we were using by calling **subRef()** on our allocated object. If this was the only object using the **apAllocator_<>** object, it would be deleted at this time. Next, we point to the same **pMem_** object that our **src** object is using, and increase its reference count. Because we never have to allocate new memory and copy the data, these operations are very fast.

Memory Access

Accessing memory is handled in two different ways. We provide both **const** and non-**const** versions of each to satisfy the needs of our clients. To access the pointer at the beginning of memory, we use:

```
T* data () { return *pMem_;}
```

When we discussed the **apAllocatorBase_<>** object, we talked about when it is appropriate to use **operator T*** and when a function like **data()** should instead be used. In **apAllocatorBase_<>**, we chose to use the operator syntax so that ***pMem_** will return a pointer to the start of our memory. In this **apAlloc<>** object, we use the **data()** method to grant access to memory, because we want clients to explicitly state their intention. **operator[]** prevents the user from accessing invalid data, as shown:

```
template<class T, class A>
T& apAlloc<T, A>::operator[] (unsigned int index)
{
  if (index >= size())
    throw std::range_error ("Index out of range");

  return *(data() + index);
}
```

Instead of creating a new exception type to throw, we reuse the **range_error** exception defined by the STL.

Object Duplication

The **duplicate()** method gives us the ability to duplicate an object, while letting both objects have separate copies of the underlying data. Suppose we have the following code:

```
apAlloc<int> alloc1(10);
apAlloc<int> alloc2 = alloc1;
```

Right now, these two objects point to the same underlying data. But what if we want to force them to use separate copies? This is the purpose of **duplicate()**, whose implementation is shown here:

```
template<class T, class A>
void apAlloc<T, A>::duplicate ()
{
  if (ref() == 1) return;  // No need to duplicate

  A* copy = clone ();
  pMem_->subRef ();  // Remove reference from existing object
  pMem_ = copy;      // Replace it with our duplicated data
}
```

Notice that this is very similar to our assignment operator, except that we use our **clone()** method to duplicate the actual memory. Instead of putting the copy functionality inside **duplicate()**, we place it inside **clone()** to allow clients to specify a custom **clone()** method for classes derived from **apAlloc<>**. This version of **clone()** does a shallow copy (meaning a bit-wise copy) on the underlying data:

```
template<class T, class A>
A* apAlloc<T, A>::clone ()
{
  A* copy = new A (pMem_->size(), pMem_->align());

  // Shallow copy
  T* src = *pMem_;
  T* dst = *copy;
  std::copy (src, &(src[pMem_->size()]), dst);
  return copy;
}
```

Under most conditions, a shallow copy is appropriate. We run into problems if **T** is a complex object or structure that includes pointers that cannot be copied by means of a shallow copy. Our image class is not affected by this issue because our images are constructed from basic types. Instead of using **memcpy()** to duplicate the data, we are using **std::copy** to demonstrate how it performs the same function.

3.2 Prototyping

Our strong recommendation is that any development plan should include some amount of time for prototyping. Prototyping has a number of advantages and can directly affect the success of a commercial software development effort. Our rules of thumb for prototyping are shown in Figure 3.5.

Prototyping Rules

✔ **Explore the hardest parts of the problem first in your prototypes.**

✔ **Use good coding practices in your prototypes.**

✔ **Document your prototypes even more heavily than actual production code, so that your design ideas are recorded.**

✔ **Experiment with different language elements to see how they affect the design and implementation.**

✔ **Take what you learn in one prototype and apply it to hone the next prototype.**

✔ **Write unit tests for your prototypes.**

✔ **Make sure that the compilers on all your platforms can predictably handle the prototypes and language constructs.**

✔ **Never distribute your prototypes as finished software products.**

Figure 3.5: Prototyping Rules

3.2.1 Why Prototyping Works

In our own commercial development efforts, we have consistently shown that by including prototyping as part of the process, the product is completed on time with full functionality. Why? Here are some of the reasons:

- **Early Visibility to Problems**. Prototypes help refine the design to produce the desired final product. More than that, prototyping is a necessary and important step in the design process. Errors can be caught during the prototyping stage instead of during actual development. Prototyping allows you to modify the design to avoid mistakes and it provides better visibility of what is required to complete the final product. Had you discovered the mistake during the development phase, it could negatively affect both the content of the product and the schedule for releasing the product.

- **Measurement of Performance and Code Size**. The intent of the prototype isn't to develop the product, but to develop ideas and a framework for the design. Good coding practices are as important here as they are for any other part of the design, including documentation and unit tests. Yes, unit tests. Otherwise, how else can you tell if the prototype is performing correctly? The unit test framework is also a good way to measure performance and code size. If a prototype is successful, it might be used as the basis for the real design. Prototypes only need to implement a small portion of the overall solution. By keeping the problem space limited, one or more features can be developed and tested in a very structured environment.

- **Assurance of Cross-Platform Compatibility**. Prototypes are also useful when the product must run on multiple platforms or on an embedded system. It might be obvious how something is designed on one platform, but the design may not work as well on others. This is especially true in the embedded platform world, because the problem is constrained by execution time and hardware resources (i.e., processor speed, memory, and the file system). Prototypes can also help decide which compiler(s) and version to use. The C++ standard library has evolved in recent years and compiler vendors are still trying to catch up. You should learn at the prototyping stage that your desired compiler will or will not work as planned. Once the compiler is chosen, you still must see if the included standard library will work, or whether a third-party version is needed.

- **Test Bed for Language Features**. Prototypes are also great for trying out new concepts or language features. This is especially true with the somewhat complex nature of templates. It is not always obvious how a final template object might look, or how it might interact with other objects. This is often found during the design phase, and some small prototypes can help guide the implementor. In our image class design, the use of templates is not necessarily obvious from the beginning.

3.2.2 Common Fears

There are a number of common fears and misconceptions about prototyping. We discuss some of the prevalent ones here.

One of the most common fears is that prototypes will be turned into the actual released software to save time and effort. This is especially true if your management is shown a prototype that looks like the desired final product. It can give the erroneous impression that the product is closer to completion than is actually the case. The problem with this scenario isn't that the prototype gave an incorrect impression, but rather that the expectations of management weren't properly set. Part of the development manager's role is to clearly set the expectations for any demonstration. Clearly explaining exactly what is being shown is part of that responsibility. If this is done well, management need not get a false impression.

Another common misconception about prototyping is that it will delay the actual design and implementation phases and result in making the product late. In actuality, prototyping is an iterative process with the design and implementation phases. By clarifying the most difficult aspects of the design, prototyping can actually result in avoiding costly mistakes and bringing the product in on time.

3.2.3 Our Image Framework Prototyping Strategy

In Chapter 2, we showed our first attempt to design an image object to handle the simple problem of generating a thumbnail image. We presented this test application to show how easy it is to design an object that solves a simple problem. Not unexpectedly, this application is totally inadequate for solving real-world problems and certainly unsuitable for our image framework. In this section, we use the prototyping strategy shown in Figure 3.6 to look at various aspects of image objects, to ensure that our image framework meets the standards of commercial software.

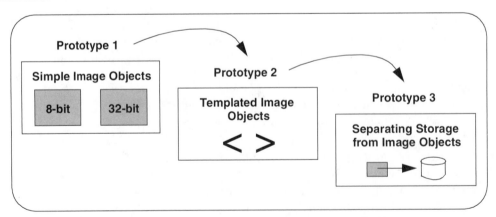

Figure 3.6: Image Framework Prototyping Strategy

We have chosen a prototyping strategy that lets us investigate three different aspects of the problem. In Prototype 1, we look at the common elements of images with different pixel types (8-bit versus 32-bit) to help us create a cleaner design. In Prototype 2, we explore whether using templates is a better way to handle the similarities between images with different pixel types. Once we started exploring templates, it became clear that there are both image data and image storage components. In Prototype 3, we investigate the feasibility of separating these components in our design.

3.2.4 Prototype 1: Simple Image Objects

Prototype 1 is designed to explore the similarities between images of different pixel types. Remember that our test application defined a pixel as an **unsigned char** to specify monochrome images with 256 levels of gray (this is frequently called an 8-bit image, or an 8-bit grayscale image). 8-bit images are still very popular in applications for security, medical imaging, and machine vision, but they represent just one of many image formats. Other popular monochrome formats define pixels with depths of 16 bits and 32 bits per pixel. The larger the pixel depth, the more grayscale information is contained. And while 8 bits may be sufficient for a security application, 16 bits might be necessary for an astronomical application. In some cases, a monochrome image sensor may produce images that contain 10 bits or 12 bits of information. However, images of these odd depths are treated as 16-bit images with the higher-order bits set to zero.

Prototype 1 explores two types of monochrome images: an 8-bit image like our test application, and a 32-bit image, as shown in Figure 3.7.

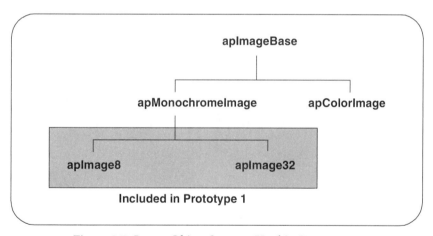

Figure 3.7: Image Object Strategy Used in Prototype 1

To be precise, our 8-bit image is represented by an **unsigned char**, and our 32-bit image is represented by an **unsigned int**. Each prototype object defines a simple class to create an image and supports one image processing operation, such as creating a thumbnail image.

Like any good prototyping strategy, we keep features from the test application that worked and add new features, as shown in Table 3.3.

Table 3.3: Features Reused and Added to Prototype 1

Reused Features	New Features
Simple construction	Uses **apAlloc<>**
Access to pixel data via **getPixel()** and **setPixel()**	Access to pixel data via **pixels()** for faster access
	thumbnail is a member function instead of a global function

The definition for **apImage8** is shown here.

```
typedef unsigned char Pel8;

class apImage8
{
public:
  apImage8 ();
  apImage8 (int width, int height);
  // Creates a null image, or the specified size

  virtual ~apImage8 ();

  int width  () const { return width_;}
  int height () const { return height_;}

  const Pel8* pixels () const { return pixels_.data();}
  Pel8*       pixels ()       { return pixels_.data();}
  // Return pointer to start of pixel data

  Pel8 getPixel (int x, int y) const;
  void setPixel (int x, int y, Pel8 pixel);
  // Get/set a single pixel

  // Image operations (only one for the prototype)
  virtual apImage8 thumbnail (int reduction) const;

  // Default copy ctor and assignment are ok
protected:
  apAlloc<Pel8> pixels_; // Pixel data
  int           width_;  // Image dimensions
  int           height_;
};
```

The definition for **apImage32** is shown here.

```
typedef unsigned int Pel32;

class apImage32
{
public:
  apImage32 ();
  apImage32 (int width, int height);
  // Creates a null image, or the specified size

  virtual ~apImage32 ();
```

```
int width  () const { return width_;}
int height () const { return height_;}

const Pel32* pixels () const { return pixels_.data();}
Pel32*       pixels ()       { return pixels_.data();}
// Return pointer to start of pixel data

Pel32 getPixel (int x, int y) const;
void setPixel (int x, int y, Pel32 pixel);
// Get/set a single pixel

// Image operations (only one for the prototype)
virtual apImage32 thumbnail (int reduction) const;

// Default copy ctor and assignment are ok
protected:
  apAlloc<Pel32> pixels_; // Pixel data
  int            width_;  // Image dimensions
  int            height_;
};
```

The first thing to notice about the **apImage8** and **apImage32** objects is that a **typedef** is used to define the pixel type. It not only offers a convenient shorthand, but it is clear in our code when we deal with pixels. And before anyone asks, we did think of calling them **apPel8** and **apPel32** instead of just **Pel8** and **Pel32**, but we resisted. You also might notice that we are using an **int** to represent the width and height of the image. Some might argue that this should be an **unsigned int**, but for a prototype, we feel it is acceptable to make things simpler.

When you ignore the image references, **apImage8** and **apImage32** are little more than a wrapper around **apAlloc<>**. This is clear when you look at a few functions:

```
apImage8::apImage8 () : width_ (0), height_ (0) {}

apImage8::apImage8 (int width, int height)
: width_ (width), height_ (height)
{ pixels_ = apAlloc<Pel8> (width*height);}

apImage8::~apImage8 () {}

Pel8 apImage8::getPixel (int x, int y) const
{ return pixels_[y*width_ + x];}

void apImage8::setPixel (int x, int y, Pel8 pixel)
{ pixels_[y*width_ + x] = pixel;}
```

Our prototype may not break any new ground when it comes to image processing, but it already shows the benefits of using our memory allocation object. Our **apImage8** constructor makes **apAlloc<>** do all the work and our calls to **getPixel()** and **setPixel()** use **operator[]** of **apAlloc<>**.

❖ COPY CONSTRUCTOR

It gets even better. We don't define a copy constructor or assignment operator, because the default version works fine. If this isn't clear, look at what our copy constructor would look like if we wrote one:

```
apImage8::apImage8 (const apImage8& src)
{
  pixels_ = src.pixels_;
  width_  = src.width_;
  height_ = src.height_;
}
```

pixels_ is an instance of **apAlloc<>** and **width_** and **height_** are just simple types. Since **apAlloc<>** has its own copy constructor we just let the compiler take care of this for us.

The **thumbnail()** method performs the same function as in our test application; however, its implementation is much cleaner. The output thumbnail image is created like any local variable, and returned at the end of the function. We saw how simple the copy constructor is, so even if the compiler creates some temporary copies, the overhead is extremely low. When we wrote the **thumbnail()** definition this time, we were careful with our naming convention. Variables **x** and **y** refer to coordinates in the original image and **tx** and **ty** refer to coordinates in the thumbnail image. So even though there are 4 nested loops, the code is still fairly easy to follow. The **thumbnail()** method is as follows:

❖ THUMBNAIL() METHOD

```
apImage8 apImage8::thumbnail (unsigned int reduction) const
{
  apImage8 output (width()/reduction, height()/reduction);

  for (unsigned int ty=0; ty<output.height(); ty++) {
    for (unsigned int tx=0; tx<output.width(); tx++) {
      unsigned int sum = 0;
      for (unsigned int y=0; y<reduction; y++) {
        for (unsigned int x=0; x<reduction; x++)
          sum += getPixel (tx*reduction+x, ty*reduction+y);
      }
      output.setPixel (tx, ty, sum / (reduction*reduction));
    }
  }

  return output;
}
```

If you compare the code for **apImage8** and **apImage32**, you find that they are almost identical. This is no great surprise, but the prototype shows this very clearly. This similarity leads to two thoughts. The first (historically) is to see how derivation can help simplify our design and maximize code reuse. The second is to see how templates can remove all of this duplicate code.

▶ **EXAMPLE**

Before templates were readily available, the image design could have been (and often actually was) handled by deriving each image from a common base class. As Figure 3.7 on page 47 indicates, we could derive our **apImage8** object from an **apMonochromeImage** object, which itself could be derived from **apImageBase**. Color images could also be handled by this framework by deriving from an **apColorImage** class. Although we aren't going to present a full solution for this type of framework, let's look at one of the issues that would arise by taking a look at the **thumbnail()** definition:

```
class apImageBase
{
public:
    ...
    virtual apImageBase thumbnail (unsigned int reduction) const;
    ...
protected:
    apAlloc<Pel8> pixels_;
    int          type_;
    int          width_;
    int          height_;
};
```

You can see there is a new variable, **type_**, which is used to track what kind of image this is. This might be just the pixel depth of the image, an enumeration, or any other unique value to specify the image. The variables **width_** and **height_** have the same definition as in our prototype, but now **pixels_** is always defined as a buffer of **Pel8**s. This is not necessarily bad, although it means that **pixels_** must be cast to different types in derived classes. And these casts should exist in only a single place to keep everything maintainable. Our **thumbnail()** function returns an **apImageBase** object, not the type of the actual image computed in the derived class. This is a common issue and is discussed at length in other books. See [Meyers98]. As this example illustrates, it takes a bit of work, but you can construct a framework that does hold together.

Moving forward, we want to investigate the use of templates in our next prototypes to figure out how the final image class should be implemented.

Summary of Lessons Learned

These are the things that worked well:

- Using **apAlloc<>** helped us eliminate our copy constructor and assignment operator, made worrying about temporary images unimportant, and greatly improved the readability of the code.

- By extending the test application to explore two different image classes, we observed that the implementations are very similar. This similarity seems to lend itself to a derivation class design, or perhaps the use of templates. It is something we need to explore in future prototypes.

3.2.5 Prototype 2: Templated Image Objects

In Prototype 1, we extended our test application to show that image objects of different types are actually very similar. Derivation is one possible option for handling this similarity, but it forces all images into a single class hierarchy. Another way to handle this similarity is by the use of templates, with the goal of simplifying the design and maximizing the amount of code reuse.

We use Prototype 2 to investigate a number of new features:

- We use templates and rewrite the image class, **apImage**, to take a template parameter **T** that represents the pixel type.

- We introduce a handle class idiom so that many **apImage<>** handle objects can share the same underlying **apImageRep<>** representation object.

- We verify that our design works with more complex image types, such as an RGB image.

Use of Templates

Foremost in this prototype is the need to verify that a template object is the correct representation to solve our problem. Our test application only handled an 8-bit monochrome image (i.e., **unsigned char**), and Prototype 1 added a 32-bit monochrome image (i.e., **unsigned int**). Due to the similarity of the **apImage8** and **apImage32** objects, it makes sense to turn it directly into a template object, as shown in Figure 3.8:

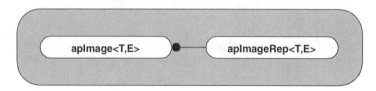

Figure 3.8: Templated Image Object Design

In Prototype 2, we introduce the *handle class idiom*, where there is a representation class that contains the data and performs all the operations, and a handle class that is a pointer to the representation class. In our prototype, **apImageRep<>** is the representation class to which the handle class **apImage<>** points.

We begin Prototype 2 by looking at the relevant parts of our **apImage<>** object from Prototype 1. It is not always clear from the outset how the prototype will be completed. Converting the **apImage<>** object into a template object gives us:

```
template<class T> class apImage
{
public:
  apImage  ();
  apImage  (unsigned int width, unsigned int height);
  ~apImage ();

  const T* pixels () const;
  T*       pixels ();

  T getPixel (unsigned int x, unsigned int y) const;
  void setPixel (unsigned int x, unsigned int y, T pixel);

  apImage<T> thumbnail (int reduction) const;
protected:
  apAlloc<T>   pixels_;
  unsigned int width_;
  unsigned int height_;
};
```

This certainly is very tidy, and with a small addition, we can use this object as a replacement for both **apImage8** and **apImage32**:

```
typedef apImage<unsigned char> apImage8;
typedef apImage<unsigned int>  apImage32;
```

Are we done? Unfortunately, templates are not always this simple. The implementation does not work correctly for **apImage8**. Let's look at the following example to understand why.

▶ **EXAMPLE** ————————————————————————————————————

Here is the original definition of **thumbnail()** from **apImage8**:

```
apImage8 apImage8::thumbnail (unsigned int reduction) const
{
  apImage8 output (width()/reduction, height()/reduction);

  for (unsigned int ty=0; ty<output.height(); ty++) {
    for (unsigned int tx=0; tx<output.width(); tx++) {
      unsigned int sum = 0;
      for (unsigned int y=0; y<reduction; y++) {
        for (unsigned int x=0; x<reduction; x++)
          sum += getPixel (tx*reduction+x, ty*reduction+y);
      }
      output.setPixel (tx, ty, sum / (reduction*reduction));
    }
  }
  return output;
}
```

❖ TEMPLATE CONVERSION

This is easily converted to a template function as shown:

✗
```
template<class T>
apImage<T> apImage<T>::thumbnail (unsigned int reduction) const
{
  apImage<T> output (width()/reduction, height()/reduction);

  for (unsigned int ty=0; ty<output.height(); ty++) {
    for (unsigned int tx=0; tx<output.width(); tx++) {
      T sum = 0;
      for (unsigned int y=0; y<reduction; y++) {
        for (unsigned int x=0; x<reduction; x++)
          sum += getPixel (tx*reduction+x, ty*reduction+y);
      }
      output.setPixel (tx, ty, sum / (reduction*reduction));
    }
  }
  return output;
}
```

It is still not obvious why it won't work correctly, until you study two lines from this function:

```
T sum = 0;
...
sum += getPixel (tx*reduction+x, ty*reduction+y);
```

If **T** is an **unsigned char**, the compiler sees this:

```
unsigned char sum = 0;
...
sum += getPixel (tx*reduction+x, ty*reduction+y);
```

The variable **sum** must have enough precision to contain the sum of many pixels. For example, if the reduction factor is 2, **sum** must be able to hold the summation of four pixels without overflowing. This condition is not true if **sum** is only an **unsigned char**. Worse, the compiler will happily accept this code without generating any errors. It is up to you and your unit tests to catch them. You might be tempted to write our first line as:

```
unsigned int sum = 0;
```

This fixes the problem for **unsigned char**, and probably works well with **unsigned int** (since images that are represented with 32 bits most likely have fewer significant bits). This fix (really more of a hack), however, does not work for many other pixel types, like **float** or **RGB**.

◄

As shown in Figure 3.8 on page 52, Prototype 2 defines **apImage<T,E>**, which has two template arguments; the second argument is how we solve the thorny issue we just discussed. The first argument, **T**, is still the pixel type, but **E** now represents the internal pixel type to use during computation. For example, the definition **apImage<unsigned char, unsigned int>** describes an image of 8-bit pixels, but uses a 32-bit pixel for internal computations when necessary. Here are some other examples:

```
typedef unsigned char Pel8;
typedef unsigned int  Pel32;

apImage<Pel8, Pel8>;  // Watch out, round off is a real possibility
apImage<Pel8, Pel32>;
apImage<Pel32, Pel32>;
```

Now for an interesting design issue. Templates do support default arguments, so we can define our prototype class as either:

```
template<class T, class E> class apImage
```

or

```
template<class T, class E = T> class apImage
```

The difference may look small, but you must consider what happens when people forget the second argument. Default arguments are best used when the developer can predict what the argument is most of the time. One would expect that the template **apImage<Pel8,Pel32>** is used more often than **apImage<Pel8,Pel8>**. But if someone writes **apImage<Pel8>** they are getting the less commonly used object. For this reason, we do not supply a default argument.

Make sure the default argument is what should be used most of the time when deciding whether to supply one for your template class.

Handle Class Idiom

The handle class idiom has been used as long as C++ has been around. See [Coplien92]. This is little more than reference counting attached to an object. It is commonplace to call the shared object the *representation object,* and to call the objects that point to them the *handle objects.* The representation class (or rep class, as it is sometimes called) contains the implementation, does all the work, and contains all the data, while the handle class is little more than a pointer to a rep class. A more in-depth discussion can be found in Stroustrup's *The C++ Programming Language, Special Edition, Section 25.7.* See [Stroustrup00].

❖ HANDLE OBJECT

In Prototype 2, `apImage<T,E>` is our handle object and points to an instance of `apImageRep<T,E>`, as shown here.

```
template<class T, class E> class apImageRep; // Forward declaration

template<class T, class E> class apImage
{
public:
  friend class apImageRep<T, E>;

  apImage (); // A null image, suitable for later assignment
  apImage (unsigned int width, unsigned int height);
  ~apImage () { image_->subRef ();}

  apImage          (const apImage& src);
  apImage& operator= (const apImage& src);
  // We need our own copy constructor and assignment operator.

  const apImageRep<T, E>* operator -> () const { return image_;}
  apImageRep<T, E>*       operator -> ()       { return image_;}
  // Allow access to the rep object

protected:
  apImage (apImageRep<T, E>* rep);
  // Construct an image from a rep instance

  apImageRep<T, E>* image_; // The actual image data
};
```

The implementation of `apImage<T,E>` is similar to our `apAlloc<T>` object, since both use reference counting. If you study the implementation, you will see it all comes down to carefully calling `addRef()` and `subRef()` in the `apImageRep<T,E>` object. Besides the obvious constructor/destructor definitions, the most important function is `operator->`. This is the crux of the object, and is how you access a method in the rep class. This operator returns a pointer to the `apImageRep<T,E>` object, so any public method can be accessed.

❖ REP CLASS OBJECT

The rep class **apImageRep<T,E>** object, which is shown here, is very similar to the templated image object shown earlier on page 52.

```
template<class T, class E> class apImageRep
{
public:
  static apImageRep* gNull ();  // A null image

  apImageRep () : width_ (0), height_ (0), ref_ (0) {}
  // Creates a null image, suitable for later assignment

  apImageRep (unsigned int width, unsigned int height);
  ~apImageRep () {}

  unsigned int width  () const { return width_;}
  unsigned int height () const { return height_;}

  const T* pixels () const { return pixels_.data();}
  T*       pixels ()       { return pixels_.data();}

  const T& getPixel (unsigned int x, unsigned int y) const;
  void     setPixel (unsigned int x, unsigned int y, const T& pixel);

  // Reference counting related
  unsigned int ref () const { return ref_;}   // Number of references
  void addRef () { ref_++;}
  void subRef () { if (--ref_ == 0) delete this;}

  apImage<T, E> thumbnail (int reduction) const;

  // Default copy ctor and assignment are ok
protected:
  apAlloc<T>   pixels_; // Pixel data
  unsigned int width_;  // Image dimensions
  unsigned int height_;
  unsigned int ref_;    // Reference count

  static apImageRep* sNull_;   // Our null image object
};
```

The first difference between the rep object and the image object (from page 52) is in the definition of the null image. In the rep object, we use a Singleton method, **gNull()**, to be our null object. We define **gNull()** as:

```
template<class T, class E>
apImageRep<T,E>* apImageRep<T,E>::gNull ()
{
  if (!sNull_) {
    sNull_ = new apImageRep (0, 0);
    sNull_->addRef ();  // We never want to delete the null image
  }
  return sNull_;
}
```

This is the same behavior as our **apAlloc<T>** object. When we attempt to allocate an object with zero elements, we actually return an object that allocates a single element. Look at what could happen if we did not define a **gNull()** object:

```
apImage<Pel8,Pel32> image;
if (image->width() == 0)
   // Null object
```

This would fail if **apImage<T,E>** contained a null pointer to the **apImageRep<T,E>** object, and we dereferenced it to get the width. An alternate, and less desirable, approach is to define an **isNull()** method to test if the pointer is null before using it, as shown:

```
apImage<Pel8,Pel32> image;
if (!image.isNull())
   // OK to use operator->
```

Null images are commonplace in applications. For example, an image operation that cannot produce a resulting image returns a null image. To eliminate the need to create many null rep images, we only need to allocate a single **gNull()**. By calling **addRef()** when the null image is created, we ensure that this object never gets deleted.

The complete source for **apImage<T,E>** can be found on the CD-ROM. Let's look at one of the constructors to reinforce that this object is little more than a wrapper:

```
template<class T, class E>
apImage<T,E>::apImage (unsigned int width, unsigned int height)
   : image_ (0)
{
  image_ = new apImageRep<T,E> (width, height);
  image_->addRef ();
}
```

❖ THUMBNAIL() METHOD

The **thumbnail()** method of **apImageRep<T,E>** now looks like this:

```
template<class T, class E>
apImage<T,E> apImageRep<T,E>::thumbnail (unsigned int reduction)
    const
{
  apImageRep<T,E>* output =
    new apImageRep<T,E> (width()/reduction,
                         height()/reduction);

  for (unsigned int ty=0; ty<output->height(); ty++) {
    for (unsigned int tx=0; tx<output->width(); tx++) {
      E sum = 0;
      for (unsigned int y=0; y<reduction; y++) {
        for (unsigned int x=0; x<reduction; x++)
          sum += getPixel (tx*reduction+x, ty*reduction+y);
      }
      output->setPixel (tx, ty, sum / (reduction*reduction));
    }
  }
  // Convert to apImage via the protected constructor
  return output;
}
```

This approach differs from our first attempt at converting **thumbnail()** to a template function (as shown on page 53). Rep classes are allocated on the heap and our handle classes can be allocated anywhere. For this reason, we must use **new** to allocate our resulting object **output**. Although our **thumbnail()** method returns an **apImage<T,E>** object, there is no explicit reference to one in the function. We did this to avoid mixing references to **apImage<T,E>** and **apImageRep<T,E>**. We end the function by executing:

```
return output;
```

The compiler converts this object into an **apImage<T,E>** object, using the protected constructor:

```
apImage (apImageRep<T,E>* rep);
```

Our handle definition is looser than some implementations, although it is sufficient for our prototype. For example, there is nothing to stop someone from creating **apImageRep<T,E>** objects directly. It is a matter of opinion as to whether this is a feature or a detriment. It highlights the fact that it is not always clear what functionality is needed when prototyping.

RGB Images

So far our prototypes have dealt with monochrome images. Our design has gotten sufficiently complex that we should look at other image types to make sure our implementation and design are appropriate. We will do that now by looking at Red-Green-Blue (RGB) images. Depending on the application, color images may be more prevalent than monochrome images. Regardless of the file format used to store color images, they are usually represented by three independent values in memory. RGB is the most common, and uses the three colors red, green, and blue to describe a color pixel. There are many other representations that can be used, but each uses three independent values to describe an image.

An RGB image can be defined as:

```
✗ typedef unsigned char Pel8;
  struct RGB {
    Pel8 red;
    Pel8 green;
    Pel8 blue;
  };
```

With this simple definition, will a statement like the following work?

```
apImage<RGB> image;
```

The answer is no. Although we defined an RGB image, we did not define any operations for it. For example, the **thumbnail()** method needs to be able to perform the following operations with an RGB image:

- Construction from a constant (**E sum = 0**)
- Summing many pixel values (**sum += getPixel (...)**)
- Computing the output pixel (**sum / (reduction*reduction)**)

Adding support for RGB images entails defining these operations. The compiler will always tell you when you are missing a function, although some of the error messages are somewhat cryptic.

While we are adding functions for an **RGB** data type, we also need to define an **RGBPel32** type so that we don't have the same overflow issue we discussed earlier. **RGBPel32** is identical to **RGB**, except that it contains three 32-bit values, rather than three 8-bit values. At a minimum, we need to define these functions:

```
// Our basic color data type (8:8:8 format)
struct RGB {
  Pel8 red;
  Pel8 green;
  Pel8 blue;

  RGB (Pel8 b=0) : red (b), green (b), blue (b) {}
};

// Internal definition during computation (32:32:32 format)
struct RGBPel32 {
  Pel32 red;
  Pel32 green;
  Pel32 blue;

  RGBPel32 (Pel32 l=0) : red (l), green (l), blue (l) {}
};

RGBPel32& operator += (RGBPel32& s1, const RGB& s2)
{
  s1.red += s2.red;
  s1.green += s2.green;
  s1.blue += s2.blue;
  return s1;
}

RGB operator/ (const RGBPel32& s1, int den)
{
  RGB div;
  div.red = s1.red / den;
  div.green = s1.green / den;
  div.blue = s1.blue / den;
  return div;
}
```

Now, we are able to define an RGB image:

```
apImage<RGB,RGBPel32> image;
```

and even write a simple application:

```
apImage<RGB, RGBPel32> p (32, 32);

// Initialize the image with some data
RGB pel;
pel.red = pel.green = pel.blue = 0;
for (y=0; y<p->height(); y++)
  for (x=0; x<p->width(); x++) {
    p->setPixel (x, y, pel);
```

```
        pel.red++;
        pel.green++;
        pel.blue++;
    }
    apImage<RGB, RGBPel32> thumbnail = p->thumbnail (2);
```

To run any real applications, we also need to define additional functions that operate on **RGB** and **RGBPel32** images. For example, the unit test we wrote for this prototype adds a few more functions to initialize and test the value of RGB pixels:

```
RGBPel32 operator+ (const RGB& s1, const RGB& s2);
RGBPel32 operator+ (const RGBPel32& s1, const RGB& s2);
bool operator==   (const RGB& s1, const RGB& s2);
```

Summary of Lessons Learned

These are the things that worked well:

- Using templates to handle different types of images took advantage of the implementation similarities and resulted in an efficient design. The use of templates is something we will keep in the next prototype when we explore separating image storage from the image object .

- Defining an RGB image type was a good way to validate that the design is flexible and can handle many image types cleanly.

Here is what did not work well:

- Using the handle idiom did not provide any obvious advantages for the design. We had hoped that reference counting in our **apAlloc<T>** class, in conjunction with our **apImageRep<T,E>** class, would simplify the design, but it didn't. We are going to reuse the handle idiom in our next prototype, to see if it makes a difference when we separate storage from the image object.

3.2.6 Prototype 3: Separating Storage from Image Objects

In Prototype 2, we introduced a handle class idiom. We put all the functionality in the rep class and used a simple handle class to access the methods in the rep class. The light-weight handle, **apImage<>**, has simple semantics, but we still ended up with a fairly complicated rep class. Since the handle class cannot be used without understanding the functionality in the rep class, we didn't meet our goal of simplifying our code.

We need to intelligently manage large blocks of memory and allow access to a potentially large set of image processing functions. Strictly speaking, the use of the **apAlloc<>** class is what manages our image memory.

So what are the advantages of keeping our handle class? It does offer an insulation layer between our client object and the object that does all the work. However, we also need another construct to hold all of the data for storing and describing the image data. The image data, such as the pixels and image dimensions, is contained within the **apImageRep<>** object, as shown:

```
apAlloc<T>   pixels_; // Pixel data
unsigned int width_;   // Image dimensions
unsigned int height_;
```

Given that our final image class will contain even more data, such as the image origin, creating an object that combines all of this data makes even more sense. Another advantage of this strategy is that, given the appropriate design, this object can be used by many different image classes. This allows applications to customize the front end and reuse the image storage object. We use Prototype 3 to separate the image storage from the actual image object by extending the handle idiom we introduced in Prototype 2.

Design for Partitioning Image Storage

The purpose of Prototype 3 is to separate the image storage from the image processing. To accomplish this, we create a class, **apStorageRep**, to encapsulate the image storage, and we define **apImage<>** to be the object that performs the image processing. We connect the two using a handle class, **apImageStorage**. The final design for Prototype 3 is shown in Figure 3.9.

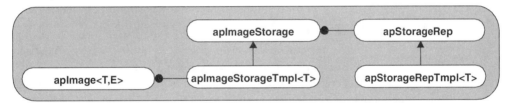

Figure 3.9: Image Object and Storage Separation Design

Note that we have introduced a new naming convention here to make it clear how these objects are related. Finding good names for closely related objects is not always easy. The C++ language does not support a class named **apImageStorage** and one called **apImageStorage<>**. The **Tmpl** suffix is added, renaming **apImageStorage<>** to **apImageStorageTmpl<T>**, to make it clear this is a templated class.

Evolution of the Design

Let's look at how we arrived at this design. Our first attempt to show how our objects are related is by extending Prototype 2, as shown in Figure 3.10.

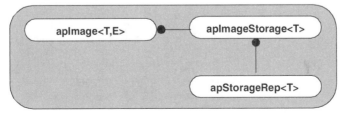

Figure 3.10: Evolution of Design (Step 1)

Although there is no inheritance in this example, the handle (`apImageStorage<T>`) and rep (`apStorageRep<T>`) classes are very closely related. Stacking them vertically in Figure 3.10 helps to show this relationship and clarifies that `apImage<T,E>` is related to the other two classes.

 If you decide to graphically depict your object relationships, take advantage of both axes to represent them.

❖ COMMON BASE CLASS

Before we start writing code, let us take one more step in improving our design. The compiler will instantiate a template object for each pixel type. Even if your users only need limited types, the image processing routines may need additional types for temporary images and the like. We have not worried about code bloat issues in our prototype, but now we need to consider how to handle them.

Memory is nothing more than a series of bytes that the user's code can access and treat as other data types. This is pretty much what **new** does. It retrieves memory from the heap (or elsewhere, if you define your own **new** operator) and returns it to the user. When coding with C, it was customary to call **malloc()**, then cast the returned pointer to the desired data type.

There is no reason why we cannot take a similar approach and handle allocation with a generic object. Our code will perform all the allocation in a base class, **apStorageRep**, and perform all other operations through a derived template class, **apStorageRepTmpl<T>**, as shown in Figure 3.11.

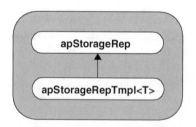

Figure 3.11: Evolution of Design (Step 2)

Image Storage Rep Objects

Given the handle idiom we have decided to use, our rep object, **apStorageRep,** will contain generic definitions for image storage, as well as the handle-specific functionality, as shown:

```
class apStorageRep
{

public:
  static apStorageRep* gNull ();
  // Representation of a null image storage.

  apStorageRep ();
  apStorageRep (unsigned int width, unsigned int height,
                unsigned int bytesPerPixel);

  virtual ~apStorageRep ();

  const unsigned char* base () const { return storage_.data();}
  unsigned char*       base ()       { return storage_.data();}
  // Access to base of memory

  unsigned int width        () const { return width_;}
  unsigned int height       () const { return height_;}
  unsigned int bytesPerPixel () const
    { return bytesPerPixel_;}
  unsigned int ref          () const { return ref_;}

  void addRef () { ref_++;}
  void subRef () { if (--ref_ == 0) delete this;}
  // Increment or decrement the reference count

  // Default copy constructor and assignment operators ok.
protected:
  apAlloc<unsigned char> storage_; // Pixel storage

  unsigned int bytesPerPixel_; // Bytes per pixel
  unsigned int width_;
  unsigned int height_;
  unsigned int ref_;            // Current reference count

  static apStorageRep* sNull_;
};
```

If you compare **apStorageRep** above with **apImageRep<>** from Prototype 2, you will find that they both offer the same functionality. The main difference is that **apImageRep<>** allocates memory as **apAlloc<T>**, where **T** is the data type, and **apStorageRep** allocates memory as **apAlloc<unsigned char>**.

Since **apStorageRep** is not a template class, let's look specifically at some of the differences, as shown:

```
apAlloc<unsigned char> storage_;
unsigned int bytesPerPixel_;
```

storage_ is defined in terms of bytes. When an object derived from **apStorageRep** wants to allocate storage, it must supply not only the width and height of the image, but also its *depth*. By depth, we mean the number of bytes it takes to store each pixel. Note that our definition does not support packed data. For example, a binary image where each pixel can be represented by a single bit still consumes the same amount of memory as an 8-bit image. This limitation is not very severe, since images often are aligned on byte boundaries by definition. And those that are not, for example 12-bit images, most likely require 16 bits of storage and fall on byte boundaries anyway. In any event, we are not going to worry about this special case now.

Once an image is constructed, we allow access to all the parameters of the object, as well as the memory pointer (as an **unsigned char**). We chose to leave the **base()** method public to allow for future functionality. We continue to use the **gNull()** definition, so we only have one instance of a null image (remember, this is an image that has a valid pointer, but has a **width()** and **height()** of zero).

Since **apStorageRep** is not a templated object, we put its definition in a header file and put much of its implementation in a source file (**.cpp** in our case). Not having it be a templated object has the advantage of giving us control of how the object will be compiled, and lets us control code bloat. For example, if this were a templated object, compilers would expect classes to be defined in a single translation unit (or by means of nested include files). This gives the decision of what to inline, and what not to, to the compiler.

By putting most of the functionality into the base class, we can have a very simple templated class, **apStorageRepTmpl<>**, that redefines **base()** to return a **T*** pointer (which matches the pixel type) instead of an **unsigned char***, as shown here.

```
template<class T>
class apStorageRepTmpl : public apStorageRep
{
public:
  apStorageRepTmpl () {}
  apStorageRepTmpl (unsigned int width, unsigned int height)
    : apStorageRep (width, height, sizeof (T)) {}

  virtual ~apStorageRepTmpl () {}

  const T* base () const
  { return reinterpret_cast<const T*> (apStorageRep::base());}
  T* base ()
  { return reinterpret_cast<T*> (apStorageRep::base());}
  // This cast is safe
};
```

Defining our **base()** method this way is an effective means of hiding the base class version of this method. As you would expect, **base()** is nothing but a safe cast of the **base()** pointer from **apStorageRep**. The base class uses **sizeof(T)** to specify the storage size of each pixel. This is passed to **apStorageRep** when it is constructed, as:

```
apStorageRepTmpl (unsigned int width, unsigned int height)
    : apStorageRep (width, height, sizeof (T)) {}
```

At this point, we are fairly satisfied with Prototype 3's design of the **apStorageRep** and **apStorageRepTmpl<>** objects. The base classes do all the real work, and the derived object handles the conversions. Unlike Prototype 2, where we let operator **new** (via **apAlloc<>**) create our pixels, in Prototype 3 we use an explicit cast to change our pointer from **unsigned char*** to **T***. In this context, casting is an efficient way to maximize code reuse. This cast is completely safe and contained within two methods.

Image Storage Handle Objects

Our handle class, **apImageStorage**, looks very similar to the **apImage<>** handle object we designed in Prototype 2. A portion of the object is shown here.

```
class apImageStorage
{
public:
  apImageStorage (); // A null image storage
  apImageStorage (apStorageRep* rep);
  virtual ~apImageStorage ();

  apImageStorage              (const apImageStorage& src);
  apImageStorage& operator= (const apImageStorage& src);
  // We need our own copy constructor and assignment operator.

  const apStorageRep* operator -> () const { return storage_;}
  apStorageRep*       operator -> ()       { return storage_;}

protected:
  apStorageRep* storage_;
};
```

The one major difference is that our handle object, **apImageStorage**, is not a template. That is because this object is a handle to an **apStorageRep** object and not an **apStorageRepTempl<>** object. The complete definition for the **apImageStorage** object can be found on the CD-ROM.

The **apImageStorage** object is not of much use to us because **operator->** allows us to access the **apStorageRep** rep object, and we really want to access the derived class, **apStorageRepTempl<>**. To accomplish this, we add an **apImageStorageTmpl<>** class that derives from **apImageStorage** as shown here.

```
template<class T>
class apImageStorageTmpl : public apImageStorage
{
public:
  apImageStorageTmpl () {}
  apImageStorageTmpl (unsigned int width, unsigned int height)
    : apImageStorage (new apStorageRepTmpl<T> (width, height))
  {}

  virtual ~apImageStorageTmpl () {}

  const apStorageRepTmpl<T>* operator -> () const
  { return static_cast<apStorageRepTmpl<T>*> (storage_);}
  apStorageRepTmpl<T>*       operator -> ()
  { return static_cast<apStorageRepTmpl<T>*> (storage_);}
};
```

Prototype 3 is a balanced design; we see that each base class has a corresponding derived template class. This symmetry is an indicator that we are getting closer to the final design.

Like our rep class, we also have to make a cast to get our **operator->** to work correctly. **static_cast<>** will safely cast the rep class (**apStorageRep**) pointer, kept by our base class, to an **apStorageRepTmpl<>** object. These casts may look complicated, but they really aren't. Two casts are needed for an **apImageStorageTmpl<T>** object to access **apStorageRepTmpl<T>**. And because of these casts, we can put most of our functionality inside base classes that are reused by all templates. Figure 3.12 shows the relationship between these two objects.

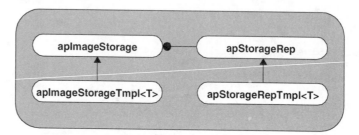

Figure 3.12: Image Object and Storage Separation Design

We are missing just one piece from this prototype. We need an object that actually performs the image processing operations on our image storage.

We chose to use **apImage<>** for this task with two template parameters:

```
template<class T, class E> class apImage
{
public:
  apImage ();
  apImage (unsigned int width, unsigned int height)
    : pixels_ (width, height) {}
  ~apImage () {}

  unsigned int width  () const { return pixels_->width();}
  unsigned int height () const { return pixels_->height();}

  const T* pixels () const { return pixels_->base();}
  T*       pixels ()       { return pixels_->base();}

  const T& getPixel (unsigned int x, unsigned int y) const;
  void     setPixel (unsigned int x, unsigned int y,
                     const T& pixel);

  // Image operations (only one for the prototype)
  apImage<T, E> thumbnail (unsigned int reduction) const;

  // Default copy ctor and assignment are ok
protected:
  apImage (apImageStorageTmpl<T>& storage);
  // Construct an image from the storage

  apImageStorageTmpl<T> pixels_;  // The actual image data
};
```

Other than its name, this object is not similar to **apImage<>** from Prototype 2. In that earlier prototype, **apImage<>** was nothing more than a handle class to the rep object. It was the rep object that did all the work. In Prototype 3, our **apImage<>** object is responsible for all of the image processing routines.

In this **apImage<>** object, all aspects of storing and maintaining the pixels are part of the storage object **pixels_**. **apImage<>** exposes only that part of the **apImageStorageTmpl<>** interface that it needs to for providing access to **width()**, **height()**, and **pixels()**. The definitions for **getPixel()** and **setPixel()** as they appear in Prototype 3 are as follows:

```
template<class T, class E>
const T& apImage<T,E>::getPixel (unsigned int x, unsigned int y)
   const
{ return (pixels_->base())[y*width() + x];}

template<class T, class E>
void apImage<T,E>::setPixel (unsigned int x, unsigned int y,
                               const T& pixel)
{ (pixels_->base())[y*width() + x] = pixel;}
```

This class structure is sufficiently complex that trying to define **operator T*** to avoid the explicit **base()** reference adds unwarranted complication. For example, we chose to define this operator in our **apAlloc<>** object because there was little confusion. But in this case, it would only spread the image functionality across three objects, giving rise to potential errors.

When we say:

```
pixels_->base()
```

it is clear we are calling the **base()** method of our rep class by means of the handle. Then, the following statement:

```
(pixels_->base())[y*width() + x]
```

becomes the lookup of a pixel, given its coordinates.

❖ THUMBNAIL() METHOD

The last method we need to look at is **thumbnail()**, and how it appears in Prototype 3 as:

```
template<class T, class E>
apImage<T,E> apImage<T,E>::thumbnail (unsigned int reduction) const
{
  apImage<T,E> output(width()/reduction, height()/reduction);

  for (unsigned int ty=0; ty<output.height(); ty++) {
    for (unsigned int tx=0; tx<output.width(); tx++) {
      E sum = 0;
      for (unsigned int y=0; y<reduction; y++) {
        for (unsigned int x=0; x<reduction; x++)
          sum += getPixel (tx*reduction+x, ty*reduction+y);
      }
      output.setPixel (tx, ty, sum / (reduction*reduction));
    }
  }

  return output;
}
```

If you removed the template references, this function is very similar to the **thumbnail()** method we designed in Prototype 1. This similarity to our very simple example means that we have a nice clean design.

Let's contrast Prototype 3's simpler version of **thumbnail()** with that in Prototype 2 to highlight the differences:

Prototype 2

```
apImageRep<T,E>* output =
  new apImageRep<T,E> (width()/reduction,
                       height()/reduction);
...
output->setPixel (tx, ty, sum / (reduction*reduction));
```

Prototype 3

```
apImage<T,E> output(width()/reduction,
                    height()/reduction);
...
output.setPixel (tx, ty, sum / (reduction*reduction));
```

The simple handle object in Prototype 2 meant our image processing routines had to access the computed images using pointers. We were able to access pixels in the current image using a normal method call, but access to a new image required access by means of the handle. In Prototype 3, access is consistent, regardless of which image we are trying to access.

Summary of Lessons Learned

These are the things that worked well:

■   Dividing the image into storage and processing pieces enhances the design. It makes accessing the **apImage<>** object very direct using the **.** operator, even though the implementation of the object is slightly more complicated.

■   Accessing image data from inside image processing routines is very clean.

■   Writing custom versions of **apImage<>** with access to the same underlying image data is very simple using the current design. This element works extremely well, and we will keep it as an integral component of the final design.

Here is what did not work well:

■   Using handles in our prototype has not shown a significant benefit to the design. **apAlloc<>** already allows the raw memory to be shared, avoiding the need to make needless copies of the data. Based on our prototypes, we have decided not to use handles in the final design.

3.3 Summary

In this chapter, we designed and implemented an object to efficiently manage memory allocation. We outlined the requirements of such an object in terms of a commercial-quality image framework. Then we designed and implemented the solution, using reference counting and memory alignment techniques to achieve those requirements. Because the solution involved heavy use of templates, we also provided a review of some of the syntactic issues with templates, including class conversion to templates, template specialization, function templates, and function template specialization.

With our memory allocation object complete, we began prototyping different aspects of the image framework design. Our first prototype explored two different types of images, 8-bit and 32-bit images, to determine if there were enough similarities to influence the design. We found that the classes were indeed very similar, and we felt that the design should be extended to include inheritance and/or templates to take advantage of the commonality.

In our second prototype, we extended our first prototype by using templates to handle the similarity among image objects. In addition, we introduced the handle class idiom, so that image objects of different types could share the same underlying representation object. Then we took the prototype one step further by exploring more complex image types, such as RGB images. We found that the use of templates resulted in an efficient design that leveraged the similarities; however, the handle idiom did not provide any obvious advantages.

In our final prototype, we explored separating the image storage component from the image object, because of the amount of data our image classes contained. We felt this strategy might allow the eventual reuse of the image storage object by various image objects. Once again, we tried to apply the handle idiom in our solution. We found that dividing the image into storage and processing pieces enhanced the design, but the handle idiom did not provide any obvious benefits.

In Chapter 4, we consider other issues for the final design of our image framework, including: coding guidelines and practices, object creation with the goal of reusability, and the integration of debugging support into the framework's design.

4

Design Considerations

In this chapter we discuss issues that should be considered at the beginning of the design process, including guidelines for coding and reusability. We also demonstrate a number of techniques for adding debugging support to your design.

4.1 Coding Guidelines

Before going much further, we should discuss naming conventions and other coding conventions or standards. This is often a controversial subject, especially when the development team is more than just a couple of people. From the standpoint of the company, having very specific coding standards is an attractive proposition. Standards can help create very uniform software that developers, as well as customers, can rely upon to describe the code. It is not uncommon to have coding standards that require more than 50 pages to describe. The more complicated the standards, the more complex the bureaucracy is that supports it, and this translates into a productivity loss. Before an organization plunges into a complicated standards document, these trade-offs should be examined to make sure the final result is positive.

From our own experience, we have found that balancing the needs of the organization without suppressing the creativity of the developers can be achieved. A standards document that addresses the most important issues, as well as guidelines for other issues, is a workable compromise. Developers can be challenged during code reviews if the software deviates from the standards, and any changes needed are agreed upon by those present. A coding standard should be thought of as a set of coding guidelines.

Guidelines should be agreed upon by the team before starting a project. If a company-wide standard exists, it should be reviewed to make sure the guidelines are applicable. Make the guidelines simple and easy to follow, and keep in mind their purpose: you want software that is readable and maintainable, and you want development to progress smoothly and efficiently. Guidelines should, at a minimum, include such items as:

- Naming conventions

- Comment rules (class, members, static members, enums, and so on)

- Header file layout

- Copyright notice and version control information

- Indentation

- Namespace usage

- Template restrictions

- Standard library usage

4.1.1 Changes to Existing Software

First, be consistent. Whatever guidelines you follow, you should strive to be consistent across all source files, or at least within a single translation unit. If you are starting a new project, all source files should meet these guidelines. If you are adding functionality to existing products, any new files should meet these guidelines. However, if you are adding functionality to an existing file, you need to examine how extensive the changes are. If the changes affect more than half of the lines of code, you should consider modifying all source lines to meet the new guidelines. But if you are making only smaller changes, such as bug fixes or simple enhancements, you are best served by adapting to whatever standard is used by the code.

For example, consider a small change you need to make to some code: the fixed coordinates are to be replaced by the actual coordinates of the image. The existing code looks like this:

```
/* Step through every pixel in the image and
   clear each pixel. */
for (int y=0; y<256; y++)
{
  for (int x=0; x<256; x++)
  {
    ...
  }
}
```

You should avoid changing the style of the code while making the changes. Instead of changing the code to look like this,

```
✗ // Step through every pixel in the image and
  // clear each pixel.
  for (int y=0; y<height(); y++) {
    for (int x=0; x<width(); x++) {
      ...
    }
  }
```

you should keep the original code consistent by making the changes like this:

```
/* Step through every pixel in the image and
   clear each pixel. */
for (int y=0; y<height(); y++)
```

```
{
  for (int x=0; x<width(); x++)
  {
    ...
  }
}
```

If you decide to change the coding style or apply other formatting changes, you should make these changes before applying any functional changes. In addition, you should make sure the formatting changes pass all applicable unit tests and system tests before making any functional changes.

Most developers (and we are no exception) like to work with a certain coding style, but that is not a sufficient reason to change any more lines of code than are necessary. Legacy code should always be viewed as fragile, and making any unnecessary changes should be avoided. We recommend using a system utility, such as **diff**, to view the changes made to a file,

```
diff version1.cpp version2.cpp
```

where **version1.cpp** and **version2.cpp** are placeholders for the files you want to compare.

If we did this for the changes mentioned earlier, the output of the **diff** would be as follows:

```
< for (int y=0; y<256; y++)
---
> for (int y=0; y<height(); y++)
5c5
<   for (int x=0; x<256; x++)
---
>   for (int x=0; x<width(); x++)
```

It is very clear what changes have been made; the < character precedes the original line of code, and the > character precedes the modified line of code. But if we use **diff** to look at the original code and the nonrecommended modifications mentioned earlier, the output would be as follows:

```
1,6c1,4
< /* Step through every pixel in the image and
<    clear each pixel. */
< for (int y=0; y<256; y++)
< {
<   for (int x=0; x<256; x++)
<   {
---
> // Step through every pixel in the image and
> // clear each pixel.
> for (int y=0; y<height(); y++) {
>   for (int x=0; x<width(); x++) {
```

The changes are much less clear in this example. These modifications would certainly complicate the review process and delay the software release.

4.1.2 Naming Conventions

What do you name a variable or a class? Do you use underscores in names, or capitalization? These are a matter of style and should be covered in the coding guidelines. Regardless of what style is applied, variable and class naming should always be descriptive. For example, instead of naming index variables **i** or **j** (a holdover from the days of Fortran) you should consider using **x** and **y** if these indices are used to represent coordinates. In this case, a single letter name is more descriptive than if these were called **xCoordinate** and **yCoordinate**. We have found that choosing short, descriptive names is better than choosing longer, even more descriptive names. When you look at our code, you will see variables **x,y** refer to coordinates, and **x0,y0** refer to the origin of the image. The first time you see this variable, you might have to look at the header file to see its meaning, but afterwards it is easy to remember.

Traditional C code has used the underscore character to construct long variable names. For example, **total_count** and **max_size** are variable names that are both descriptive and readable. But just as readable are names like **totalCount** and **maxSize**. We prefer to use capitalization, but both methods work better as names than **totalcount** and **maxsize**. Consider a better example: compare **bigE**, and **big_e**, and **bige**.

Naming conventions are numerous. We will look at two sets of them in a little more detail: one is the set of conventions used in this book, while the other is popular among Microsoft developers.

The Microsoft convention defines class names using the prefix **c**. For example, the Microsoft Foundation Classes (MFC) contains the classes **CPen**, **CBrush**, and **CFont**. Our code examples use an **ap** prefix to avoid name collisions with other classes, as in the examples **apRect** and **apException**. If we had used the Microsoft convention, we would have wanted to call our classes **CRect** and **CException**, but both are already defined in the MFC (and probably countless other C++ libraries). Feel free to choose whatever prefix you want, but it is important to distinguish class names (and structs) from other identifiers.

Namespaces were added to the language to prevent name collisions, but aside from their use in the standard C++ library, we have seen little use of this feature elsewhere. There is a common habit among developers to effectively disable namespaces by adding **using namespace std;**. We do not recommend this approach. Namespaces are important. It is not difficult to get into the habit of writing **std::** when you want to access a feature from the standard library. For a nice description of how to safely migrate software toward using namespaces, see [Sutter02].

Member variables should also be distinguishable from other variables, such as local variables or arguments. The Microsoft convention adds two pieces of information to a variable name. The first is an **m_** prefix to indicate a member variable, and the second group of letters, such as **str**, indicates the type of variable. Examples include:

```
m_bUpdatable         boolean
m_nQuery             short
m_lCollatingOrder    long
```

```
m_strConnect          CString
m_pvData              void* pointer
```

Our convention is to add a simple underscore _ suffix to identify member variables. While not as descriptive as the other convention, it also doesn't tie our variable name to a specific data type. The variable name without the underscore remains available for other uses, such as a local variable. We also apply this convention to internal class names that are included in the API, but are never called directly by the API's clients.

Using the underscore suffix, the variables from the previous example become:

```
updatable_
query_
collatingOrder_
connect_
data_
```

Here's a simple example:

```
class apExample {
public:
  apExample (int size) : size_ (size) {}
  int size () const { return size_;}
private:
  int size_;
};
```

Our convention also includes a few other rules, as shown in Table 4.1.

Table 4.1: Naming Conventions

Type	Convention	Example
enumerations	**e** prefix	**eNone, eStandard**
static variables	**s** prefix	**sOnly_**
static functions	**g** prefix	**gOnly()**

We can demonstrate all of these rules in the following simple example:

```
class apExample {
public:
  enum eTypes {eNone, eSome, eAll};
  static apExample& gOnly()
    { if (!sOnly_) sOnly_ = new apExample();
      return *sOnly_;}
  eTypes type () const { return type_;}

private:
  static apExample* sOnly_;
  eTypes type_;

  apExample () : type_ (eNone) {}
};

apExample* apExample::sOnly_ = 0;
```

This object may not do anything interesting, but it does show that with just a few simple rules, a piece of code can become quite readable. **apExample** is a singleton object. Access to member functions is through **gOnly()**, which returns a reference to the only instance of **apExample**.

One last area we mention is template type arguments. Expressive names for templates are nice, but they consume a lot of space. Consider this example, where we define the copy constructor:

```
template<class Type,class Storage>
class apImage
{
   apImage (const apImage<Type,Storage>& src);
   ...
};

template<class Type,class Storage>
apImage<Type,Storage>::apImage
(const apImage<Type,Storage>& src)
{
   ...
}
```

Because there is so much repetition of type names in the syntax, you can use shorter names, yet the clarity isn't compromised. We can simplify the above example by doing this:

```
template<class T,class S>
class apImage
{
   apImage (const apImage<T,S>& src);
   ...
};

template<class T,class S>
apImage<T,S>::apImage (const apImage<T,S>& src)
{
   ...
}
```

In this example, the expressive names only increased the complexity of the code. We prefer the single letter names, although we occasionally use two letter names (i.e., **T1**, **S1**).

Note that in Standard Template Library (STL), the template parameter names are very long because they form an API, and the use of long names is very descriptive.

4.1.3 Indentation

Indentation is also a controversial issue. If you are designing a class library that you intend to sell to other developers, consistent indentation across all files is expected. However, if you are developing an application where only in-house developers have access to the sources, you can relax this standard to keep the indentation style consistent across a file (instead of ideally across all sources). Like we demonstrated earlier, modifications to an existing indentation style should be avoided unless most of the contents of a file are being rewritten.

Otherwise, many unnecessary changes result that could delay releasing the code, as each difference has to be examined and tested.

We strongly recommend using program editors that can be configured to many desired styles, reducing the number of keystrokes necessary to use any particular style. For example, our preferred style is:

```
void function (std::string name)
{
  if (test) {
    doSomething (name);
    doSomethingElse ();
  }
  else
    doNothing ();
}
```

This is the K&R (Kernighan & Ritchie) style, with indentation of two spaces. It is a compact style with the goal of keeping the code readable but dense. We prefer using spaces rather than tabs, since it is more platform- and editor-independent. It is much more difficult to make the style platform-independent if tabs are used. For example, software displayed under Microsoft Developer Studio might have tabs every two spaces, but your favorite Unix editor might have tabs every eight spaces (and printers often print plain text files assuming a tab size of eight). Not only will the display look strange, but if you edit the code on both platforms, you will not be happy with the results.

4.1.4 Comments

Yes - and the more the better! Comments are almost always a good thing, as long as they accurately represent what the code does. Someone unfamiliar with a piece of software will usually look at the comments before looking at the code itself. And just like it takes some time to learn how to write good software, it does take time to learn how to write good comments. It is not the length of the comments, or the style in which you write them; rather it is the information they contain. Comments are more than just a written explanation of what the software does. They also contain thoughts and ideas that the developer noted while the code was being written. A casual observer may not understand the complexity of a block of code or the limitations that were added because of scheduling or other factors.

Block comments are usually placed at the beginning of the file or before any piece of code that is not obvious. The length is not important, as long as the block comment conveys:

- What the code does.
- How the code works.
- Why it was written this way.

We will discuss our recommendations for header file comments in the next section, but first, look at an example of right ways and wrong ways to document.

✗
```cpp
void apCache::clear (eDeletion deletion)
{
  Cache::iterator i;
  for (i=cache_.begin(); i!=cache_.end();) {
    apCacheEntryBase* entry = i->second;
    if (deletion == eAll || entry->deletion() == eAll ||
        entry->deletion() == deletion) {
      delete (i->second);
      cache_.erase (i++);
    }
    else
      ++i;
  }
}
```

Taken out of context, it is not clear what this code does. From the member name, **apCache::clear**, one could deduce that this code is deleting information from a cache object, but it requires a bit of study to figure out what this code is doing in all cases. Developers write code like this all the time. When it was written, it was very clear to the developer how and why it was written this way. But to other observers, or perhaps even the developer after a few weeks, the subtleties of this code might be lost. Now let's look at this example again, but with a very concise comment:

```cpp
void apCache::clear (eDeletion deletion)
{
  // Delete some or all of our objects. This loop is different
  // because we can't delete the iterator we're on.
  // See Meyers, Effective STL, Item 9
  Cache::iterator i;
  for (i=cache_.begin(); i!=cache_.end();) {
    apCacheEntryBase* entry = i->second;
    if (deletion == eAll || entry->deletion() == eAll ||
        entry->deletion() == deletion) {
      delete (i->second);
      cache_.erase (i++);
    }
    else
      ++i;
  }
}
```

This comment does not attempt to explain the purpose of every line of code, but it does describe why this iterator loop differs from most others. It even includes a reference to a better description of the problem.

There is no need to comment something that is obvious, such as the following:

```cpp
apRGBTmpl& operator= (const T& c)
{
  red   = c;
  green = c;
  blue  = c;
  return *this;
}
```

Even taken out of context, it is clear that this member function sets the color components of an RGB pixel to the same value.

Comments should also be added to single lines in order to clarify what is happening, or remind the reader why something is being done. It is a good idea to use this for conditional statements, as shown:

```
void function ()
{
  if (isRunning()) {
    ...
  }
  else {
    // We're not running so use default values
    ...
  }
}
```

It is very clear after the conditional statement what the block of code is doing, but this thought might be lost when the **else** code is reached. Adding a comment here is a good idea just to get the readers mind back in sync with the code.

Each file should have comments at the beginning containing any copyright information required by the company. Even if you are writing software for yourself, you should get in the habit of adding a standard block to all files. Following this, you should have at least a one-line description of what the file contains. Our files look like this:

```
//   bstring.cpp
//
//   Copyright (c) 2002 by Philip Romanik, Amy Muntz
//   All rights reserved. This material contains unpublished,
//   copyrighted work, which includes confidential and proprietary
//   information.
//
//   Created 1/22/2002
//
//   Binary string class
```

The copyright block is often much longer than this, but it is surprising how much proprietary software contains no copyright information at all. If you are in the business of writing commercial software, no software you create should be missing this block. Even free software contains an extensive copyright notice, an assignment of rights, and a list of any restrictions placed on the code.

Adding a line to tell when the file was created helps to distinguish older implementations from one another. Developers will often add a change list to describe all changes made to the file since it was created. There is nothing wrong with this, although its use has dwindled since version control systems have become popular.

4.1.5 Header File Issues

Header files describe the public and private interface of an object. You should strive to make header files consistent and descriptive of all public member functions. It is also useful to describe most private members, as well as member variables. Whenever there is confusion about what a piece of code does, the header file can be consulted to describe the purpose of each function and the meaning of each variable.

Include guards will prevent a header file from being included more than once during the compilation of a source file. Your symbol names should be unique, and we recommend choosing the name based on the name of the file. For example, our file, **cache.h**, contains this include guard:

```
#ifndef _cache_h_
#define _cache_h_
...
#endif // _cache_h_
```

Lakos describes using redundant include guards to speed up compilation. See [Lakos96]. For large projects, it takes time to open each file, only to find that the include guard symbol is already defined (i.e., the file has already been included). The effects on compilation time can be dramatic, and Lakos shows a possible 20x increase in compilation times when only standard include guards are used.

Since the header file is the public interface to an object, it makes sense to document each member function here with a simple description. We also recommend adjusting the alignment of similar lines of code to make it easy to see the differences. For example, here are two inline member functions:

```
bool lockImage   () const { return storage_.lock ();}
bool unlockImage () const { return storage_.unlock ();}
// Lock/unlock our image state (and our storage)
```

Aligning your code in this way also makes it easier to spot mistakes in the code. It is very clear when you use the following formatting:

```
bool isNull        () const { return storage_.isNull();}
int  ref           () const { return storage_.ref();}
int  bytesPerPixel () const { return storage_.bytesPerPixel();}
int  rowSpacing    () const { return storage_.rowSpacing();}
```

It is much harder to read the very same statements in this different format:

✗
```
bool isNull () const { return storage_.isNull();}
int ref () const { return storage_.ref();}
int bytesPerPixel () const { return storage_.bytesPerPixel();}
int rowSpacing () const { return storage_.rowSpacing();}
```

In these examples, we didn't include any documentation because the member name and inline definition are self-describing. Other member functions, however, may need more documentation. A comment should describe not only what a function does, but also its parameters and side effects. For example:

```
int substitute (std::string src, std::string replacement,
                bool replaceAll = false);
//Description  String replacement of our internal string
//Parameters   src            String to replace
//             replacement    Replacement string
//             replaceAll     false to replace only first occurrence
//Returns      Number of replacements made, 0 if none
```

A consistent ordering of functions in a class definition is also important. It makes it easier to find and locate functions while looking at a header file. For each class, we use the following order:

- **public class members**
  constructors
  copy and assignment operators
  simple set/get methods
  other methods

- **protected class members**
  member functions
  member variables

- **private class members**
  member functions
  member variables

For any class that does not require a user-written copy constructor or assignment operator, place a comment in the header file stating that it was a conscious decision to omit it. The absence of either a copy constructor or a comment saying that one is not necessary is a warning sign that the object needs to be checked.

4.1.6 Restrictions

The C++ standard defines the capabilities of the language, but just because a compiler allows a certain syntax or feature, does not mean that you should be using it. Organizations and projects have very good reasons, such as multi-platform or legacy concerns, to restrict the use of features.

The compiler used to produce a piece of software, or any tool used for development, should be controlled during the development and maintenance cycle of a project. You must not just change to a more recent version of the compiler without the same amount of testing done for a general release. It is very common for software released on multiple platforms or embedded platforms to use a specific language subset. With multi-platform releases, you are faced with designing to the least-common denominator (i.e., you build to the most restrictive features of each compiler). With embedded platforms, you have to deal with memory and performance issues that may force certain features to be avoided.

A good example is exception handling. As the C++ standard library has evolved, so have many semi-compatible or outright incompatible library versions out there. But replacing these older libraries has a cost associated with it. And, since the performance of exception handling can vary greatly on different platforms (see *Item 15* in [Meyers96]), your organization may decide that exception handling should not be used.

Templates are another issue. When compilers first started to support templates, the level of support varied greatly by compiler vendor. Even today, some compilers have limitations regarding function templates and partial specialization. We were quite surprised when we took some of our code samples and compiled them on different platforms. We found that some compilers were able to figure out which template function or conversion to apply, while others gave up because of ambiguity. It turns out that the ambiguous template instantiation error is the correct behavior, according to the C++ standard. The standard describes a scoring method to deduce template parameters and to decide which template to instantiate. If there is more than one template definition producing an equally good score, an error is produced because of the ambiguity. For example, consider this function template:

```
template<class T1, class T2, class T3>
void add2 (const T1& s1, const T2& s2, T3& d1)
{
  d1 = s1 + s2;
}
```

It is obvious what this function is doing, and we need to use these templates for built-in types (like **unsigned char** or **int**). In order to get well-defined results from some of our image processing functions, we use functions like **add2()**. But there is no way to say that this template should only be applied to built-in types. Our code defines an RGB data type (**apRGB<>**) to specify the contents of a color pixel. So, elsewhere in the code we have defined the following function:

```
template<class T1, class T2, class T3>
void add2 (const apRGBTmpl<T1>& s1, const apRGBTmpl<T2>& s2,
           apRGBTmpl<T3>& d1)
{
  ...
}
```

This version of **add2()** adds the red, green, and blue components separately to the output pixel (we aren't showing the definition now because we have to deal with some special overflow issues that we have not yet introduced). So now consider this snippet of code:

```
int s1, s2, d1;
apRGB<int> rgb1, rgb2, rgb3;
...
add2 (s1, s2, d1);
add2 (rgb1, rgb2, rgb3);
```

It is pretty obvious to us what should happen; however, compilers that comply with the C++ standard will generate an error, because both templates are considered equally good for many data types. Our workaround is using a macro to selectively compile code and to define specific versions, such as those shown below:

```
void add2 (int s1, int s2, int& d1);
void add2 (int s1, int s2, unsigned char& d1);
void add2 (int s1, int s2, unsigned short& d1);
```

Another issue involving the use of templates or the C++ standard library is code bloat. Every instantiation of a template comes at a cost, because the compiler must produce a different implementation for each template object or function. Stroustrup shows how to use template specialization to help reduce code bloat when the template parameters are pointers. See [Stroustrup00]. In his example, template parameters for a class **Vector**, such as **Vector<Shape*>** and **Vector<char*>**, share a partial specialization, **Vector<T*>**. This method can prove very effective for curbing code bloat, since containers of pointers are very common.

But even with such ways to curb the size of applications using templates, some organizations will simply choose to avoid the issue by eliminating or restricting the use of templates. For example, a single instance of **std::vector<void*>** can be used to handle a list of pointers. The main disadvantage of this is that casting will be needed when pointers are extracted from this container. It does not have to be a maintenance nightmare if all access to this object happens from a single function to handle the cast:

```
class apImageList{
public:
   ...
   const apImage* operator[] (unsigned int index) const
   { return reinterpret_cast<const apImage*>(list_[index]);}
private:
   std::vector<void*> list_;
};
```

We could use the same template instantiation many times with complete safety, because access to the container passes through the necessary casting. Any use of casting should be documented in the code to explain why it is done.

4.2 Reusable Code

As software evolves through the addition of new features or routine maintenance, the *intent* of the original software tends to change. By intent we mean the original purpose and design of the software. Well-designed software should facilitate future design changes without breaking the existing system. For example, in our image framework, we certainly don't want the whole system to break if we define a 32-bit grayscale image type when the system already supports an 8-bit grayscale image. Adding a binary (i.e., 1-bit) image type is another story; some major design changes are required in order to support this type. Poorly designed software can make any small design change difficult or impossible to implement.

In this section we discuss *reusable* software components. By reusable, we mean not just software that can be used on multiple projects and/or platforms, but also software that can serve multiple purposes in the same application. A component's reusability does not guarantee a well-designed or cleanly written object, but it certainly increases the odds of being such. It is not uncommon to have developers whose entire mission is to develop reusable components for an organization or group.

To see what we mean, let us look at a well-known and well-designed reusable component: the string object in the Standard Template Library. String classes have been around since the beginning of C++. The **std::string** class is an elegantly designed package that has almost everything you could need. But even with this functionality, you don't have to search too hard to find somebody who thinks the library has too little functionality or, conversely, too much functionality. Let's use this class to explore the issues surrounding reusable software.

Reusable software solves a generic problem. It should address the needs of a company, workgroup, or class of applications. For example, the standard library string class is globally generic. It not only handles character manipulation of char-sized data, it can also work with characters of various sizes:

```
typedef basic_string<char> string;
typedef basic_string<wchar_t> wstring;
```

We will discuss this issue in more detail later when we talk about coding for internationalization, but suffice it to say, a character is frequently larger than what a **char** can store. From the standpoint of the **std::string** class (or more precisely, the **std::basic_string** class), a string is simply an array of characters whose size can be specified by the user. The class makes no other assumptions about what is contained. This raises an interesting question. Can nulls or other binary characters be embedded in a **std::string**? The answer is yes. The string class maintains the length separate from the actual character data, so that **length()** and **size()** return this value rather than calling something like **strlen()**. The class appends a trailing null character, so that **c_str()** returns a C-like string, but this does not corrupt any data you wrote. We will explore a binary string class shortly.

Let us assume that the standard library did not exist and we were forced to design our own string class. What functionality would it support and what limitations would we impose? There is no single correct answer, because you have to consider a number of factors:

■   Does binary data need to be encoded?

■   Is multi-byte character encoding acceptable, or is Unicode necessary?

■   Can C-style string functions be used to provide some of the needed functionality?

■   What kind of insertion and extraction operations are required?

The answers to these questions may not be obvious until you examine how and where you could use a string class. Let's face it, if no string class existed at all, software would still get written, and it might look like this:

```
char* append (const char* src1, const char* src2)
{
  char* dst = new char [strlen(src1) + strlen(src2) + 1];
  strcpy (dst, src1);
  strcat (dst, src2);
  return dst;
}
```

Writing a reusable string class is not the difficult part, since strings are very well understood. Sure, there may be performance and efficiency issues, but these are fairly easy to observe and correct. The hard part is deciding how extensive an object to create. If the object of your design is to create a general purpose string class for a class library you want to sell, customers will expect a feature-rich object. For example, the **CString** class from the Microsoft Foundation Class has almost 100 public member functions and operators. With all these functions, it is not inconceivable that some of these functions have never been used in any real application, other than in the unit test code to validate the class.

At the other extreme, you can write a string class that does only what is necessary to get the job done as follows:

```
class apString
{
public:
  apString  (int size);
  ~apString ();
  apString  (const apString& src);
  apString& operator= (const apStringc& src);
  int size () const;
  char& operator[] (int index);
private:
  char* p_;
};
```

Is this a string class? Yes it is, but as you can see it does very little. Such an object may prove invaluable in one application, but we do not consider it reusable because it does not do anything very useful. Let's extend our definition of reusable code to include the following attributes:

- Provides useful and generic functionality.

- Can be described in a few sentences using concrete terms. If you can describe an object in simple terms, it will tend to be a simple object. For example, we can describe a string class by saying, "An object that manipulates character arrays, replacing C-style string functionality in most applications."

- Makes few assumptions about how or when the class can be used. For example, what if our string class only worked on strings with fewer than 100 characters? Or, what if the class only supported the storage of letters but no numbers? All designs have some limitations, but these limitations should not limit the object's general-purpose use.

4.2.1 The Economics of Reusability

Believe it or not, reusable code is expensive to develop and maintain. Once a reusable component exists, it is "free" to use, and hopefully pays for itself many times over. But the path to reusable software isn't free. There is a lot more to the process than just designing and implementing the code. For example, what happens when the software is used by two developers and one of them wants to change the interface? Should it be easy to add new member functions? Who is responsible for preventing the object from getting too complex?

If maintenance and enhancement responsibilities fall to the development team of an application, it makes sense for the responsibilities of reusable components to fall to a similar group. Larger organizations can potentially allocate one or more resources to develop, maintain, and enhance reusable components. This is the very charter of this group and their success or failure depends on getting their peers to adopt and use the software they create. Think of this group as third-party developers with a big advantage. Since you share the same employer, you ultimately share the same goals. And it is much more likely that you can talk to the developers directly if necessary.

Smaller groups can handle the management of reusable components internally. If the software is only used within a single group, a single individual can be charged with maintaining the code, just like any other piece of software. The group's manager can act as the clearing house for requests and decide when it is appropriate to make changes.

The process is more interesting for mid-sized organizations that consist of more than one development team. Each team has different schedules and requirements, and there is no centralized group to manage the shared software. Control of the reusable code should belong to a team created from members of all the separate development groups. One developer from each group should act as spokesperson for his/her group to ensure that changes and enhancements will not negatively impact their project. Having multiple developers from the same project attend these meetings is discouraged, because it tends to slow down and complicate the process. After all, you don't want an entirely new bureaucracy to develop that will slow down your development cycle. This group should be led by a development manager or project manager to keep it on track.

Here are some common situations you might be faced with. Imagine there are two development project teams, team A and team B, that are each using the same reusable components.

- Team A discovers that some enhancements are needed to continue to use a reusable component in their product. There is sufficient time to make these changes before the next release. Team B, however, has no desire to see any changes made to their software base.

- Team A makes a small bug fix to the reusable component and commits the change to the source control system. Team B unknowingly uses this version and strange problems appear in their application.

- The group in charge of reusable components approves a number of enhancements. However, the developer in team A charged with making these changes cannot complete the task because of other schedules and commitments. Team B is facing a deadline and needs these enhancements ASAP.

These issues are not unique to reusable software components, but they can create situations that cannot be resolved by a single development team. In the first example above, configuration management software can allow team B to use the current version of a component while team A uses a different version. These changes can consist of a combination of new functionality, extensions to existing functionality, or bug fixes. Whatever the reason, no changes to the software should be made by team A without the knowledge and approval of team B. Version control is very important for reusable components, so much so that using timestamps or other simple methods to select which version of software to use may not be sufficient. For this reason, we recommend adding version or release tags to new versions. This treats an internally developed component the same way as one purchased from a third-party source. It also impresses on the team the notion that changes to a reusable component should happen at the same frequency as one would expect new versions of third-party libraries.

The second issue can be caused by assuming that the most recent version of a component is always the one to select. The solution to this problem is easy: don't make this assumption. This is no different than taking a new compiler or library update from a vendor and assuming it will work. However, this scenario can easily happen because most changes made to mature software involve fixing bugs. If we had developed the standard library string class internally, who would not just want to use the most recent version when it becomes available? We sometimes place more trust in something or someone than we should. Consider this simple function as part of a reusable component:

```
bool isValid (const std::string& src)
{
  for (int i=0; i<src.size(); i++)
    if (!isalpha(src[i]))          // Verify [a-z,A-Z]
      return false;
  return true;
}
```

Because this is such a simple function, it is clear that `isValid()` will return true if the string only consists of alphabetic characters, or is a null string. However, developers seldom look at the actual source code unless they suspect a problem. Instead, they consult the header file for the function declaration and the associated documentation. In this case, the header file contains:

```
bool isValid (const std::string& src);
// Returns true if the string contains only alphabetic characters
```

Perhaps you have already recognized the issue: by comparing the description in the header file with the actual function, there is an undocumented behavior when a null string is passed. The function will return **true**, but the documentation says nothing about this. The big question is: will a developer make use of this undocumented functionality? The answer is: you have no idea. The chance of this happening increases as more projects start using this code.

Now let us assume that the person maintaining the `isValid()` function makes an enhancement to the function as shown:

```
bool isValid (const std::string& src)
{
  if (src.size() == 0)
    return false;
  for (int i=0; i<src.size(); i++)
    if (!isalnum(src[i]))          // Verify [a-z,A-Z,0-9]
      return false;
  return true;
}
```

By examining this function you will see that two changes have been made. The first is to specify the behavior for null strings. A null string will now return false. Second, this function now considers alphanumeric characters to be part of a valid string. The documentation is also changed to either:

```
    bool isValid (const std::string& src);
✗   // Returns true if the string contains only alphanumeric characters
```

or:

```
bool isValid (const std::string& src);
// Returns true if the string contains only alphanumeric characters.
// Returns false for null strings.
```

We certainly hope the change looks more like the second possibility, so that the documentation better reflects what the function actually does. It would not surprise us if the documentation continues to ignore the behavior of null strings. This can happen because documentation changes do not always occur when changes are made to the code. Many developers will argue that the code itself is the documentation, and any documentation included in the header file is just a synopsis of what the function does. We won't get into this issue right now because it will only get us off track.

Let us look at what happens when a newer version of `isValid()` is available in a software update. The decision to use the updated version of `isValid()` will most likely be made based on the function's accepting alphanumeric characters and not just alphabetic characters. Even if the update includes information regarding the behavior of nulls, this change can easily fall through the cracks and not get noticed. It may not even be obvious to the developer if this special null case is even an issue. When multiple teams use the same piece of reusable code, it is possible that all the developers on team A will use the null behavior of `isValid()` while team B never does. If the person responsible for maintaining `isValid()` is part of team B, they may change the null behavior of `isValid()`, thinking it has no effect on the code, when in actuality it could greatly affect team A.

The real costs of creating a reusable component are now becoming clear. A piece of software goes through a number of steps before it becomes a reusable component. For smaller organizations, it all starts with the creation of a piece of software that solves a particular problem, but may be generic enough to be used in other places. Once it is recognized as a possible reusable component, a set of well-defined steps should be followed:

1. Proposal. A short proposal should describe the overall functionality, and explain why this component is necessary to the project and why it can be used by other projects. A short example of how the code is used is helpful. At this stage, the proposal is only meant to see if there is enough interest in the component.

2. Approval and assignment of a maintainer (most likely the developer) and the group to review it.

3. Review of the interface.

4. Unit test review and other automated tests.

5. Documentation. In addition to functional and design documentation, you should also include change logs, such that any changes made are documented in a text file.

6. Initial check-in.

Binary String Class

A binary string class may not sound very interesting until you realize all the uses there are for it. If we renamed our example to be something like "object streaming" or "object persistence," it might appear more important. To achieve either goal, software is needed to collect and manipulate binary streams of data. These data streams can represent anything from image data to the contents of objects. We aren't going to tackle a complete object persistence mechanism here, but we will show you one important reusable component.

To be more precise, our binary string object manages tagged data. By this we mean that every item written to our stream consists of two parts. The first part is a *tag*, which specifies the type of data written, and is followed by the data itself. A raw binary stream of data can be difficult to decode, especially if its format is modified over time. Tagging the data makes it easier to interpret and allows anyone to read a stream of data, even when its meaning is not known. Our object, **apBString**, tags data in the following formats:

- Byte (signed, 1 byte)
- Word (signed, 2 bytes)
- Integer (signed, 4 bytes)
- Unsigned Integer (unsigned, 4 bytes)
- Float (4 bytes)
- Double (8 bytes)
- String
- Data
- **apBString**

The tag field is one byte and precedes the data. Most tagged formats are pretty obvious, because they follow the way the underlying data types are stored in memory. A string is written as a length (4 bytes), followed by the string data. A data block is written in the same way and is used to represent arbitrary data. **apBString** objects can also be nested inside of other **apBString** objects, allowing this object to encapsulate other binary objects. It is this behavior that paves the way for object streaming. The definition of **apBString** is shown here.

```
typedef unsigned char   Pel8;    // 1-byte
typedef unsigned short Pel16;    // 2-bytes
typedef int            Pel32;    // 4-bytes   (unsigned)
typedef unsigned int   Pel32s;   // 4-bytes   (signed)
class apBString
{
public:
  apBString  ();
  ~apBString ();

  apBString            (const apBString& src);
  apBString& operator= (const apBString& src);

  size_t     size () const { return string_.size();}
  const void* base () const { return string_.c_str();}
  // Return pointer, and size of our data

  void rewind () { offset_ = 0;}
  // Reset our output pointer to the beginning

  bool eof () const { return offset_ >= string_.size();}
  // Return true if the stream is at the end
```

```
      bool match () const { return match_;}
      // Return true if all extraction resulted in a match between
      // the requested data type and the stored data type

      const std::string& str () const { return string_;}
      // Acess to our underlying string data

  // Insertion operators
    apBString& operator<< (Pel8    b);
    apBString& operator<< (Pel16   w);
    apBString& operator<< (Pel32s l);
    apBString& operator<< (Pel32   l);
    apBString& operator<< (float   f);
    apBString& operator<< (double d);
    apBString& operator<< (const std::string& s);
    apBString& operator<< (const apBString& bstr);

      void append (const void* data, long size);

      // Extraction operators
    apBString& operator>> (Pel8&   b);
    apBString& operator>> (Pel16&  w);
    apBString& operator>> (Pel32s& l);
    apBString& operator>> (Pel32&  l);
    apBString& operator>> (float&  f);
    apBString& operator>> (double& d);
    apBString& operator>> (std::string& s);
    apBString& operator>> (apBString& bstr);

      bool fetch (const void*& data, unsigned int& size);

      std::string dump ();
      // Ascii dump of data, from the current offset
  private:
    std::string  string_;
    int          offset_;
    bool         match_;

      enum eTypes {eNone=0, ePel8=1, ePel16=2, ePel32s=3, ePel32=4,
                   eFloat=5, eDouble=6, eString=7, eData=8, eBstr=9};
      // Supported datatypes. These values can never be changed but
      // more can be added

      apBString  (const void* data, unsigned int size);

      void add (eTypes type, const void* data, unsigned int size);
      // Add the specified data to our buffer

      const void* extract (eTypes& type);
      // Return a pointer to the next data type and return its type.
      // Returns null if you attempt to read past the end

    Pel8        readPel8   (const void* p);
    Pel16       readPel16  (const void* p);
    Pel32s      readPel32s (const void* p);
    Pel32       readPel32  (const void* p);
    float       readFloat  (const void* p);
    double      readDouble (const void* p);
    std::string readString (const void* p);
      // Read a particular quantity from our string.

      std::string dumpBString (unsigned int indent);
      // Text dump the contents from a single BString
};
```

The complete source code can be found on the CD-ROM. Our binary string is stored as a `std::string` object. As we mentioned early in this section, `std::string` makes no assumptions regarding the data it contains. A trailing null character is often written at the end of the data so that code that calls the `c_str()` method can treat it as a C-style string. Note that if the data contains a null character, you'll need to use the `data()` method instead.

Let us look at how a variable of type `Pel16` is treated. First, there needs to be a way to add data to our binary string:

```
apBString& apBString::operator<< (Pel16 w)
{
  add (ePel16, &w, sizeof (w));
  return *this;
}

void apBString::add (eTypes type, const void* data,
                     unsigned int size)
{
  // Append the type
  Pel8 t = static_cast<Pel8>(type);
  string_.append (reinterpret_cast<char*>(&t), sizeof (Pel8));

  // Append the data
  string_.append (reinterpret_cast<const char*>(data), size);
}
```

Most of our insertion operators, `operator<<`, call a private method `add()` to actually append data to our string (which calls the `append()` method of `std::string`). The extraction operator, `operator>>`, is much more complicated. When it reads data from the stream, it first reads the tag to figure out what kind of data is in the stream, and then tries to convert this quantity to a `Pel16` and return it. The current offset in the string is stored in `offset_`, and this allows `string_` to be parsed without having to modify it, as shown:

```
apBString& apBString::operator>> (Pel16& w)
{
  eTypes type;
  w = 0;

  bool match = false;
  const void* p = extract (type);
  if (p == 0) return *this;

  switch (type) {
  case ePel8:
    w = readPel8 (p);
    break;
  case ePel16:
    w = readPel16 (p);
    match = true;
    break;
  case ePel32s:
    w = (Pel16) readPel32s (p);
    break;
  case ePel32:
    w = (Pel16) readPel32 (p);
```

```
    break;
  case eFloat:
    w = (Pel16) readFloat (p);
    break;
  case eDouble:
    w = (Pel16) readDouble (p);
    break;
  case eString:
    w = (Pel16) atoi (readString(p).c_str());
    break;
  default:
    // Unsupported type. We don't have to do anything
    break;
  }

  match_ &= match;
  return *this;
}
```

This function checks the data type of the next member in the stream using the **extract()** method, and attempts to read and then convert the data to a **Pel16**. This is true for the **String** data type as well, because the **atoi()** function is called to convert the string to an integer quantity. Data types that cannot be converted to a **Pel16**, our **eData** (block of binary data) and **eBStr** (binary string) type, return 0. The extraction operator also keeps track if the data type read in the stream exactly matches the requested data type. You can query the **match()** method to see if any previous extraction required a conversion. Depending upon the application, a data mismatch can imply that the data is corrupted. Note that **apBString** does not detect whether an overflow occurs during extraction, because data is typically extracted to variables of equal or larger size.

So, how reusable is **apBString**? In general terms, it is a very basic building block to manage binary data that satisfies all of our definitions for a reusable object. But, as we have designed it, it is only portable on machines with the same memory architecture. Our class copies data, byte for byte, into our binary string. If we use **apBString** on a machine in little-endian format (the low-order byte is stored in memory at the lowest address, such as with Intel processors), it cannot be read properly on a big-endian machine (the high-order byte is stored in memory at the lowest address, such as with Sun SPARC). We could have chosen to address the endian issue in our design by making sure all of our string data was written in the chosen endian format; however, that was not one of our design guidelines. In this regard, **apBString** is not reusable between different types of machines. The code is portable, but the data files are not.

4.3   Designing in Debugging Support

During software development, a good debugger, when combined with a seasoned developer, allows software to quickly evolve from its initial state to release-quality code. The debugger provides the tools to examine the state of the running software, while the developer provides the insight on how to interpret this information. But debuggers aren't always available when you need them. For example, your software may be in the hands of a customer and you only have a limited description of a problem, and are not able to reproduce it. In this section, we discuss some strategies for getting the information you need from your software.

Besides using software debuggers, profilers, and other tools, you can also insert statements to log information during the debugging phase. This information is subsequently written to the console, file, or other device for later review; or, it is simply discarded.

There are advantages and disadvantages to adding your own debugging code. The biggest advantage is that you are in total control. You can decide if your code waits for specific conditions to occur or if it generates reams of information immediately. This lets you detect many timing-related bugs that would otherwise be almost impossible to diagnose.

One of the biggest disadvantages, however, is that debugging code is not present in production releases. Sometimes this results in timing-related bugs that appear only in the production version of the software.

It is important to remove debugging statements from production releases. Debugging messages can expose sensitive information regarding the product's implementation. In the hands of competitors, this information can yield a wealth of information. Depending upon the nature of the application, we have found that some debugging information, such as customer-specific timing issues or details, is too sensitive to share with the rest of the company.

Many people handle the debugging statements issue in code that looks very similar to this:

```
#ifdef DEBUG
std::cerr << "Some debugging messages" << std::endl;
#endif
```

During development, the makefile will define the variable **DEBUG** to compile the debugging code into the application. Production releases do not define this variable, effectively removing all of this code from the product.

In this section, we present a strategy for handling debugging information that is:

■ Present in the software, including production releases.

■ Requires little or no overhead when not in use.

■ Generates selective amounts of debugging information, depending on the need.

First, we design a generalized debugging stream. Next, we create destination objects, called *sinks*, for the debugging output. Once we have the destinations, we create an object to control the amount of debugging information that is actually output to those destinations. Finally, we extend our debugging environment to allow remote access to objects through an object registry.

Figure 4.1 illustrates the components that make up our debugging environment.

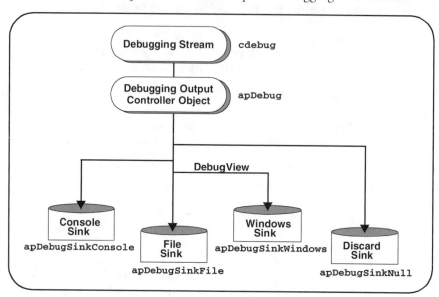

Figure 4.1: Debugging Environment Overview

4.3.1 Creating a Generalized Debugging Stream

When we add debugging code to our application, we usually write information to a standard stream, such as **std::cout** or **std::cerr** (or C-style **stdout**, **stderr**). This is useful, but we will do it one better by creating a new stream whose purpose is reserved for debugging. This leaves the standard streams available for casual debugging purposes. For in-depth information on streams, see [Langer00].

If you want to continue using **std::cout**, it is possible to redirect this stream if you need to create a permanent copy. We can temporarily redirect **std::cout** to a file, **redirect.txt**, with the following code:

```
#include <iostream>
#include <fstream>
...
  std::cout << "This should be written to the console" << std::endl;

  std::ofstream file ("redirect.txt");
  std::streambuf* oldbuf = std::cout.rdbuf (); // Save
  std::cout.rdbuf (file.rdbuf());

  std::cout << "This should be written to the file" << std::endl;

  std::cout.rdbuf (oldbuf); // Restore
  std::cout << "This should be written to the console" << std::endl;
```

To create a more permanent solution, we really want to dedicate a stream to send debugging information. Then we can write statements such as:

```
cdebug << "Debugging stream message" << std::stream;
```

where **cdebug** is our new debugging stream.

The C++ standard stream library consists of a very full set of classes to allow streams to be created and manipulated. However, the classes can be very complicated to use and understand. Fortunately, we do not have to jump in and completely understand **std::ostream** and everything that goes with it. We can choose a subset that meets our needs. Since this is only being used in debug mode, we can afford to choose a solution that is not optimized for performance. This is an especially good trade-off if the solution is easy to understand and implement.

To create our new debugging stream, **cdebug**, we first create regular static objects. In our header file, we declare the objects at global scope, as shown:

```
extern apDebugStringBuf<char> debugstream;
extern std::ostream cdebug;
```

We then define them in our source file, as shown:

```
apDebugStringBuf<char> debugstream;
std::ostream cdebug (&debugstream);
```

cdebug is an instance of **std::ostream** that connects a stream with our string buffer object. **debugstream** is our global stream buffer object (an instance of **apDebugStringBuf<>**, which is defined on page 100) that forwards the stream data to the appropriate destination, called a sink. (Sinks are fully described on page 96.)

Let's look at the following example:

```
cdebug << "This line goes to our null sink" << std::endl;

debugstream.sink (apDebugSinkConsole::sOnly);
cdebug << "This line goes to std::cout" << std::endl;

apDebugSinkConsole::sOnly.showHeader (true);
cdebug << "Also to std::cout, but with a timestamp" << std::endl;

apDebugSinkFile::sOnly.setFile ("test.txt");
debugstream.sink (apDebugSinkFile::sOnly);
cdebug << "This line goes to test.txt" << std::endl;

apDebugSinkFile::sOnly.showHeader (true);
cdebug << "Also to test.txt, but with a timestamp" << std::endl;
```

If you look at the file, **test.txt**, it will contain:

```
This line goes to test.txt
Mon Apr 22 19:42:24 2002: Also to test.txt, but with a timestamp
```

If you execute these lines again, you will see two additional lines in the file because we append data, rather than overwriting it.

4.3.2 Creating Sinks

We are now ready to create objects that will hold the information from the debugging stream. These objects are called sinks. A *sink* is the ultimate destination for a stream of information, so it nicely describes what our object does.

Our base class, **apDebugSink**, defines the basic interface that any derived sink object must implement. Its definition is shown here.

```
class apDebugSink
{
public:
  apDebugSink ();

  virtual void write (const std::string& str) = 0;
  virtual void write (int c) = 0;
  // Write a string or character to our debugging sink;

  virtual void flush () {}
  // flush any stored information for this type of sink.

  virtual std::string header () { return standardHeader();}
  // By default, we emit a standard header when headers are enabled

  void showHeader (bool state) {  enableHeader_ = state;}
  // Set the state of whether a header is written

protected:
  std::string standardHeader ();

  bool enableHeader_; // true writes header when buffer is flushed
};
```

apDebugSink is very simple. The **write()** method adds a string or character to our debugging stream with optional buffering. Derived classes can override **flush()** to emit any stored characters in the object. Although we do not make any assumptions regarding buffering, the intent is to buffer one line of information at a time. A timestamp, or other information, can be prepended to each line before it is output. Derived classes can call **header()** to retrieve the value of the header before outputting a line of debugging information. Unless overridden, **header()** will display just the time by calling **standardHeader()**, whose implementation is shown here.

```
std::string apDebugSink::standardHeader ()
{
  std::string header;

  // Fetch the current time
  time_t now = time(0);
  header += ctime (&now);
  header.erase (header.length()-1, 1); // Remove newline written
  header += ": ";

  return header;
}
```

In our framework, we define four different types of sinks: null, console, file, and windows.

❖ NULL SINK

We define **apDebugSinkNull** to discard any characters passed to it and to do nothing further. This is a useful way to shut off the stream. **apDebugSinkNull** is also the default sink when you construct a debugging stream, **cdebug**. The definition of **apDebugSinkNull** is shown here.

```cpp
class apDebugSinkNull : public apDebugSink
{
public:
  static apDebugSinkNull sOnly;

  virtual void write (const std::string& str) {}
  virtual void write (int c) {}

private:
  apDebugSinkNull ();
};
```

We only need a single instance of each sink, so we have defined a static instance, **sOnly**. In previous prototypes, we used a function, **gOnly()**, to access our singleton object. In this case, however, we are directly constructing the static object because we will be passing it around by reference. This is obvious when we look at how sink objects connect with the **cdebug** stream.

The remaining lines of code contained in the source file are as follows:

```cpp
apDebugSinkNull apDebugSinkNull::sOnly = apDebugSinkNull ();

apDebugSinkNull::apDebugSinkNull () {}
```

❖ CONSOLE SINK

apDebugSinkConsole writes a stream of characters to **std::cout**. Its definition is shown here.

```cpp
class apDebugSinkConsole : public apDebugSink
{
public:
  static apDebugSinkConsole sOnly;

  virtual void write (const std::string& str);
  virtual void write (int c);
  virtual void flush ();

protected:
  virtual void display (const std::string& str);
  // Output the string. Derived classes can override this

  apDebugSinkConsole ();
  virtual ~apDebugSinkConsole ();

  std::string buffer_;
};
```

❖ FILE SINK

apDebugSinkFile writes a stream to a specified file. Its definition is shown here.

```
class apDebugSinkFile : public apDebugSinkConsole
{
public:
  static apDebugSinkFile sOnly;

  void setFile (const std::string& file);
  // Set/change our file name. The stream is flushed before the
  // file name is changed.
private:
  virtual void display (const std::string& str);

  apDebugSinkFile ();
  virtual ~apDebugSinkFile ();

  std::string file_;
};
```

As you can see, **apDebugSinkFile** actually derives from **apDebugSinkConsole**. We do this because the only difference between these objects is where the data is written when the internal buffer, **buffer_**, is flushed.

Flushing a Sink

Flushing data from the internal buffer occurs in the following cases:

■ When an entire string is output

■ When a newline (i.e., **\n**) character is written to the buffer

■ When the object is destroyed

■ When the file name is changed

■ When **flush()** is called

The implementation of **flush()** is as shown:

```
void apDebugSinkConsole::flush ()
{
  if (buffer_.size() == 0)
    return;

  if (enableHeader_)
    buffer_ = header() + buffer_;

  // Add a trailing newline if we don't have one
  // (we need this when we shut down)
  if (buffer_[buffer_.length()-1] != '\n')
    buffer_ += '\n';

  display (buffer_);
  buffer_.clear ();
}
```

Since **flush()** does all the work of formatting the buffer, **display()** becomes very simple, as shown:

```
void apDebugSinkConsole::display (const std::string& str)
{
  std::cout << str;
}

void apDebugSinkFile::display (const std::string& str)
{
  if (file_.size() == 0)
    return;

  // Open the file in append mode. The dtor will close
  // the file for us.
  std::ofstream output (file_.c_str(), std::ios_base::app);
  if (!output)
    return;     // The file could not be opened. Exit

  output << str;
}
```

Although these sink objects are intended to be used by our stream object, they can also be used independently, as shown in the following lines of code:

```
for (int i=0; i<10; i++)
  apDebugSinkConsole::sOnly.write ('0' + i);
apDebugSinkConsole::sOnly.write ('\n');
```

This code outputs "**0123456789\n**" to **std::cout**.

❖ WINDOWS SINK

Let's look at one more useful sink before we leave this topic. If you are developing under Microsoft Windows, there is a useful function, **OutputDebugString()**, that outputs a string to the debugger if one is running. And, thanks to a great piece of freeware called **DebugView**, which is provided on the CD-ROM included with this book, you can view these strings whenever you want, even in release builds. Adding a new sink to support this type of output is easy. Its definition is shown here.

```
class apDebugSinkWindows : public apDebugSinkConsole
{
public:
  static apDebugSinkWindows sOnly;
  virtual void display (const std::string& str);
};

apDebugSinkWindows apDebugSinkWindows::sOnly = apDebugSinkWindows();

void apDebugSinkWindows::display (const std::string& str)
{ OutputDebugString (str.c_str());}
```

If there is no application or system debugger, then **OutputDebugString()** just makes a simple check; the overhead is negligible.

4.3.3 Connecting a Sink to a Stream

We are now ready to connect our sink object to a stream. If you study the standard library, you will find the **std::basic_stringbuf<>** class. This object manages an array of character elements for a stream object. What we want to do is derive an object from **std::basic_stringbuf<>** that uses our sink objects as the actual storage of the stream data. This is actually quite simple. If no storage buffer is allocated by the **std::basic_stringbuf<>** object, the object will call the virtual function **overflow()** with every character it attempts to save in its storage:

```
int_type overflow (int_type c);
```

where **int_type** is defined as the character type that the object handles.

We need to override this function to insert characters into our **apDebugSink** object, as shown:

```
template<class T, class Tr = std::char_traits<T>,
class A = std::allocator<T> >
class apDebugStringBuf : public std::basic_stringbuf<T, Tr, A>
{
public:
  apDebugStringBuf (apDebugSink& s = apDebugSinkNull::sOnly)
                 : sink_ (&s) {}
  ~apDebugStringBuf () { sink_->flush();}

  typedef typename std::basic_stringbuf<T, Tr, A>::int_type int_type;

  int_type overflow (int_type c) {
    if (c != traits_type::eof())
      sink_->write (c);
    return traits_type::not_eof(c);
  }

  void sink (apDebugSink& s) { sink_ = &s;}
  // Change our sink

private:
  apDebugSink* sink_;
};
```

This object looks confusing because of how the stream library is written, but it is actually very powerful. With this object, we can write to any kind of **apDebugSink** object (file, console, null, or windows) without worrying about the details.

When the **apDebugStringBuf<>** object is constructed, we default to using the **apDebugSinkNull** object to discard all debugging output. If you recall from page 95, **cdebug** is created as a static instance of **apDebugStringBuf<>**, as shown:

```
apDebugStringBuf<char> debugstream;
std::ostream cdebug (&debugstream);
```

4.3.4 Controlling Debugging Output

Our debugging stream, **cdebug**, gives us a place to write debugging information and the flexibility to control where this information is sent. We still need more control over what information is generated. In the simplest case, we want something like:

```
if (some condition) cdebug << "debugging" << std::endl;
```

Sometimes the **condition** is complicated and depends upon certain run-time conditions; other times, the **condition** relates to the desired amount of debugging output. We are going to explore the usefulness of this latter case.

We can define an object, **apDebug**, to keep track of the current amount of debugging detail to be generated. Its definition is shown here.

```
class apDebug
{
public:
  static apDebug& gOnly ();

  int   debug   ()      { return debug_;}
  int   debug   (int d) { int cur = debug_; debug_ = d; return cur;}
  // Get/set the global debugging level

  bool isDebug (int level) { return debug_ >= level;}
  // Returns true if this level is enabled for debugging.

private:
  static apDebug* sOnly_;
  int debug_;

  apDebug ();
};
```

debug_ is an integer value that indicates the amount of debugging output to generate. We use the convention of the higher the number, the more detail to include. Whenever the debugging level of a piece of debugging code is greater than or equal to the current debugging level, the debugging code should be executed. We can automate this decision by constructing a clever macro. In general, we avoid macros, but this case really needs one:

```
#ifdef NODEBUG
#define DEBUGGING(level,statements)
#else
#define DEBUGGING(level,statements)             \
  if (apDebug::gOnly().isDebug(level)) {        \
    statements                                  \
  }
#endif
```

The macro, **DEBUGGING**, is disabled if the symbol **NODEBUG** is defined during compilation. This makes it easy to remove all debugging code from your application with a simple change to your makefile. You can treat this macro just like a function:

```
DEBUGGING(level, statements);
```

where **level** is the debugging level of these statements, and **statements** is one or more C++ statements that should be executed when **debug_ >= level**. In case you aren't used to the syntax of macros, the **** characters at the end of some lines indicate that the macro continues on the next line. Using this character allows us to make the macro look more like lines of code.

Note that our symbol, **NODEBUG**, is different than the **NDEBUG** symbol, which is used by compilers to indicate when assertions should be included in a build. We want our debugging interface to be included in production builds during testing and early releases, so we use a separate symbol, **NODEBUG**, for this purpose. If we used **NDBEUG** for both purposes, we could not have our debugging support included without assertions also being present.

One big downside to using macros is interpreting error messages during compilation. Macros are expanded, meaning that one line of your source code actually becomes many lines. If an error is found while compiling the macro, some compilers may or may not report the correct line of the error. And for those that do, you may still be left with some fairly cryptic messages. Here's another example:

```
DEBUGGING(1, cdebug << "This is level 1" << std::endl; );
DEBUGGING(2, {
  for (int i=0; i<10; i++)
    cdebug << "This is line " << i << std::endl;
});
```

In this example, we use the **{** and **}** braces to further make our macro look more like code. While this isn't strictly necessary, we think it improves the readability of the code. If the debugging level in **apDebug::gOnly()** is still zero (from the previous example), then neither of the above statements will execute. Once the macros are expanded, the above code is equivalent to the following statements:

```
if (0 >= 1) {
  first debugging statement ...
}
if (0 >= 2) {
  second debugging statement ...
}
```

Although these statements add extra bytes to the application, they add very little overhead when they are inactive. Activating either or both of these lines is easy:

```
apDebug::gOnly().debug (1);  // Debug level set to 1
apDebug::gOnly().debug (2);  // Debug level set to 2
```

We recommend that you define what the various debugging levels mean when using this technique. We also recommend that you use a limited number of values to keep things simple, as shown in Table 4.2.

Table 4.2: Debugging Levels

Debugging Level	Meaning
0	Debugging disabled
1	Error or exceptional condition
2	Timing details or execution summaries
3-8	User-defined usage
9	Show internal state

We can extend this technique to change the meaning of a debugging level by using the specific bits instead of the value. And, if an integer does not contain enough bits to contain all your combinations, you can modify **apDebug** to use a **std::bitset** to store an arbitrary number of bits, as follows:

```
class apDebug
{
public:
  static apDebug& gOnly ();

  bool  debug   (int pos) { return debug_.test (pos);}
  bool  debug   (int pos, bool value)
  { bool cur = debug_.test (pos);
    if (value)
      debug_.set (pos);
    else
      debug_.reset (pos);
    return cur;
  }
  // Get/set the global debugging level

  bool set   (int pos)
  { bool cur = debug_.test (pos); debug_.set (pos); return cur;}
  bool clear (int pos)
  { bool cur = debug_.test (pos); debug_.reset (pos); return cur;}
  // Set/clear a specific bit and return the old state

  void reset () { debug_.reset ();}
  // Turns off all debugging

  bool isDebug (int pos) { return debug_.test (pos);}
  // Returns true if this level is enabled for debugging.

private:
  static apDebug* sOnly_;
  std::bitset<32> debug_;      // 32 is an arbitrary value

  apDebug ();
};
```

In this implementation, instead of setting a debugging level, you are setting a specific bit to enable or disable a specific debugging feature. Our earlier example now looks like:

```
DEBUGGING(0, cdebug << "This is bit 0" << std::endl; );
DEBUGGING(1, {
  for (int i=0; i<10; i++)
    cdebug << "bit 1. This is line " << i << std::endl;
});
```

It can be hard to remember the meaning of each bit, so we recommend you use an enumeration to manage them as shown. Bits are numbered starting with zero.

```
enum {
  eGUIDebug     = 0, // GUI debugging
  eImageDebug   = 1, // Image operations
  eStorageDebug = 2, // Image storage operations
  ...
};
apDebug::gOnly().reset ();                  // Disable all debugging
apDebug::gOnly().set (eImageDebug);      // Enable bit-1
DEBUGGING(eImageDebug, cdebug << "Image Debugging Enabled";);
```

4.3.5 Accessing Objects Indirectly Through an Object Registry

Debugging allows you to monitor what the application is doing. It is a much more difficult task to design a full-featured remote debugger. In this section, we discuss how to access an object indirectly through a simple object registry. This registry can be used to develop debuggers running either on the same machine or on a remote machine.

If you only ever have one instance of an object, accessing it would be easy. We are very fond of using a **gOnly()** method to reference a singleton object, and this reference is available throughout the application. For example, enabling debugging using the **apDebug** object we presented in the previous section is as easy as:

```
apDebug::gOnly().set (eImageDebug);
```

The problem is more complicated when multiple instances of an object exist. Without some listing of all objects in existence, you cannot easily communicate with a specific instance. An object registry consists of two parts, as shown in Figure 4.2.

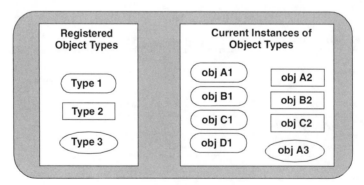

Figure 4.2: Object Registry

The first part tracks what kinds of objects are registered, with one entry per object type. The second part tracks the current instances of the specific object types. With such a registry, we can quickly see if an object type is contained in the registry, and, if so, the specific instances of the object that exist.

► EXAMPLE

Years ago when we first learned C++, it was common to see examples such as:

```
class Object
{
  Object ();
  virtual ~Object ();

  virtual void dump (ostream& out) {} // Dump the object state
  ...

};

class apImage : public Object
{
  ...
};
```

All objects were derived from a common base class (**Object** in this case), which provided one or more services to the object. This included virtual functions that would dump the state of the object, or persist or recover the object from a stream. Even trivial objects were derived from this base class because it was believed that all objects should offer a minimum set of services. Before you knew it, every object was derived from at least one other object, and multiple inheritance issues became a real headache.

Fortunately, those days are behind us. Our design gives the developer the choice of whether an object should be registered, on both an object or instance basis. We also keep it simple so that you can use only the functionality you need. This design is shown in Figure 4.3.

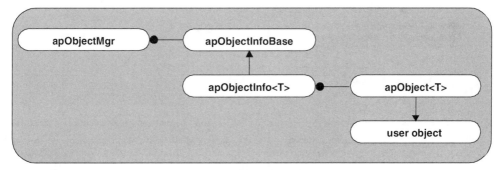

Figure 4.3: Object Registry Design

The classes work together as follows:

- **apObjectMgr** manages a list of all object types that are using our debugger interface.

- **apObjectInfoBase** is the base class that you derive objects from when you want an object that keeps track of all instances of a specific type.

- **apObjectInfo<T>** keeps track of all object instances for a specific type.

- **apObject<T>** is the base class that you derive objects from when you want an object to have remote debugging capability.

- **user object** is an object that must be derived from **apObject<T>** if the user wants it to be available for remote debugging.

❖ COMMON BASE CLASS

Every object that enters the registry must derive from a common base class, because we need to maintain a list of objects in the registry. The base class allows us to track all instances of the object as well as do some basic control. We start by designing a singleton object for each object that we want to track. Using the **gOnly()** method to access the object also means that it is only created the first time the object is created. Like we have done in other examples, we split the objects into a common non-template object and a template object, as follows:

```
class apObjectInfoBase
{
public:
  typedef std::map<void*, char> INSTANCEMAP;

  apObjectInfoBase () : debug_ (0) {}

  int  debug ()        { return debug_;}
  void debug (int d) { debug_ = d;}
  bool isDebug (int level) { return debug_ >= level;}

  void addInstance    (void* obj) { mapping_[obj] = 1;}
  void removeInstance (void* obj) { mapping_.erase (obj);}
  // Add/remove an object from our instance list

  virtual std::string process (const std::string& command) = 0;
  // Command processor.

  virtual std::string dump () = 0;
  // Returns a list of managed objects

protected:
  int          debug_;   // Debug level for this object
  INSTANCEMAP mapping_; // List of all current objects
};
```

apObjectInfoBase uses a **std::map** object to keep a list of all instances of a particular object. By storing the object as a **void*** pointer, as opposed to a native pointer, we are able to keep our solution generic. But why did we use a **std::map** object when a **std::vector** object would also work, as would a **std::list** object? We define **mapping_** as a **std::map<void*, char>**, where **void*** is the key (the address of the object), and **char** is the value (an arbitrary number). The purpose of **mapping_** is to be a list of object pointers. We chose a **std::map** object because it can efficiently handle additions and deletions and do all the work for us. For example, look at the code that adds or removes an object instance from this list:

```
void addInstance    (void* obj) { mapping_[obj] = 1;}
void removeInstance (void* obj) { mapping_.erase (obj);}
```

Not only are they very simple, but these insertions and deletions are also extremely fast. By using a **std::map** object, we do waste a little space because we store a **char** that we always ignore. **std::map** has the additional benefit of limiting the list to one instance of each object; this is a good choice, since we only track one instance of each debuggable object.

Keep in mind that there are many alternatives to using **std::map**. It is easy to spend too much time researching the problem in hopes of finding the most efficient STL component. For example, we could have also chosen to use **std::set**, as this matches the requirements of our object very closely. With so many components to choose from, this can take longer than it takes to implement the entire object. If you have not used many STL components, you will soon discover that you end up using only a small subset of objects. This is not a bad thing. For commercial software, this can give you an edge. While some teams are crafting the "perfect solution," you already have a solution implemented and working.

 Thoroughly understanding and reusing a small subset of STL components can give you a competitive advantage in getting a working solution quickly.

Figure 4.4 shows our favorite subset of STL components.

Recommended STL Components

✔ Use std::string for working with strings.

✔ Use std::vector for a 1D array with fast random access to the elements.

✔ Use std::list for a 1D array with efficient insertion and deletion.

✔ Use std::map for storing key, value pairs.

Figure 4.4: Recommended STL Components

Our base class, **apObjectInfoBase**, also contains a debugging interface very similar to the **apDebug** object we presented earlier. In this implementation, we use the **debug_** variable as a level, rather than as a sequence of bits. The class also defines pure virtual methods **process()** and **dump()**. **dump()** produces a human readable description of the object. **process()** is a general interface that we can use for remote debugging. To use this functionality, however, we still need one instance for every object type. That is exactly what the **apObjectInfo<>** class provides:

```
template <class T>
class apObjectInfo : public apObjectInfoBase
{
```

```
public:
  static apObjectInfo<T>& gOnly ();

  const std::string& name () const { return name_;}

  virtual std::string process (const std::string& command);

  virtual std::string dump ();
private:
  static apObjectInfo<T>* sOnly_;
  std::string name_;

  apObjectInfo ();
};
```

The template argument, **T**, for **apObjectInfo<>** is the name of the object type we want to debug. In addition to being a singleton object and defining our usual **gOnly()** function, **apObjectInfo<>** also provides an implementation for the pure virtual methods in **apObjectInfoBase**, as shown:

```
template <class T>
std::string apObjectInfo<T>::dump ()
{
  std::string str;
  char buffer[16];

  INSTANCEMAP::iterator i;
  for (i=mapping_.begin(); i != mapping_.end(); i++) {
    sprintf (buffer, " %d", i->first);
    str += buffer;
  }
  return str;
}
```

Our object maintains a list of all instances, so the **dump()** method produces a list of instances by address. We could have made the default implementation of **dump()** do much more, like display the object details of each instance, but this goes beyond the scope of **apObjectInfo<>**. If we didn't restrict ourselves to a minimal representation of this object, we would have added some means of iterating on all the instances of the object. This would give the client the ability to access any instance. Besides, **dump()** is more of a debugging aid to monitor how many instances exist.

We should be spending our time deciding what **process()** does. When we first considered **process()**, we didn't know exactly what the function should do, so we wrote a stub function instead:

```
template <class T>
std::string apObjectInfo<T>::process (const std::string& command)
{
  //TODO
  return "";
}
```

During development, label incomplete functions with **//TODO** (or some other comment) to make sure it gets revisited later.

As the stub function indicates, a command string is sent to **process()** for processing and any result is returned as a string. Both the argument and return type are strings, because we want to keep the interface very generic. Using strings comes at a price, because the command string must be parsed each time to decide what to do.

❖ GENERIC STRING PARSING

Writing a generic parsing routine isn't difficult. We place it in a class, **apStringTools**, to serve as a namespace for similar string functions. Our parsing function takes a string and a list of terminator characters and returns two strings: one containing the next token in the string, and the other containing the remaining string data. The header file contains:

```
typedef struct apToken
{
  std::string parsed;
  std::string remainder;
} apToken;

class apStringTools
{
public:
  ...
  static apToken sParse (const std::string& str,
                         const std::string& term = sStandardTerm);

  static std::string sStandardTerm;
  // Standard terminators (space, tab, newline)
};
```

Our implementation uses only **std::string** functions to accomplish the parsing. The **find_first_of()** and **find_first_not_of()** methods are used to determine where the next token is located, and **substr()** divides the string into two pieces, as shown:

```
// Note. The first character in the string is a space
std::string apStringTools::sStandardTerm = " \t\r\n";

apToken apStringTools::sParse (const std::string& str,
                               const std::string& term)
{
  apToken result;

  // Skip over leading terminators
  size_t start = str.find_first_not_of (term);
  if (start == str.npos) {
    // The entire string only contains terminator characters
    return result;
  }
```

```
        // Find the first command
        size_t end = str.find_first_of (term, start);
        if (end == str.npos) {
          result.parsed = str;
          return result;
        }

        // Extract the first command
        result.parsed = str.substr (start, end-start);

        // Return the rest of the string (after the terminators)
        size_t next = str.find_first_not_of (term, end);
        if (next != str.npos)
          result.remainder = str.substr (next);

        return result;
      }
```

❖ COMMAND PARSER

With this function, we can now write a simple command processor to parse our string. We support three functions.

■ **list** returns a space-separated list of instances of this object. A unique identifier is returned for each instance (the hex address of the object).

■ **execute <string>** calls the **process()** method for each instance and passes it the remaining string.

■ **to <instance> <string>** calls the **process()** method of a specific instance and passes it the remaining string. The instance should match the identifier returned by the **list** command.

A **process()** method to support these commands with simple **if** statements is shown here.

```
      template <class T>
      std::string apObjectInfo<T>::process (const std::string& command)
      {
        // Parse our command
        apToken token = apStringTools::sParse (command);

        INSTANCEMAP::iterator i;
        std::string result;         // Our result string
        char buffer[16];            // Buffer for sprintf()

        if (token.parsed == "list") {
          // "list" Returns list of all instance addresses
          for (i=mapping_.begin(); i != mapping_.end(); ++i) {
            sprintf (buffer, "%x ", i->first);
            result += buffer;
          }
        }
        else if (token.parsed == "execute") {
          // "execute <command>" Send the remaining string to instances
          for (i=mapping_.begin(); i != mapping_.end(); ++i) {
            T* obj = reinterpret_cast<T*>(i->first);
            result += obj->process (token.remainder);
            result += " ";
          }
        }
```

```
    else if (token.parsed == "to") {
      // "to <instance> <command>" Send remaining string to a
      // specific instance. Matching is by string because the list
      // command returns a list of strings
      apToken instance = apStringTools::sParse (token.remainder);
      for (i=mapping_.begin(); i != mapping_.end(); ++i) {
        sprintf (buffer, "%x", i->first);
        if (instance.parsed == buffer) {
          T* obj = reinterpret_cast<T*>(i->first);
          result += obj->process (instance.remainder);
        }
      }
    }
    else {
      // Unknown command. Don't do anything
    }
    return result;
  }
```

If you had a large number of commands to support, you could make the parsing faster by using some shortcuts. For example, we can rewrite the comparison portion of our previous example to group commands by their length, as shown:

```
switch (token.parsed.size()) {
case 2:
  if (token.parsed == "to") {
    // 'to' processing
  }
  break;
case 4:
  if (token.parsed == "list") {
    // 'list' processing
  }
  break;
case 7:
  if (token.parsed == "execute") {
    // 'execute' processing
  }
  break;
default:
}
```

This example may look unimpressive, but imagine what would happen if you had 50 commands and implemented **process()** with this style. Instead of performing 50 comparisons in the worst case, you would probably perform no more than 10 to 15.

Perhaps a better solution when you have many commands to process is to use a **std::map** object to map the command name (a string) to a function or object that handles the request. This solution is beyond the scope of this book, but the idea is to define the following inside **apObjectInfo<>**:

std::map<std::string /*command*/, apCommandProcessor*> mapping_;

We have not defined **apCommandProcessor**, but we would derive one object from **apCommandProcessor** for every command we want to handle. Once **mapping_** is built with the data, either during static initialization or by means of an initialization function, it can be used to start processing commands.

Before going any further, let us review how using templates has drastically improved the design. Before templates, we might have used macros to construct the equivalent of the `apObjectInfo<>` object. Macros are workable for short definitions, but for anything longer than a few lines, they can be difficult to follow and maintain.

For example, a macro to declare, but not define the object, is as shown.

```
#define CREATEINSTANCECLASS(classname)                        \
class apObjectInfo_##classname : public apObjectInfoBase      \
  {                                                           \
  public:                                                     \
    static apObjectInfo_##classname gOnly ();                 \
    virtual std::string process (const std::string& command); \
    virtual std::string dump ();                              \
  private:                                                    \
    static apObjectInfo_##classname* sOnly_;                  \
    apObjectInfo_##classname ();                              \
  };
```

To create an object similar to `apObjectInfo<T>`, we do as follows:

```
CREATEINSTANCECLASS(T);
```

where **T** is the name of the object of which you want to track the instances. This creates an object `apObjectInfo_T`. Another macro is still needed to supply the definition of the object. If templates did not exist, we would still exploit macros to avoid duplicate code. It is our experience that writing a macro for the first time is not too difficult, especially if you already have the class design. The real trouble begins when you later try to extend or correct problems with it. This happens because it is hard to visualize the function when it is written in macro format. The merging operator inside macros (i.e., **##**) also reduces the readability a great deal.

❖ OBJECT REGISTRY

We have two more pieces to go. `apObjectInfo<>` contains information about each instance of a particular object. We still need a way to keep track of each `apObjectInfo<>` in existence. This is also a singleton object, which represents the overall object registry:

```
class apObjectMgr
{
 public:
  typedef std::map<std::string, apObjectInfoBase*> OBJMAP;

  static apObjectMgr& gOnly ();

  std::string dump ();
  // Text dump of all objects in use

  void debugMessage (const std::string& header,
                     const std::string& msg);
  // Generate a debug message to cdebug

  void add (const std::string& name, apObjectInfoBase* obj);
  // Add an object to our list

  apObjectInfoBase* find (const std::string& name);
  // Returns a pointer to a specific apObjectInfoBase, or 0
```

```
private:
  static apObjectMgr* sOnly_;
  apObjectMgr ();

  OBJMAP mapping_;   // List of all managed classes
};
```

mapping_ takes the name of an object to a pointer and maps it to the singleton object that manages it. This is not a pointer to an **apObjectInfo<>** class, but to its base class, **apObjectInfoBase**.

debugMessage() is a general purpose function that you can use to write to the **cdebug** stream. It does nothing more than write a header (which is particular to an object type) and a message, as shown here.

```
void apObjectMgr::debugMessage (const std::string& header,
                                const std::string& msg)
{ cdebug << header.c_str() << msg.c_str() << std::endl; }
```

The **add()** method adds a new object type to our registry. We can see how it is used by looking at the **apObjectInfo<>** constructor:

```
apObjectInfo<T>::apObjectInfo<T> ()
{
  // Setup our object name. This is compiler and platform
  // dependent so this function can be modified to create
  // a more uniform string
  name_ = typeid(T).name();

  // Add this class to our apObjectMgr list
  apObjectMgr::gOnly().add (name_, this);
}
```

Since **apObjectInfo<>** is a singleton object, this constructor only runs once. We use **typeid()** to specify the object name to use in the registry. Keep in mind that **typeid()** is compiler and platform dependent so the value of this string may surprise you. For example: in Microsoft Visual Studio on a Windows platform, using **typeid()** for an object, **apTest**, returns **class apTest**. On a FreeBSD system using gcc (version 2.95.3), it returns **6apTest.** For our purposes this is fine because the string is unique on any platform.

There is no **subtract()** method in this object, because once an object is first constructed, it always stays in **mapping_**. Our singleton object is only destroyed when the application closes, so there is no need to remove an item from our map.

find() does nothing more than return a specific pointer to an **apObjectInfo<>** object, as shown here.

```
apObjectInfoBase* apObjectMgr::find (const std::string& name)
{
  OBJMAP::iterator i = mapping_.find (name);
  if (i == mapping_.end())
    return 0;
  return i->second;
}
```

In many applications, **find()** is not needed, since you can deal directly with a specific instance of **apObjectInfo<>** (for example, **apObjectInfo<apTest>**). **apObjectMgr** has a minimalistic design. For example, if you wanted to send a command to the command processor of each object manager (which will in turn send it to each instance), you could add a method such as this:

```
std::string apObjectMgr::process (const std::string& command)
{
  std::string result;
  OBJMAP::iterator i;
  for (i=mapping_.begin(); i != mapping_.end(); ++i) {
    result += i->second->process (command);
    result += " ";
  }
  return result;
}
```

❖ DEBUG OBJECTS BASE CLASS

Now that we have a top-level registry object, as well as one that can track all the instances of an object, we need to add some functionality to the objects themselves. We do this by creating a base class for all objects that need debugging. By writing it as a template class, the compiler will enforce the data types for us. We will keep the interface very simple.

```
template <class T>
class apObject
{
public:
  enum eOptions {eNone=0, eTrackInstance=1};

  apObject (eOptions options = eTrackInstance);
  virtual ~apObject ();

  int  debug ()       { return apObjectInfo<T>::gOnly().debug();}
  void debug (int d) { apObjectInfo<T>::gOnly().debug(d);}
  bool isDebug (int level)
  { return apObjectInfo<T>::gOnly().isDebug(level);}
  // Interface to apObjectInfo<T> to simplify our code

  void debugMessage (const std::string& msg);
  // Output a debug Message.

  virtual std::string header () const;
  // The header string printed before any debugging messages

  virtual std::string process (const std::string& command);
  // Command processor for a specific instance
};
```

Objects that you write will derive from **apObject<>**, so it helps to remember this when you decide what functionality **apObject<>** should have. Although we assume that all object instances of a particular object type will use this debugging interface, we can exclude certain objects from our object list by passing **eNone** to the constructor.

The constructor and destructor are shown here.

```
template <class T> apObject<T>::apObject (eOptions options)
{
  // Add ourself to our instance list if enabled
  if (options & eTrackInstance)
    apObjectInfo<T>::gOnly().addInstance (this);
}

template <class T> apObject<T>::~apObject ()
{ apObjectInfo<T>::gOnly().removeInstance (this);}
```

The methods **debug()** and **isDebug()** are simple wrappers to the corresponding methods in **apObjectInfo<>**. **debugMessage()** is a wrapper function that sends a message and header, via **header()**, to our debugging stream.

```
template <class T>
void apObject<T>::debugMessage (const std::string& msg)
{
  apObjectMgr::gOnly().debugMessage (header(), msg);
}

template <class T>
std::string apObject<T>::header () const
{
  const T* obj = static_cast<const T*> (this);

  char buffer[32];
  sprintf (buffer, " (0x%0x): ", obj);
  std::string h = apObjectInfo<T>::gOnly().name();
  h += buffer;
  return h;
}
```

process() is the method most objects should override. When we showed a sample command processor earlier, we defined an **execute** command to send a string to all object instances. **process()** is the method that will receive that string, do some processing, and return a result string. **process()** is not a pure virtual function, and will return an empty string if not overridden. You can see an example where **process()** is overridden to output a debugging string in the unit test for debugging on the CD-ROM.

Our debugging registry is somewhat heavy, in that there are many template objects that are created to manage the interface. This registry is not designed to be used by all objects in a system. Rather, it is suitable for higher-level objects that are complex or contain a lot of information, such as an image object. Often there will be from just a couple to a few hundred instances of an image in existence at any one time. All told, there may be no more than ten to twenty objects that require this type of interface. You certainly do not want or need this interface for a simple class like:

```
class apSum
{
public:
  apSum : sum_ (0)        {}
  void   sum (double d) { sum_ += d;}
  double sum () const   { return sum_;}
private:
  double sum_;
};
```

4.4 Summary

In this chapter, we explored other aspects that need to be considered for our final design. They included such coding guidelines as naming conventions, comment styles, indentation style, and header file rules. These are often passionately debated issues, and we offered practical advice to selecting a workable set of guidelines. Next, we discussed reusability and what that means for the design of objects. We also touched briefly on some of the functional and testing issues that arise with reusable components.

And finally, we spent much time discussing a debugging environment that could be integrated into the design of the framework. It offers many advantages, the main one being that it is present in production releases, but requires little overhead. This environment included a generalized debugging stream that outputs debugging information, as controlled by a separate **apDebug** object, to various sinks (or destinations). During our design and implementation, we explored STL components that were useful in the solution. We extended the environment to allow remote access to objects through an object registry, which is capable of handling many objects.

In Chapter 5, we take a look at the system-level issues that may affect the final image framework design. These issues include multithreaded and multiprocess designs, as well as strategies for using exceptions. We also take the time to explore run-time and compile-time issues, and their effects on performance as it relates to the design. Finally, we touch on adding support for future expansion into non-English and double-byte languages.

5

System Considerations

In this chapter we discuss issues that influence high-level software design. In addition to covering C++ issues like exception handling and virtual functions, we discuss such system considerations as multithreading and internationalization

5.1 Multithreaded and Multiprocess Designs

Modern operating systems, and most embedded systems, support multiple processes or threads. A *process* is a standalone application that performs a particular purpose. A process can be as complicated as a word-processing package like Microsoft Word, or as simple as the following "Hello World" application:

```
#include <iostream>
int main ()
{
  std::cout << "Hello World" << std::endl;
  return 0;
}
```

Each process is insulated from all others, even in the case of multiple instances of the same application. As an application designer, you typically do not need to concern yourself with the details of what other applications or even what the operating system is doing. However, this does not imply that different processes cannot work in unison to perform a task. In this section, we explore how partitioning a problem into many separate pieces can create a solid design that helps decrease the development time and increase the robustness of your application.

Unlike processes, *threads* are not insulated from each other. A process can consist of one or more threads that in many ways behave like separate processes. You can write a thread as though it exists by itself, but the operating system does not treat it this way. All threads in a process share the same memory space, which has both positive and negative effects. This means that the developer needs to decide when threads can and should be used to improve performance and reliability. Even if the operating system does not support threads natively, it is possible to use third-party packages to get this functionality.

The techniques we discuss here are also applicable to *embedded systems*. The dynamics of embedded systems are different from those of full-blown operating systems, such as Microsoft Windows or the many UNIX variations. Most embedded systems are deterministic, meaning they have the ability to guarantee a certain response time or processing rate. They usually support processes and threads. Embedded systems often have a very simple user interface, or none at all. In addition, they often have limited memory and other resources. And, significantly, they are designed to run indefinitely without requiring rebooting.

To use threads and processes successfully, you must be able to communicate between them, which is referred to as *interprocess communication*. Although the functionality differs among operating systems, we concern ourselves with the most important components:

- Creating and controlling threads
- Synchronizing access to common resources using threads (Section 5.1.2 on page 126)
- Communicating between processes (Section 5.1.3 on page 133)

In our discussion of these features, we focus on ways to improve reliability and decrease development time. We only use features if they offer a clear advantage for commercial software development. Consequently, we also talk about when these features should be avoided.

5.1.1 Threads

Threads are one of the first elements to consider when designing an application. Many applications lend themselves well to this mechanism, and threads are widely available on most platforms. Still, we must consider whether or not to incorporate threads into a design. Debugging and correcting problems in a multithreaded application is usually more difficult than in a non-threaded application.

▶ **EXAMPLE** ───

Let's look at a completely hypothetical threaded application that is woefully inadequate, but demonstrates our point:

```
int step     = 0;  // Our current processing step
int analyzed = 0;  // Our current analysis step

void thread1 ()
{
  while (true) {
    processingStep1 ();
    step = 1;
    processingStep2 ();
    step = 2;
    resetProcessing ();
  }
```

```
    }

void thread2 ()
{
  while (true) {
    if (step != analyzed) {
      switch (step) {
      case 1:
        analyzeStep1 ();
        analyzed = 1;
        break;
      case 2:
        analyzeStep2 ();
        analyzed = 2;
        break;
      }
    }
  }
}
```

In this example, we create two functions, **thread1()** and **thread2()**, which run in separate threads. Assume that when the application starts, these two functions start executing. The first thread performs two different processing steps, resets itself, and then performs these steps again. The second thread analyzes the results from each processing step. When the application starts, **thread1()** will run and do whatever processing is needed for step 1. **thread2()** will wait until the processing is complete and will analyze it. This process continues with step 2, and then the whole process repeats itself.

The first question you might ask is, "Will this application work?" The best answer we have for you is that we have no idea. There is no explicit control over the threads. It is up to the underlying system to define how and when these threads will execute.

Threads are often written as functions that never end, because a thread usually does not end. The thread's lifetime is the same as the application itself. This is why we ignore the issues surrounding starting and stopping threads in our example.

Full-blown operating systems, such as Microsoft Windows and many UNIX versions, offer a *fully preemptive multithreaded environment*. The operating system takes care of how and when each thread receives a slice of processing time. In other words, **thread1()** and **thread2()** can be written with very little knowledge about what the other thread function is doing.

At the other end of the spectrum are *cooperative multithreaded environments*. In this environment, you must control when one thread stops and another thread runs. While this offers complete control over the switching from one thread to another, it also means that, if poorly written, one thread can consume 100% of the processor time. Cooperative multithreading is often found in small embedded systems or as third-party libraries for platforms that have no native multithreading.

If you have the choice, use the preemptive model to ensure that *deadlocks* are minimized. A deadlock is a situation where no thread can continue executing, causing the system to effectively hang. Besides, you can always use thread priorities to make a preemptive multithreaded system behave like a cooperative system. On some systems, a high priority thread simply gets more processing time than lower priority threads. On other systems, a lower priority thread gets no processing time while a higher priority thread is running.

❖ POSIX

The number of threading APIs has fortunately become much smaller in recent years. IEEE Standard 1003.1 (also known as POSIX) is available and defines a complete interface to thread functionality, including control and synchronization. The specification is available online (currently located at **http://www.opengroup.org/onlinepubs/007904975/ toc.htm**). On most platforms with native thread support, a POSIX interface is available (on Win32 platforms, for example, a fairly complete interface can be found at **http:// sources.redhat.com/pthreads-win32**).

POSIX is complicated and somewhat intimidating. In keeping with our desire to keep things simple, we wrap the C interface in a simple class to handle our threading needs. If this simple interface is insufficient for your needs, you can extend it as necessary. We are not offering this sample as a class that can be used in all circumstances, but you may be surprised at how useful it is. We present two versions of this object: one for POSIX for UNIX platforms, and one for Win32 for Microsoft platforms. We keep our operating system-specific versions in different directories that are accessed by a top-level include file. The file hierarchy is:

```
/include
    thread.h
    /win32
        thread.h
    /unix
        thread.h
```

The top-level version of **thread.h** loads the implementation-specific version of **thread.h**, or defines a default implementation of **apThread**. Although there is a pthreads compatibility library available on Microsoft Windows, we have chosen to use native Win32 calls because it is a simpler interface and is only going to be used in the Win32 environment. The Microsoft Win32 version of **thread.h** is as shown.

```
class apThread
{
public:
  apThread () : threadid_ (-1) {}
  ~apThread () {if (threadid_ != -1) stop();}

  int threadid () const { return threadid_;}

  bool start ()
  {
   threadid_ = _beginthreadex (NULL, 0, thread_, this,
                CREATE_SUSPENDED,
                (unsigned int*) &threadid_);
   if (threadid_ != 0)
     ResumeThread ((HANDLE)threadid_);
   return (threadid_ != 0);
```

```
    }
    // Start the thread running

    bool stop ()
    {
     TerminateThread ((HANDLE) threadid_, -1);
     return true;
    }
    // Stop the thread

    bool wait (unsigned int seconds = 0)
    {
     DWORD wait = seconds * 1000;
     if (wait == 0) wait = INFINITE;
     DWORD status = WaitForSingleObject ((HANDLE) threadid_, wait);
     return (status != WAIT_TIMEOUT);
    }
    // Wait for thread to complete

    void sleep (unsigned int msec) { Sleep (msec);}
    // Sleep for the specified amount of time.
  protected:
    int threadid_;

    static unsigned int __stdcall thread_ (void* obj)
    {
     // Call the overriden thread function
     apThread* t = reinterpret_cast<apThread*>(obj);
     t->thread ();
     return 0;
    }

    virtual void thread () {
     _endthreadex (0);
     CloseHandle ((HANDLE) threadid_);
    }
    // Thread function, Override this in derived classes.
  };
```

Unlike previous examples where we define a base class and derive one or more implementations, only a single version of **apThread** is defined. If this file is included on a Win32 platform, the symbol **WIN32** is defined, so that the class definition comes from **win32/thread.h**. On UNIX platforms that support pthreads, the makefile defines **HasPTHREADS** so that the file **unix/thread.h** is included. If neither is true, or the symbol **AP_NOTHREADS** is defined, the default implementation is used. If there was no default implementation, any objects derived from **apThread** will fail to compile.

apThread is very easy to use. You can derive an object from **apThread** and then override the **thread()** member function. This function will execute when **start()** is called and continue executing until the application is finished, or the **stop()** method is called. The default implementation has the following behavior:

- **start()**, **stop()**, and **wait()** always signal failure.
- **sleep()** returns immediately.

Obviously this is not the desired behavior, but without thread support you cannot expect the application to run properly. We originally thought about defining **start()** like this:

```
    bool start () { thread(); return true;}
```

Doing so would cause nothing but trouble. If threading is not supported, the call to **thread()** will never complete, and hence **start()** will never return. It is much safer to just return **false** and hope the application fails gracefully.

 If you are building multithreaded applications on Microsoft Windows, remember to compile against one of the multithreaded run-time libraries.

The **stop()** method should be used very sparingly. Thread termination is very abrupt and can easily cause locking issues and other resource leakage. You should always provide a more graceful way to terminate your threads, such as using a flag to specify when a thread can safely shut down. The full UNIX and Win32 implementations can be found on the CD-ROM.

Let's look at the **start()** and **stop()** methods for UNIX and Win32 implementations.

❖ MICROSOFT WIN32

The Microsoft Win32 API is as shown.

```
bool start () {
  threadid_ = _beginthreadex (NULL, 0, thread_, this,
                              CREATE_SUSPENDED,
                              (unsigned int*) &threadid_);
  if (threadid_ != 0)
    ResumeThread ((HANDLE)threadid_);
  return (threadid_ != 0);
}

bool stop () {
  TerminateThread ((HANDLE) threadid_, -1);
  return true;
}
protected:
  int threadid_;

  static unsigned int __stdcall thread_ (void* obj) {
    apThread* t = reinterpret_cast<apThread*>(obj);
    t->thread ();
    return 0;
  }
```

❖ UNIX

The pthreads implementation for UNIX is as shown.

```
bool start () {
  int status;
  status = pthread_create (&threadid_, NULL, thread_, this);
  return (status == 0);
}

bool stop () {
  pthread_cancel (threadid_);
  return true;
```

```
    }
  protected:
    pthread_t threadid_;

    static void* thread_ (void* obj) {
      apThread* t = reinterpret_cast<apThread*>(obj);
      t->thread ();
      return 0;
    }
```

With the implementation details hidden, let's look at a simple example:

```
  class thread1 : public apThread
  {
    void thread ();
  };

  void thread1::thread ()
  {
    for (int i=0; i<10; i++) {
      std::cout << threadid() << ": " << i << std::endl;
      sleep (100);
    }
  }

  int main()
  {
    thread1 thread1Inst, thread2Inst;
    thread1Inst.start ();
    thread2Inst.start ();

    thread1Inst.wait ();
    thread2Inst.wait ();
    return 0;
  }
```

Two worker threads are created: each prints ten lines of output and then exits. Beyond that, it is difficult to predict what will actually be output. In addition, what will be output also depends upon the platform on which it runs. On Microsoft Windows, for example, the output is very orderly, as shown:

```
  2020: 0
  2024: 0
  2020: 1
  2024: 1
  2020: 2
  2024: 2
  2020: 3
  2024: 3
  2020: 4
  2024: 4
  2020: 5
  2024: 5
  2020: 6
  2024: 6
  2020: 7
  2024: 7
  2020: 8
  2024: 8
```

```
2020: 9
2024: 9
```

However, you can't rely upon the behavior of the operating system to control the output. For example, if **sleep(100)** is removed from the **thread()** definition, the output changes to be as shown:

```
2020: 0
2020: 1
2024: 0
2024: 1
2024: 2
2024: 3
20242020: 2
2020: 3
2020: 4
2020: 5
2020: 4
2024: 5
2024: 6
2024: 7
2024: 6
2020: 7
2020: 8
2020: 9
: 8
2024: 9
```

When the operating system decides to switch from one thread to another, it is usually after a thread has consumed a certain amount of processing time. This can happen any time, including in the middle of executing a line of code. If each thread was completely independent of the others, this would not be an issue. But even in our simple example, both threads use a common resource: they both generate output to the console.

This example highlights the primary challenge when using threads. It is imperative that access to shared resources be carefully controlled. A shared resource can be more than just an input/output stream or file. It might be something as simple as a global variable that can be accessed by many threads. As the number of threads increases, the complexity of managing them increases as well. You might wonder why we always seem to encapsulate a functionality like threads into its own class. After all, if your application only ever runs on a single platform, you might consider using the native API calls directly. But encapsulation does serve another important purpose. In addition to ensuring that all users of our thread object get the same behavior, encapsulation allows us to use our debugging resources to observe what is happening. Most thread problems occur with missing or incorrect synchronization, an issue we will talk about shortly. But another common problem occurs when the thread itself goes out of scope and closes. Consider this example:

```
class thread: public apThread
{
  void thread () {
    while (true) {
      ...
    }
  }
}
```

```
};

int main()
{
  thread thread1;
  thread1.start ();
  {
    thread thread2;
    thread2.start ();
  }
  ...
}
```

thread2 goes out of scope when the closing brace is reached, causing the thread to stop running. Before you say that you would never write code like this, you need to realize how easy it is to write code that results in such behavior. For example:

■ One or more **apThread** objects is controlled by another object that goes out of scope.

■ An exception is thrown, and the **apThread** object goes out of scope during stack unwinding.

One solution to the scoping problem is to allocate **apThread** objects on the heap with operator **new**. While you can be very careful not to delete heap-based objects prematurely, remembering to delete them at all is another matter. It is not uncommon for bad coding practices like this to surface in multithreaded code. Single-threaded applications often rely on the operating system to cleanly shut down an application, and therefore this issue is ignored. These practices do not work with multithreaded applications unless the lifetime of all threads is the same as that of the application itself.

This demonstrates yet another benefit of encapsulating a thread in **apThread**. Your **apThread**-derived object can control the object lifetime of other components that exist only to serve a thread. Although you can do this inside the constructor and destructor of your derived object, we recommend overriding **start()** and **stop()** and taking care of it there. Doing so in these functions delays the construction and destruction of other components until they are needed, rather than when the **apThread** object is constructed.

We recommend that Singleton objects be used for threads that persist for the entire lifetime of an application. Construction happens when the object is first referenced, presumably when the application begins execution.

 Use Singleton objects for threads that persist for the entire lifetime of the application.

Let's look at the following example:

```
class thread: public apThread
{
public:
  static thread& gOnly();
```

```
    void thread ();
  private:
    static thread* sOnly_;
    thread ();
  };
```

When the application starts:

```
    thread::gOnly().start ();
```

it causes the thread to be constructed and begin execution.

Applications that use threads, especially those that frequently create and destroy them, should be watched closely to detect problems during development and testing. You must make sure that global resources, such as heap, are properly allocated and freed by threads to prevent serious problems later. Heap leakage is one of the easier problems to find, but it usually takes more time to fix. You are far better off assuming that your thread has a memory problem than assuming that it does not. If you take this stance during the design, you will be very sensitive to memory allocation and deallocation. If your design calls for many threads to execute the same piece of code, you should account for this in your unit tests by creating at least as many threads as you expect to use in the actual application.

 If many threads are required for a piece of code, make sure your unit tests include at least as many threads as you expect in the actual application.

The execution of many threads consumes more than just heap memory. Other resources, both system- and user-defined, must be monitored to make sure they are properly allocated and freed. This is easy if you encapsulate your resources inside a Singleton object to manage them. Besides the obvious advantage of having a single point where resources are allocated and freed, the resource manager can keep track of how many, and to whom, each resource is allocated. If all the resources become exhausted, the list maintained by the resource manager can be examined to track down the culprit.

5.1.2 Thread Synchronization

It is uncommon for threads in an application to be completely independent of each other. After all, if they were truly independent, they could be separate processes. Let's look at the example we first used when threads were introduced:

```
    class thread1 : public apThread
    {
      void thread ();
    };

    void thread1::thread ()
    {
      for (int i=0; i<10; i++) {
        std::cout << threadid() << ": " << i << std::endl;
        sleep (100);
```

```
    }
  }

  int main()
  {
    thread1 thread1Inst, thread2Inst;
    thread1Inst.start ();
    thread2Inst.start ();

    thread1Inst.wait ();
    thread2Inst.wait ();
    return 0;
  }
```

This example creates two threads that both write to **std::cout**. The output from this example cannot be predicted because thread execution is dependent upon the operating system. The line that outputs information to the console:

```
std::cout << threadid() << ": " << i << std::endl;
```

is not *atomic*. This means that this line of code is not guaranteed to run as a unit because the operating system scheduler may switch control to another thread, which might also be sending output to **std::cout**. Unless you really understand how the scheduler works on your platforms, you should assume that no operation is atomic. This really isn't an issue until you start using threads that share resources. Resources can be:

- Any type of I/O, including console and file I/O.

- Hardware resources, such as timers, image acquisition, or image buffers.

- Any global variable, such as reference counts, queues, or object lists.

Shared resources can also be less tangible things like *bandwidth*, the amount of information your application can send or receive per unit of time. For example, many threads can simultaneously request information from sockets, such as fetching web pages or other information. Most operating systems can manage hundreds or thousands of simultaneous connections and will patiently wait for information to arrive. The management is not the problem, but the timely receipt of information is. If the machine running your application needs a constant stream of information, you may find that you are trying to access more information than you have available bandwidth to receive.

Before we discuss how to use synchronization to control access to shared resources, let us discuss something you should never (or almost never) do. Most operating systems can give an application almost complete control of a system. For example, a process can be made to consume most of the processor time, while other processes are made to wait. A single thread can be made to run such that no other thread will execute. This is extremely dangerous. If you are considering doing this because your existing machine is not fast enough, you probably should consider running on a faster machine. After all, if a machine can only execute **N** instructions per second and you must run **N+1** instructions, no amount of optimization will help you. More likely, the current design is lacking the techniques to make the pieces interact properly.

Threads can be made to interact nicely with each other by synchronizing access to any resources that are shared. Most operating systems support many types of synchronization objects, but we will only discuss one of them. The big difference among most synchronization methods is their scope. By scope, we mean whether shared resources can be accessed by different threads in the same process, different processes, or even different machines. Remember, the larger the scope, the more overhead that must be paid in order to use it. By restricting ourselves to communication between threads, we can add synchronization with very little cost.

❖   APLOCK

As we did when we presented threads, we will show two implementations of **apLock**: POSIX for UNIX platforms and Win32 for Microsoft platforms. The file hierarchy looks the same:

```
/include
    lock.h
    /win32
        lock.h
    /unix
        lock.h
```

The locking metaphor is very descriptive of what this object does. When one thread obtains a lock, all other threads that wish to obtain the lock must wait for it to be freed. As with **apThread**, the top-level version of **lock.h** loads the appropriate version of **lock.h**, or a default version if necessary.

```
// Decide which implementation to use
// Defining AP_NOTHREADS will use the default implementation in
// applications where threading isn't an issue.

#if !defined(AP_NOTHREADS) && defined(WIN32)
#include <win32/lock.h>
#elif !defined(AP_NOTHREADS) && defined(HasPTHREADS)
#include <unix/lock.h>
#else

class apLock
{
public:
  apLock  ()        {}
  ~apLock ()        {}

  bool lock   () { return true;}      // Get the lock
  bool unlock () { return true;}      // Release the lock
};

#endif
```

One **apLock** object is constructed for each resource whose access must be limited to one thread at a time. The default version always returns immediately as though the lock/unlock operation were successful. We can modify our previous example to include locking by creating a global object to control access to the console. To work correctly, the lock must be obtained before something is written to the console, and then unlocked when finished.

```
apLock consoleLock;
class thread1 : public apThread
{
  void thread ();
};

void thread1::thread ()
{
  for (int i=0; i<10; i++) {
    consoleLock.lock ();
    std::cout << threadid() << ": " << i << std::endl;
    consoleLock.unlock ();
    sleep (100);
  }
}

int main()
{
  thread1 thread1Inst, thread2Inst;
  thread1Inst.start ();
  thread2Inst.start ();

  thread1Inst.wait ();
  thread2Inst.wait ();
  return 0;
}
```

The differences from our previous example are:

```
apLock consoleLock;
...
    consoleLock.lock ();
    std::cout << threadid() << ": " << i << std::endl;
    consoleLock.unlock ();
...
```

When this snippet of code executes, you will no longer see lines of output broken by output from another thread. It will produce output similar to this:

```
2020: 0
2024: 0
2020: 1
2024: 1
2024: 2
2020: 2
2024: 3
2020: 3
2020: 4
2024: 4
2020: 5
2024: 5
2024: 6
2020: 6
2024: 7
2020: 7
2020: 8
2024: 8
2020: 9
2024: 9
```

If this were actual production code, we never would have defined **consoleLock** as a global object. We probably would not use a Singleton object either, because **consoleLock** is used only for console I/O. The best solution is to define an **apLock** object in a class that manages console I/O. For instance, we could modify our debugging stream interface (see Section 4.3.1 on page 94) to include a lock so that the **cdebug** stream is synchronized between threads.

To simplify the locking and unlocking required to use **consoleLock**, we can take advantage of a technique called Resource Acquisition Is Initialization, also referred to as RAII. To use this method, we define a simple wrapper object that guarantees the lock will be freed when the object is destroyed. We create a new object, **apConsoleLocker**, to manage and own the lock as shown.

```
class apConsoleLocker
{
public:
  apConsoleLocker ()  { consoleLock_.lock();}
  ~apConsoleLocker () { consoleLock_.unlock();}

private:
  static apLock consoleLock_;

  // Prohibit copy and assignment
  apConsoleLocker                (const apConsoleLocker& src);
  apConsoleLocker& operator= (const apConsoleLocker& src);
};
```

Our example, continued from the previous page, now looks like this:

```
...
    {
      apConsoleLocker lock;
      std::cout << threadid() << :  << i << std::endl;
    }
...
```

The use of braces is very important, as the destruction of **apConsoleLocker** is what releases the lock so that other threads can use the resource that the lock controls. If you do not want the lifetime of your **apConsoleLocker** object to match that of the function it is defined in, you can use braces to control its lifetime.

The full UNIX and Win32 implementations are found on the CD-ROM, but the important sections are shown here. For our UNIX implementation with pthreads, we use a *mutex object* (named because it coordinates mutually exclusive access to a resource). Since only one thread at a time can own a mutex, this mechanism solves our problem nicely. Microsoft Windows has mutex support as well, but it also allows them to be used between processes. A slightly faster solution is to use a *critical section*, which performs the same job as a mutex, but can only be used within the same process.

❖ UNIX

The pthreads definition on UNIX is as shown.

```
class apLock
{
public:
  apLock  ()      { pthread_mutex_init (&lock_, NULL);}
  ~apLock ()      { pthread_mutex_destroy (&lock_);}

  bool lock () const
  { return pthread_mutex_lock (&lock_) == 0;}

  bool unlock () const
  { return pthread_mutex_unlock (&lock_) == 0;}

private:
  mutable pthread_mutex_t lock_;
};
```

❖ MICROSOFT WIN32

The Microsoft Windows Win32 API is as shown.

```
class apLock
{
public:
  apLock  ()      { InitializeCriticalSection (&lock_); }
  ~apLock ()      { DeleteCriticalSection (&lock_);}

  bool lock () const
  { EnterCriticalSection (&lock_); return true;}

  bool unlock () const
  { LeaveCriticalSection (&lock_); return true;}

private:
  mutable CRITICAL_SECTION lock_;
};
```

We made **lock()** and **unlock()** into **const** methods so that they can be used without restriction. To do this, we made our underlying synchronization object **mutable** so we could avoid any casts. When writing code like this, pay particular attention to the destructor to make sure it doesn't become the weakest part of your object. Your destructor must clean up after itself. It is a mistake to leave this task up to the operating system when the application terminates.

Our discussion of synchronization is not complete until we discuss deadlocking. Deadlocking occurs when many threads hold locks on one or more resources, while attempting to obtain locks to other resources held by other threads. Consider this example:

```
apLock lock1, lock2;
void thread1 ()
{
  ...
  lock1.lock ();
  // Do something
  lock2.lock ();
  ...

}
```

```
void thread2 ()
{
  ...
  lock2.lock ();
  // Do something else
  lock1.lock ();
  ...
}
```

The following conditions will cause a deadlock:

- **thread1** locks **lock1**.

- **thread2** locks **lock2**.

- **thread1** waits for **lock2** to be released so it can be acquired.

- **thread2** waits for **lock1** to be released.

Both of these threads are now deadlocked and will never exit. While it is possible to write a **lock()** method that will time out if the lock cannot be obtained, you are still faced with an undesired situation (for pthreads, see **pthread_mutex_trylock()**; for Win32, see **TryEnterCriticalSection()** or **WaitForSingleObject()**). A better solution is to avoid deadlock conditions completely. Don't be fooled into thinking that you need many threads and many synchronization objects before you need to worry about deadlocks. If one thread forgets to release a synchronization object, you can easily face a partial deadlock when another thread waits for that lock.

You will decrease the chances of a deadlock condition if you minimize the amount of code that must execute while you possess a lock. Consider these two examples:

Example 1

```
consoleLock.lock();
for (int i=0; i<10; i++)
  std::cout << i;
std::endl;
consoleLock.unlock();
```

Example 2

```
std::ostringstream output;
for (int i=0; i<10; i++)
  output << i;
output << std::endl;
consoleLock.lock();
std::cout << output.str().c_str();
consoleLock.unlock();
```

In Example 1, the console is locked while data is computed and written to the stream. In Example 2, the output data is computed first, then the lock is obtained for the shortest amount of time possible. Although this example is trivial, it does demonstrate how you can make simple changes to improve the dynamics of your application.

Use locking around the smallest section of code possible. This will improve readability and reduce the chances of deadlock conditions.

It may not be enough to simply reduce the chances for deadlocks; rather, using a simple rule can ensure that deadlocks are impossible. If each thread always locks items in the same order (such as, first lock A, then B, then C, ...), deadlocks can be completely avoided. Of course, such a strategy may involve more extra work than you are willing to do. See [Nichols97].

Now that we understand the issues of locking and unlocking, we can show a generic interface to the RAII technique. There are two steps: first we construct a global **apLock** object (see page 128) to control access to a resource; then, we define a class, **apLocker**, that locks the lock when it is constructed and unlocks the lock when it is destroyed. **apLocker** is shown here.

```
class apLocker
{
public:
  apLocker (apLock& lock) : lock_ (lock)  { lock_.lock();}
  ~apLocker () { lock_.unlock();}

private:
  apLock& lock_;

  // Prohibit copy and assignment
  apLocker            (const apLocker& src);
  apLocker& operator= (const apLocker& src);
};
```

If you are not careful, you may discover that you are adding locking in places that do not need them. This may not break any code, but it can become confusing, or worse, cause an exhaustion of available locks. In Prototype 3 (see page 60) we used handles to take advantage of reference counting to minimize image duplication. But what happens if the representation objects are used by multiple threads? There is a potential bug inside **apStorageRep** because the reference count manipulation is not thread safe, as shown:

```
void addRef () { ref_++;}
void subRef () { if (--ref_ == 0) delete this;}
```

Although a statement like **ref_++** looks trivial, there is no guarantee that it is atomic. But before you go and rewrite this code to add locking, you need to understand how your application will use it. Although it is possible for multiple threads to create this situation, it is unlikely to occur. In this particular example, a bug is created if **addRef()** is called after **subRef()** has already decremented **ref_** and deletes the object. This is no different than an application that attempts to use an object that goes out of scope. The problem is not missing locking; it is poor design. If an object must persist beyond the scope of a thread, it should be created and owned by a different thread that will not go out of scope. Please keep in mind that the Standard Template Library (STL) is not guaranteed to be thread safe.

5.1.3 Processes

Depending upon the application, a problem can sometimes be divided into separate distinct pieces. Before all these pieces are committed to being separate threads, you should also consider if they should be separate processes. A *process* has its own address space and is completely insulated from other processes. In a multithreaded application, for example, an error in a thread can cause an entire application to shut down. However, an error in one process will not cause another process to shut down.

To help you decide if you should be adding a thread or another process to your application, you should study what resources are needed and whether the application needs any information in a timely fashion. Choose threads when there is a tight coupling of resources, especially when timing is important. It is less clear-cut when there is a loose coupling between functions. For example, suppose an application generates a large volume of data by servicing requests by means of sockets or the Internet. Summary information is then written to a log file for each request. Every few minutes some statistics must be computed based on these results. If we implement this using only threads, it can be done without much difficulty, as follows:

- One or more threads process requests, as usual.

- Relevant summary information is computed by these threads.

- Periodically, a separate thread runs to compute the actual statistics. This thread copies the existing statistics and resets them, so that summary information can be built up for the next interval.

Let's see how this changes when we use separate processes for the implementation:

- One or more threads process requests, as usual.

- A summary record is written after each request to a file.

- Periodically, the summary file is renamed so that new summary records are written to a different file.

- Another process detects this file rollover, extracts information from each summary record, and computes the necessary statistics.

This solution is clearly more work, but does it result in a more reliable solution? Although we left out many details, the answer is probably yes. There are two distinct pieces here: a request processor and a log analyzer, and they have separate requirements. We haven't said anything about throughput, but it is possible that requests for an imaging application must be processed at the rate of 50 or more requests per second. With other types of application, rates can be as high as hundreds or thousands of requests per second. The generation of statistics happens at a much slower rate; from every few minutes to every few hours. By writing the summary information to a file, we can share the necessary information so that these statistics can be computed by a separate process.

Now let us consider what happens when an error condition occurs. If we used threads to implement our solution, an error in one thread can cause the entire application to shut down. Any incremental calculations will be lost and the application must be restarted. If we use separate processes to implement our solution, a failure of one process will not interfere with the other. The operating system will happily continue executing one of the processes, even though the other has stopped running. If the request processor dies, no data will be written to the summary file until it begins running again. The statistics process can still analyze this information and generate reports. If the statistics process dies, the requests will be processed and summary information will build up in one or more files for later processing.

Another advantage of using processes to implement this solution is the well-defined interface between the two pieces. There are only so many ways that information can be transferred from one process to another. And in each of them, you transfer a discrete amount of information. Whether you are using the file system, sockets, or pipes, one process can transmit information to another process. This destination can also be on another machine entirely, but that is beyond the scope of this book. The point is that a rigid interface develops between the processes. If more information must be exchanged at a future point, this interface will be modified. With threads, there is a tendency for these interfaces to get blurred, because exchanging information is as easy as setting a variable.

5.2 Exception Handling

Exception handling was once a largely documented but unsupported feature in many compilers. Those days are behind us. If you haven't read Stroustrup's chapter on exception handling, you definitely should. See [Stroustrup00]. Here we discuss practices that will help you to use exception handling efficiently and to avoid its overuse.

❖ BRIEF OVERVIEW

Exception handling can be summarized in a simple example:

```
int main()
{
  try {
    // Your application goes here
  }
  catch (...) {
    std::cerr << "Exception caught" << std::endl;
    return 1;
  }
  return 0;
}
```

By placing your application inside a **try()** block, the listed exceptions can be caught. In this case, all exceptions are caught. This is not uncommon inside **main()** because it acts as the last chance to catch an exception. If no exception handler is defined, **std::terminate()** is called, which then calls **abort()**. You can use **throw** to generate an exception, using a built-in class or one of your own, as shown:

```
throw std::overflow_error ("Out of range");
```

This uses the standard library **overflow_error** class for the exception. This class takes a string, containing whatever information you want, during construction. We can modify our example slightly to catch specific errors:

```
int main()
{
  try {
```

```
      // Your application goes here
   }
   catch (std::exception& ex) {
     std::cerr << "Standard Library exception caught: " << ex.what()
               << std::endl;
     return 1;
   }
   catch (...) {
     std::cerr << "Exception caught" << std::endl;
     return 1;
   }
   return 0;
}
```

The order in which you list **catch()** blocks is very significant, because the first matching block will execute. In this example, we are catching any object of type **std::exception** — we also catch any exception derived from this class. If the **throw** statement above is executed, the following will be displayed to **cerr**:

```
   Standard Library exception caught: Out of range
```

❖ EXCEPTIONS IN CONSTRUCTORS AND DESTRUCTORS

In general, you can generate exceptions or catch them whenever you want. However, the use of exceptions in constructors and destructors requires care to avoid heap or resource leakage, or unexpected program termination.

The function of a constructor is to create and initialize an object. Since a constructor does not return a value, you may have wondered what your application can do when an error is detected during construction. Because constructors are not intended to fail, throwing an exception is a reasonable strategy. This strategy allows you to place code at a higher level, where it can best be decided how to handle the error. What happens is that, even though the object may not be completely constructed, the destructor is called for all class members that were fully initialized before the exception is thrown. As a result, the object is brought back to the state it was in before the object was constructed.

To prevent heap or resource leakages when an exception is thrown inside a constructor, you should use the Resource Acquisition Is Initialization (RAII) technique we discussed on page 130. By wrapping a resource object inside another object, it is guaranteed that the resource's destructor will be called if the resource object was constructed before an exception is thrown. The resource's destructor will release the resource and return the system to the state it was in before the original constructor was ever called. If you do not use this technique, you can't guarantee that an exception thrown from within a constructor will not cause a heap or resource leak. For detailed information, see [Stroustrup00].

Generating exceptions within a destructor must be avoided. To see why, let's consider what happens when an exception is thrown. A catch handler is written to handle an exception and continue execution. Objects constructed inside the **try()** block are destroyed when the exception is caught. If any of these destructors were to generate an exception of their own, the system would be in a hopeless state because there is no way to know what the proper course of action should be. If this condition actually happens, the application calls **terminate()**. Unless you write a custom termination handler, **abort()** is called and the application shuts down. As a matter of practice, exceptions should never be called from within a destructor unless you catch them before they propagate outside the destructor.

❖ CATCHING EXCEPTIONS

Regardless of how much or how little you use exception handling, you need to take some steps to catch any errors before they cause your application to terminate. Even if your code does not use exception handling, the standard library does. At the very least your application needs to have a top-level catch handler, as we showed above. We recommend two additions to your top-level catch handler. The first is to catch specific types of errors before your catch-all handler does. Your application should make every attempt to restart itself, or gracefully fail, before you give up and terminate the application. The second addition is to include another catch handler as a backup to the first. Adding too much logic in the first catch handler can actually trigger another exception. The backup catch handler should attempt to write error information to an error log or console, exit, and then if possible restart the application.

To get in the habit of having a top-level catch handler, you should put your application code in a function other than **main()**. This will make it easier to add an exception handling scheme to suit your needs, as shown.

```
#include "debugstream.h"

int yourMain (int restart)
{
  // Your main function goes here
}

int catchMain()
{
  int retval    = 0;
  bool running = true;
  int restart   = 0;  // Restart count
  while (running) {
    try {
      // Run the application
      retval = yourMain (restart);
    }
    catch (std::exception& ex) {
      cdebug << "catchMain: Standard Library exception caught: "
             << ex.what() << ". Restarting ..." << std::endl;
      restart++;
      // Add code to decide if we should fail instead of restarting
    }
    catch (...) {
      cdebug << "catchMain: Unknown exception caught" << std::endl;
      retval = 1;
      running = false;
    }
  }

  cdebug << "catchMain: Stopping with exit code " << retval
         << std::endl;
  return retval;
}
```

```
int main()
{
  // Set up our debug stream
  debugstream.sink (apDebugSinkConsole::sOnly);
  apDebugSinkConsole::sOnly.showHeader (true);

  return catchMain ();
}
```

In this example, **yourMain()** is the function that runs your application. It takes a parameter, **restart**, that lets the application know if this is the first time it is run, or whether the system is restarting after an error. Many applications are written with an event loop, so restarting the application after an error is certainly possible. Your application code can attempt to restart the application and preserve as much state information as possible. For instance, your application might display an error message that tells the user an error has occurred, and allows them to decide whether to continue using the application without restarting it.

The call to **yourMain()** is wrapped in a **try** block. We have shown two **catch** statements: one for standard library exceptions, and a catch-all for any others. You can add **catch** statements for other categories of errors, especially for exceptions that you define. In our example, we restart the application after any standard library exception is caught. Please keep in mind that global and static objects are not reinitialized after an exception is caught and **yourMain()** is called again. You must explicitly reinitialize any global and static objects to prevent subtle bugs from appearing in subsequent runs of **yourMain()**. We could have defined the variable **restart** to be a **bool**, but then the application would not know how many times the application was restarted. By using an **int**, the application can decide what should happen if the application is restarted too many times. For example, if we define **yourMain()** to be:

```
int yourMain (int restart)
{
  throw std::overflow_error ("Out of range");
  return 0;
}
```

the application will go into an infinite loop and send countless error messages to the console. This is clearly not what should happen, and you can rectify this situation inside **yourMain()** or **catchMain()**.

Before you think the design issues of a top-level catch handler are resolved, you must consider what happens if an exception is caught in **catchMain()**, which throws an exception. In our example, the catch handlers are short and simple. In reality they may be much more complicated, and we must assume that exceptions might be thrown within them. We recommend adding a second level of exception handling by splitting **catchMain()** into two pieces, as shown:

```
int primaryMain()
{
  int retval   = 0;
  bool running = true;
  int restart  = 0;  // Restart count
```

```
   while (running) {
     try {
       // Run the application
       retval = yourMain (restart);
     }
     catch (std::exception& ex) {
       cdebug << "primaryMain: Standard Library exception caught: "
              << ex.what() << ". Restarting ..." << std::endl;
       restart++;
       // Add code to decide if we should fail instead of restarting
     }
     catch (...) {
       cdebug << "primaryMain: Unknown exception caught" << std::endl;
       retval = 1;
       running = false;
     }
   }

   cdebug << "primaryMain: Stopping with exit code " << retval
          << std::endl;
   return retval;
}

int catchMain()
{
   try {
     // Run the application
     return primaryMain ();
   }
   catch (...) {
     cdebug << "catchMain: Unknown exception caught" << std::endl;
     return 1;
   }

   return 0;
}
```

We have moved the functionality that was in **catchMain()** into a new function
primaryMain(). The new **catchMain()** function calls **primaryMain()** but catches all
errors. No recovery is attempted. In this example, we write a string to **cdebug** and exit. In
production code, it is best to save the state of the application in such a way that it uses as
few resources as possible. The only reason the catch handlers inside **catchMain()** are used
is if some kind of catastrophic failure has occurred.

❖ CATCHING MEMORY ALLOCATION ERRORS

What happens if a call to **operator new** fails because there is insufficient memory? A
user-defined error handler function will be called if one is defined. Otherwise,
std::bad_alloc() is called. A handler function is set by calling
std::set_new_handler() with a pointer to the function. If all you want to do is generate
an error when there is insufficient heap, the solution is simple:

```
void newHandler ()
{
   cdebug << "memory allocation failure" << std::endl;
   throw std::bad_alloc ();
}
```

```
int main ()
{
  std::set_new_handler (newHandler);
  ...
}
```

Once **newHandler()** is established as our error handler, it will be called when any heap allocation fails. The interesting thing about the error handler is that it will be called continuously until the memory allocation succeeds, or the function throws an error. If you were to write the function as:

```
void newHandler () {}
```

your application will be effectively dead if a heap allocation error occurs. Since no error is thrown by the handler, the allocation will be attempted again once **newHandler()** is done, which will simply fail again.

If you decide to use global handlers, such as **std::set_new_handler()**, you should only use them in top-level functions. These handlers should not be defined in resusable pieces of software because this prevents your application from using these features. If your global handlers only deal with one or more special cases in your application, remember to call the previous handler function to deal with any cases you do not process.

In our original handler there is a danger of triggering another heap allocation error when writing to the I/O stream (using our **cdebug** stream). Issues like these should always be considered when writing global handler functions. To solve this problem, we create a Singleton object, **apHeapMgr**, to catch heap errors and also attempt some limited recovery.

We want to try and recover from a heap allocation error, and the best way to do this is to reserve a block of heap memory when the application starts. The idea is that the handler releases this heap memory when an error occurs, allowing the allocation to succeed. This technique doesn't solve all heap-related problems, but if the size of the reserve buffer is large enough, at least the application can continue running. And, if you can't continue running, it is very important to notify users and give them a chance to save the state of the application before another error occurs. Heap exhaustion does not just happen when there is no more heap memory available. If heap becomes fragmented, it is very possible that an allocation of the desired size is not possible. The **apHeapMgr** Singleton object (because we have only one instance of it) is defined here.

```
class apHeapMgr
{
public:
  static apHeapMgr& gOnly ();

  int  allocate (int desiredSize);
  void release  () { cleanup();}
  // Allocate or release the heap memory. This can be done
  // manually or in response to a low memory condition.
  // allocate() returns the number of bytes reserved

  void automatic (bool state) { state_ = state;}
  // When set to true (the default), a low memory condition
  // will automatically release any reserved memory.
```

```
private:
  static void newHandler ();
  // Our memory handler when new cannot allocate the desired memory

  static apHeapMgr* sOnly_;

  apHeapMgr ();

  void releaseMemory (); // Release reserve memory
  void cleanup ();        // Release our reserve and unhook our handler

  new_handler oldHandler_; // Previous handler
  bool        state_;      // true if we will automatically release memory
  bool        nested_;     // Detects if newHandler() is nested
  int         size_;       // Amount of memory (bytes) in reserve
  char*       reserve_;    // Reserve memory we keep
};
```

newHandler() is a static method that is the actual error handler. **allocate()** is used to
create the reserve memory buffer. The desired size is passed as an argument. To be safe, the
reserve buffer is obtained using a while loop, reducing the desired size by half until the
memory allocation is successful. Once the reserve buffer is obtained, **newHandler()** is set as
the error handler function. **release()** is the opposite of **allocate()**, and will release any
memory buffer and deactivate the error handler. **automatic()** directly controls when the
reserve buffer may be used. When set to **true** (the default), the reserve buffer is freed when
a heap allocation error occurs. Setting the state to **false** disables the error handler, putting
the user in charge of when the reserve buffer can be released.

The source code can be found on the CD-ROM, but the error handler function is repeated
here.

```
void apHeapMgr::newHandler ()
{
  if (apHeapMgr::gOnly().nested_) {
    // We have recursed into our handler which is a catastrophe
    throw std::bad_alloc ();
  }

  apHeapMgr::gOnly().nested_ = true;

  if (apHeapMgr::gOnly().state_) {
    // Free our memory if we have not already done so
    if (apHeapMgr::gOnly().reserve_) {
      apHeapMgr::gOnly().releaseMemory ();
      apHeapMgr::gOnly().nested_ = false;
      return;
    }
  }

  cdebug << "Throwing bad_alloc from newHandler" << std::endl;
  apHeapMgr::gOnly().nested_ = false;
  throw std::bad_alloc ();
}
```

This is a static function, so we must use the Singleton object, **apHeapMgr::gOnly()**, to
reference it. A flag, **nested_**, is used to see if **newHandler()** was called during the
execution of **newHandler()**. This recursion means our error handler has itself generated an

allocation error. At this point, it is unsafe to do anything other than throw an error and exit. If the reserve buffer is available and we are allowed to automatically release it (**state_** is **true**), the buffer is freed and the handler ends. In all other cases **std::bad_alloc()** is thrown after an error message is generated.

❖ USING EXCEPTION SPECIFICATIONS

We have not used exception specifications in our production code. The specifications are instructions to the compiler regarding what exceptions a function can throw. For example:

```
    void function() throw (apException1);
```

This specification says that **function()** can throw only **apException1** or an exception derived from **apException1**. **apException1** can represent any exception, either user-defined or system-defined. Other possibilities are:

```
    void function();            // All exceptions can be thrown
    void function() throw ();   // No exceptions can be thrown
```

You would think that we would be endorsing these specifications as a way to improve your code. Unfortunately, there are a couple of issues that prevent us from doing so.

The first issue is that specifications are not completely checked at compile time. If your code throws an exception that is not listed in your specification, a function called **std::unexpected()** is called. If you do not define your own function by way of **std::set_unexpected()**, the application will terminate. That is an extremely harsh thing to do, and it does not matter if you have a catch-all handler defined in your code. In addition, you are somewhat limited in what your **std::unexpected()** function can do. For example, you can certainly do this:

```
    void myUnexpected ()
    {
      std::cout << "myUnexpected" << std::endl;
    }

    void willthrow () throw ()
    {
      throw std::overflow_error ("Out of range");
    }

    int main()
    {
      std::set_unexpected (myUnexpected);
      try {
        willthrow ();
      }
      catch (...) {
        std::cout << "catch-all" << std::endl;
      }
      return 0;
    }
```

You might be surprised at what happens. In this example, a **willthrow()** function is called, which is defined not to throw any errors. However, it does throw an exception. **willthrow()** is wrapped in a **try** block to catch all errors. **set_unexpected()** is first called to install our handler, **myUnexpected()**, to run instead of **std::unexpected()**. This example will do one of the following things:

- Fail to compile or generate warnings, because **willthrow()** violates the exception specification
- Compile, execute, and display **myUnexpected** on the console, and then **std::terminate()**
- Compile, execute, and display **catch-all** on the console.

The behavior is compiler-specific and should be documented in the release notes of whatever C++ compiler you are using. However, this discrepancy makes it unusable for multi-platform products. Obviously, the desired solution is to have the compiler detect and flag all invalid exception specifications. If this were the case, we would probably be using this feature. You might expect that the catch-all will run, but this is contrary to what exception specifications are all about. If the compiler can only determine at run-time that a compiler specification has been violated, it must shut down the application or call your handler function first.

Can exceptions be thrown from within our handler function? The answer is yes, an error can indeed be thrown. The problem is that this exception must be listed in every exception specification that may be traversed until the exception is caught. If this is not done, the application will call **std::terminate()**. For a large system, this amounts to adding an exception specification to every function, unless you understand the dynamics of your application perfectly. It is also important that you catch all exceptions within your destructor; otherwise, **std::terminate()** will be called as well in this case.

If you do plan on using exception specifications, read the documentation carefully. On Microsoft Windows systems, for example, each thread maintains its own **std::unexpected()** function. You must call **std::set_unexpected()** after any thread is created. Our rules for handling exceptions are shown in Figure 5.1.

Exception Rules

✔ **Document in your comments every exception a function can throw.** It is a good coding practice to tell your users which exceptions can be thrown by a function.

✔ **Use the RAII technique to manage resources and to guarantee that there is no resource leakage during exception processing.**

✔ **Install a system-wide catch-all handler to catch any exceptions you might have missed.** This function should attempt to restart the application or perform an orderly shutdown.

✔ **Never ever let an exception leak from a destructor.**

✔ **Only use global handlers, such as `std::set_new_handler()`, in top-level functions.**

Figure 5.1: Exception Rules

5.2.1 Designing Your Own Exception Framework

So far we have reviewed how exceptions work and some of the potential pitfalls you should watch for in your code. An application should define its own set of exceptions that define application-specific error conditions. Reusing standard library exceptions is one possibility, if they map nicely to existing exceptions. For example, **std::overflow_error** is an excellent choice for a generic overflow error. It is non-specific, but it also takes a string that can detail the source of the error. The disadvantage of using both application-specific (your own) and standard library exceptions is that your catch handlers become more complicated, because you need to deal with both of them.

Designing your own exception framework is not difficult because little information needs to be carried with an exception. A string is usually sufficient to detail the specific error. To address this issue of having two different exception frameworks (your own and standard library exceptions), we derive our **apException** base class from **std::exception**. The base class defines a virtual function, **what()**, that returns a string describing the error, as shown.

```
class apException : public std::exception
{
public:
  apException (std::string name)
    : std::exception (), name_ (name) {}

  virtual ~apException () {}

  virtual const char* what () const
  { return name_.c_str();}

protected:
  std::string name_;
};
```

We don't recommend that you derive exceptions directly from **std::exception** because there is no way to separate standard library exceptions from your own. Adding your own base class, like **apException**, allows you to write code to only catch your own exceptions, such as:

```
try {
  ...
}
catch (apException& ex) {
  // Our exception
}
catch (...) {
  // Some other exception
}
```

But you can also write code, to catch your own exceptions, as well as standard library ones, like this:

```
try {
  ...
}
catch (std::exception& ex) {
  // Our exception or any standard library exception
}
catch (...) {
  // Some other exception
}
```

Derive an object from apException for each type of exception you expect to have in the application.

For example, suppose your imaging application frequently verifies that the coordinates passed to a function are correct. Using **std::out_of_range** error is not appropriate because this error is not specific enough. We can derive an object, **apBoundsException**, to handle this error condition, as shown here.

```
class apBoundsException : public apException
{
public:
  apBoundsException (std::string name="")
    : apException ("apBoundsException: " + name) {}
};
```

We have written **apBoundsException** so that any additional information is optional. The name of the exception is pretty specific so that the string information is not necessary. In this example:

```
try {
  throw apBoundsException ("Hello");
}
```

```
catch (apBoundsException& ex) {
    std::cout << "caught " << ex.what() << std::endl;
}
```

we display the message, caught apBoundsException: Hello on the console. And because of the virtual what() function, this line of output is identical if the catch block is any of the following:

```
catch (apBoundsException& ex) { ... }
catch (apException& ex) { ... }
catch (std::exception& ex) { ... }
```

5.2.2 Avoiding Exception Abuse

Exceptions are often overused. Let's look at an example:

```
char getPixel (int x, int y)
{
  if (x < 0 || x >= width() ||
      y < 0 || y >= height())
    throw apBoundsException ("getPixel");
  ...
}
```

There is nothing wrong with this example at first inspection. If the caller passes invalid arguments to getPixel(), it throws apBoundsException(). But let's look at how this function might be used:

```
int sum ()
{
  int total = 0;
  for (int y=0; y<height(); y++) {
    for (int x=0; x<width(); x++) {
      total += getPixel (x, y);
      ...
    }
  }
  return total;
}
```

If you wrote sum(), would you include a try/catch block? And if you did, you might write one of the following:

```
int sum1 ()
{
  int total = 0;
  try {
    for (int y=0; y<height(); y++) {
      for (int x=0; x<width(); x++) {
        total += getPixel (x, y);
      }
    }
  }
  catch (apBoundsException& ex) {
    cdebug << ex.what() << std::endl;
  }
  return total;
}
```

```
int sum2 ()
{
  int total = 0;
  for (int y=0; y<height(); y++) {
    for (int x=0; x<width(); x++) {
      try {
        total += getPixel (x, y);
      }
      catch (apBoundsException& ex) {
        cdebug << ex.what() << " at " << x << "," << y << std::endl;
      }
    }
  }
  return total;
}
```

sum1() wraps the entire function in a single **try** block. If an exception occurs, it prints a message and returns the current total. **sum2()** wraps each call to **getPixel()**, which allows the error message to be more clear. An exception will print a message and the loops will continue to run.

sum2() is the most effective at trapping errors but is also the slowest, since the **try** block is set up **width()*height()** times. As we have written these functions, an exception will never be thrown because the loops never deliver invalid coordinates. In this case, it makes no sense to incur the expense of a catch handler on every iteration.

Consider a function's purpose before adding exception support. You may find a more optimal place to add the exception.

Low-level functions are not good candidates because they are called frequently. In our example, a better solution is to call the exception where it is generated, as shown here.

```
class apImage
{
  ...
  char getPixel (int x, int y);
  //Description Fetch the contents of a single pixel.
  //           No exceptions are thrown. This is the responsibility
  //           of the caller.
  //Parameters x,y are the 0-based coordinates of the pixel
  //Returns    Pixel value at (x,y). Returns 0 if the coordinates
  //           are invalid.

  int sum ()
  //Description Compute the sum of all pixels in the image
  //Returns     Sum of all pixels.
};
```

You must document your exception strategy. In our example, it is very clear from the comments what **getPixel()** does. It states that exceptions are not thrown, and that **0** is returned if invalid coordinates are passed. **sum()** does not say anything about exceptions because none are thrown; and the reason none are thrown is that **sum()** knows as much information about the size of the image as **getPixel()** does.

Sometimes it makes sense to consider whether it is appropriate to even use exceptions.

 Consider whether or not exceptions are the appropriate mechanism before routinely adding them.

For example, if we eliminate exception support from our previous example, it makes this code much simpler, as shown here.

```
char apImage::getPixel (int x, int y)
{
  if (x < 0 || x >= width() ||
      y < 0 || y >= height())
    return 0;
  ...
}

int apImage::sum ()
{
  int total = 0;
  for (int y=0; y<height(); y++) {
    for (int x=0; x<width(); x++) {
      total += getPixel (x, y);
    }
  }
  return total;
}
```

In this case, it really makes sense to eliminate exception support in **getPixel()** since the caller can easily determine if the coordinates are valid. In **apImage::getPixel()** above, the function returns **0** if the coordinates are invalid. This is a silent check, meaning that no error is generated if this is ever true. If **getPixel()** is used properly, this condition will never be relevant.

C-style functions typically use the return value to indicate an error condition, as shown here.

```
FILE* fp = fopen ("file", "r");
if (fp == NULL) {
  ...
}
```

Is there anything wrong with doing this? Absolutely not. After all, if you use **std::ifstream** to read from a file, it doesn't throw an exception if the file does not exist. Exceptions are intended for exceptional cases; that is, cases that are not expected in the normal course of execution. Trying to open a nonexistent file might be considered a fatal error in some applications, but in general, an application should always test to see if the operation succeeds. Before you call **throw** from a function, you should consider whether the error is really an exception. We prefer to do things like this:

```
bool compile (...);
//Description Compile our data into a fast, binary format.
//Returns     true if the compilation was ok, false on failure
```

or perhaps:

```
std::string compile (...);
//Description Compile our data into a fast, binary format.
//Returns     null string on success, else error description
```

❖ WHEN TO USE EXCEPTIONS

It seems like we are finding lots of reasons not to use exceptions. So, when should they be used? If it is very unusual for a function to fail, you might consider using an exception. One of the disadvantages of functions that return status is that you have to check the status. If you have a large nesting of functions, this means that checks must be performed at every level.

Another good time to use exceptions is when a number of processing steps are treated as one unit. For example, consider a machine vision system that receives a signal of some sort, takes a picture (acquiring an image), and then processes and subsequently analyzes the image. If you take a high-level look at these steps, each step must be completed before the next step can begin, as follows:

```
bool inspect ()
{
  try {
    acquire ();
    process ();
    analyze ();
  }
  catch (apException& ex) {
    ... //Report error
    return false;
  }
  ...
  return true;
}
```

Let's look at the **process()** step and what it might do:

```
void process ()
{
  int i;
  bool ok;
  for (i=0; i<nFilterSteps; i++) {
    ok = filterImage (i);
    if (!ok) throw apException ();
  }

  for (i=0; i<nMorphSteps; i++) {
    ok = morphImage (i);
    if (!ok) throw apException ();
  }
}
```

In our example, **process()** performs a number of image filtering steps, followed by a number of image morphology steps. An error at any step during this processing is considered a fatal error for the application. The functions, **filterImage()** and **morphImage()**, however, are low-level image processing routines that return their status instead of throwing exceptions, because this is handled by the application.

If you look at the **inspect()** function, we have the opposite behavior. We catch any errors during processing and return the overall status as a **bool**. This makes sense because whoever calls **inspect()** is interested in the result, and it is up to **inspect()** to catch and handle any relevant exceptions. We did not try to catch all errors here because we are expecting only errors derived from **apException** (or application-specific errors) to be thrown. If a different exception is thrown while **inspect()** is running, it will be caught by a higher-level catch handler; probably the one installed when the application started. For instance, what would happen if a memory error is thrown (**std::bad_alloc**)? **inspect()** would not know how to handle this condition, but some other piece of code will, and that is why we only catch those errors we know how to handle.

Another appropriate time to use exceptions is when an unrecoverable error occurs deep inside a program, such that it cannot be handled at that level. For example, if a low-level function runs out of memory trying to allocate a temporary buffer, there is little that can be done. If you do not catch this exception yourself, the application's top-level catch handler will catch the error. However, your routine has the opportunity to log this error, perhaps to the console or to a log file, and then generate a more specific error that describes what happened. When you implement your top-level catch handler, reserve a memory buffer that can be released when the user needs to save the state and restart the application. The information describing the error can help the development team decide if this is indeed a memory error, or another type of bug in the system.

5.2.3 Using Assertions

Assertions are conditional statements that test for abnormal conditions and terminate the program, should they be false. Assertions are typically used only during debugging, when the symbol **NDEBUG** is not defined (see **assert.h** for details). During production builds, **NDEBUG** is defined and these statements effectively do nothing.

If your development environment does not have the notion of debugging versus production builds, you do not want to use assertions. An assertion will not only stop the system, it will also display details about where the error occurred, as shown:

```
void process (apImage* p)
{
  assert (p);
  ...
}
```

If a null pointer is passed to **process()**, the assertion will be false and the application will terminate. Presumably this statement is here as a check, because **process()** must be called with a valid pointer. During testing when the assertion is active, this statement is an effective means of finding aberrant code. But if null is passed to the production build, the behavior is unclear.

In debug builds, use assertions to enforce whatever restrictions you place on a function. If the comments for a function describe certain requirements that must be true, assertions are an excellent way to guarantee this. We can modify the **getPixel()** function we showed earlier, as follows:

```
char apImage::getPixel (int x, int y)
{
  assert (x >= 0 && x < width());
  assert (y >= 0 && y < height());

  if (x < 0 || x >= width() ||
      y < 0 || y >= height())
    return 0;
  ...
}
```

At first glance this function may appear flawed. After all, if **assert()** is used to make sure the coordinates are valid, why do we test it again? Just remember what happens if this is a production build. The assertions are missing in this case, and there is nothing to enforce the coordinate values. Whether you need both of these checks depends a lot on the application and how well it is tested. It is extremely difficult to completely test an application.

Keep in mind that the debugging version of the software differs in more ways from the production version than just the addition of assertion statements. Often the debugging software has different timing characteristics or other behavioral differences that can mask bugs that may actually exist in the production version.

We offer you the following guidelines for using assertions in Figure 5.2.

Assertion Rules

✔ When you add assertions, do not remove any existing checks in the function.

✔ In new functions that you write, use assert() rather than other checks to enforce argument constraints.

✔ Consider writing your own assertion macros that will throw an exception, rather than calling abort(). This gives your application a chance to restart if you have a top-level catch handler.

✔ Never put code required for your application in assert(). These statements will not be compiled when NDEBUG is defined, as is typically the case for production builds.

Figure 5.2: Assertion Rules

5.3 Compile-Time Versus Run-Time Issues

If you have ever recompiled your code on a newer version of a compiler or on a different platform, you will quickly discover that there are new errors and warnings produced. These errors are a result of the level of compile-time checking your compiler is performing. You will particularly notice these errors with templates, because compilers sometimes have problems deciding what to do when presented with conflicting specifications.

Unfortunately, compilers cannot perform all checks at compile time. Some must be deferred until run time, such as casting references with **dynamic_cast<>** or exception specifications (see page 142). The design of the application is also important. For example, virtual function calls require one or more run-time lookups to determine which function to call.

Your designs will be more robust if you can shift as much burden as possible to your compiler. You need to pay careful attention to any warnings that are issued because they can identify design weaknesses or potential problems. Many developers consider all warnings as extraneous messages. This practice, however, allows certain mistakes into the production code.

5.3.1 Compiler Issues

When you build your application to run across many platforms, you will certainly encounter issues with the different compilers. Each compiler handles the code differently according to its features and quirks. Even if your application is only intended for a single platform, you still have to consider compiler issues, because compiler enhancements, patches, and other upgrades are frequently required, thus changing the compilation environment.

❖ COMPILER WARNINGS

Let's look at an example of some potentially dangerous code and the warnings it produces using a variety of compilers:

```
 1:  #define SIZE 5000
 2:  #define N   500000
 3:
 4:  int main()
 5:  {
 6:     int i = SIZE * N;        // Overflows an integer
 7:     long l = 0;
 8:     unsigned long ul = 0;
 9:
10:     if (l > ul) {}           // signed/unsigned mismatch
11:     return 0;
12:  }
```

This sample code is provided only as a test for the compilers; we don't use it anywhere in our image framework. The issues it raises, however, are ones that everyone encounters at some point during development. For example, there are two real problems evident in lines 6 and 10.

In line 6:

```
int i = SIZE * N;
```

seems fine until you look at the values of **SIZE** and **N**. For 32-bit integers, **SIZE*N** does not fit. To correct this problem you can use an **unsigned int** (appropriate in this example), or you can use a larger signed quantity. This, however, will not fix the problem on many embedded platforms where integers are only 16 bits. In line 10:

```
if (l > ul)
```

there are problems when the value of **l** is negative. The compiler converts the signed quantity to unsigned and then makes the comparison. For example, if we rewrite this example as:

```
long l = -1;
unsigned long ul = 0;
if (l > ul)
  std::cout << l << " is greater than " << ul << std::endl;
```

you will see:

```
-1 is greater than 0
```

displayed on the console.

There are also two smaller issues in our example. In line 6, the variable **i** is set but never referenced. Most often this occurs when other code that used the variable is removed during the course of development. This condition can also indicate that the function is unfinished. The second issue is at line 12; the file has no newline character at the end of it. Some compilers will generate a warning if the last line of the file is an actual line of code.

So, what happens when this code is compiled? Let's take a look at the output of a few different compilers.

❖ GNU GCC

The GNU compiler, gcc, was tested on various platforms (Solaris, FreeBSD, and AIX) and performance was identical on each one. With version 2.95.3 of gcc, no warnings are reported. On version 3.0.3, gcc reports the following:

```
main.cpp:49:1: warning: no newline at end of file
```

But that is using the compiler with no arguments (**g++ main.cpp**). If we use "**g++ -Wall main.cpp**" to enable all warnings, we see:

```
main.cpp: In function `int main()':
main.cpp:39: warning: comparison between signed and unsigned integer
   expressions
main.cpp:35: warning: unused variable `int i'
main.cpp:49:1: warning: no newline at end of file
```

❖ SUN NATIVE COMPILER

With Sun's native compiler, there were no warnings.

❖ SGI IRIX

The SGI native Irix compiler reports the following:

```
cc-1061 cc: WARNING File = compilertest.cpp, Line = 52
  The integer operation result is out of range.
  int i = SIZE * N;        // Overflows an integer
            ^


cc-1001 cc: WARNING File = compilertest.cpp, Line = 66
  The source file does not end with a new-line character.
  }
    ^


cc-1174 cc: WARNING File = compilertest.cpp, Line = 52
  The variable "i" was declared but never referenced.
  int i = SIZE * N;        // Overflows an integer
      ^
```

❖ MICROSOFT VISUAL C++

Microsoft Visual C++ (versions 6 and 7) produce the following:

```
main.cpp(48): warning C4307: '*' : integral constant overflow
main.cpp(52): warning C4018: '>' : signed/unsigned mismatch
```

All of this tells us what we already know: different compilers produce varying amounts of output. Most compilers have a myriad of command-line flags adding even more dimensions to this problem. We have a rule for standardizing the level of code quality across platforms.

 All production code should compile cleanly, using the highest level of detection. For gcc, use the -Wall command-line flag; for Microsoft Visual C++, use /W4 (warning level 4).

Let's review each of the warning messages. We have a few comments about each type of warning. For line 6:

```
int i = SIZE * N;
```

some compilers classified this as a warning. Other compilers, such as the native Sun compiler, didn't list any warnings. Even though we are responsible for avoiding overflow errors, in our opinion, all compilers should have flagged this problem as an error, so that it must be fixed before the code will compile. For example, if **i** had been defined as a **short** or **char**, the odds of a problem like this occurring are much greater.

For line 10:

```
if (1 > ul)
```

some compilers generated a warning. If **1** must remain a signed quantity and **ul** an unsigned quantity, then you need to cast one of the quantities so that they are of the same type. Often this type of problem arises innocently because the signed variable is used only as a counter, as shown in the following brief example:

```
for (int i=0; i<N; i++) {
    ...
    if (i > ul) ...
}
```

Our signed quantity, i, cannot be negative, so the comparison is always valid. It is easy to write code like this, because the alternative:

```
for (unsigned int i=0; i<N; i++) ...
```

makes the line more complicated. Besides, the loop may perform both signed and unsigned comparisons, making this a moot point. However, our recommendation is that you should modify your code to make the intent clear when you see warnings like these during compilation.

The other warnings that were generated were obvious: adding a newline at the end of the file and getting rid of the variable that was never referenced. Some compilers tend to be very picky, with warnings that seem unimportant. But, even if they are unimportant on a relative scale, they do clutter the output, making it more difficult to spot real problems. So, even if the warning seems trivial, such as a missing newline at the end of a file, you should make the change so you will never have to see that warning again. Besides, if you follow our rule for production code, all warnings have to be fixed before the code is considered for release.

❖ COMPILER ERRORS

Most errors found by the compiler are coding errors that must be fixed. The error messages themselves, however, are sometimes non-specific messages like "syntax error." If the source of the error is not obvious, you can start by following these simple steps.

1. Make sure your brackets are balanced. Indenting your code makes this easier to diagnose.

2. Make sure all statements end with a semicolon, ;.

3. Comment out offending lines and see if the error message goes away. Sometimes the mistake is actually on a different line than that indicated by the error message.

4. Study any macro definitions carefully for mistakes.

In rare cases, some errors are caused by the compiler itself. Perhaps the best example of this is how compilers handle templates. When templates were first introduced, they were used in very well-defined ways. As compilers began to support features such as function templates, inconsistencies started to appear. Let's look at a problem we encountered during prototyping of the image framework:

```
template<class T1, class T2, class T3>
void add2 (const T1& s1, const T2& s2, T3& d1)
{ d1 = s1 + s2;}

template<class T> class apRGBTmpl
{
```

```
public:
  T red;
  T green;
  T blue;

  apRGBTmpl () : red(0), green(0), blue(0) {}
};

template<class T1, class T2, class T3>
void add2 (const apRGBTmpl<T1>& s1, const apRGBTmpl<T2>& s2,
           apRGBTmpl<T3>& d1)
{
  d1.red   = s1.red   + s2.red;
  d1.green = s1.green + s2.green;
  d1.blue  = s1.blue  + s2.blue;
}

int main()
{
  apRGBTmpl<unsigned char> rgb1, rgb2;
  apRGBTmpl<long> rgb3;
  add2 (rgb1, rgb2, rgb3);   // Fails to compile on win32 MSVC7
  return 0;
}
```

The first definition of the template function **add2()** appears as if it is nothing more than a wrapper around a trivial line of code. However, the use of function templates like this allows us to handle the often ignored image processing issue of overflow. This definition of the **add2()** function template can be used in lots of ways, such as:

```
long l1, l2;
short s1, s2, s3;
add2 (s1, s2, s3);
add2 (s1, s2, l1);
add2 (l1, l2, s1); // Possible overflows here
```

Later in our example, we show a trivial implementation of an RGB pixel type, **apRGBTmpl<>**. This object is more complex than the simple RGB structure we used in earlier prototypes because we provide numerous arithmetic operations as part of the design. We define a version of **add2()** that takes arbitrary **apRGBTmpl<>** objects, so that we can write statements like the one defined in **main()**:

```
apRGBTmpl<unsigned char> rgb1, rgb2;
apRGBTmpl<long> rgb3;
add2 (rgb1, rgb2, rgb3);
```

Because we have two different template function definitions for **add2()**, the compiler must decide which one to use. As our comment indicates, Microsoft Visual C++ generates the following errors:

```
error C2667: 'add2' : none of 2 overloads have a best conversion
error C2668: 'add2' : ambiguous call to overloaded function
```

The compiler is unclear as to which template should be used. This is the correct behavior according to the C++ standard. The big problem with errors like this is that there is little you can do once you get them. In fact, we had to apply some workarounds to address this problem, as you will see in Chapter 6.

We have also found that many compilers are quite lax regarding syntax for templates. If you experiment with a particular compiler, you may find it accepts certain syntax that violates the ISO C++ standard. Partial template specialization is one area where support is missing from many compilers. This is an example of the issues you will uncover during prototyping. Remember, you are not coding to the standard as much as you are coding to the conformance of the compilers on your target platforms. If your development includes multiple platforms, this means you are effectively designing for the least common denominator.

5.3.2 Run-Time Issues

You have the ability to directly control run-time issues through the design of your application. In this section, we look at some compile-time constructs that also have a run-time component. We also look at performance issues to see how some commonly used C++ techniques can greatly affect execution time.

❖ COMPILE-TIME CONSTRUCTS

The compiler can't always detect all errors at compile time. Sometimes, the compiler detects errors at run time and throws an exception. Some constructs, such as exception specifications (see Section 5.2 on page 135), require both compile-time and run-time checks. If an exception is thrown and the specification is invalid, then **std::unexpected()** is called and the application terminates (the proper behavior). You must define **std::unexpected()** such that it can identify that the error condition occurred. Even if you are careful about defining exception specifications, there is nothing to prevent another developer (or even you) from writing software that violates this specification. And, you must do extensive testing to make sure your specifications are correct. These complexities are just some of the reasons we recommend you do not use this construct.

Another run-time issue that occurs is when casting is performed using **dynamic_cast<>**. This construct is useful for doing a downcast; that is, converting an object from its current type to that of a derived object. Consider this simple example:

```
class apImage
{
public:
  apImage () {}
  virtual void f () {}
};

class apColorImage: public apImage
{
public:
  apColorImage () {}
  virtual void f () {}
};

class apGrayImage: public apImage
{
```

```
public:
  apGrayImage () {}
  virtual void f () {}
};
```

In this example, we define a base class, **apImage**, and derived classes, **apColorImage** and **apGrayImage**. When **dynamic_cast<>** is used correctly, it converts a pointer or reference to a derived class, and it looks something like this:

```
apImage imageInstance;
apImage& imageRef = imageInstance;
apColorImage colorInstance;
apColorImage& colorRef = colorInstance;

apImage& upcast = colorRef;
apColorImage& downcast1 = dynamic_cast<apColorImage&> (upcast); // ok
```

This cast converts a reference from an **apImage&** to an **apColorImage&**. But when this example is changed to try to convert an object from one derived type to another, or from a base class instance to a derived type, we run into problems, as follows:

```
apColorImage& downcast2 = dynamic_cast<apColorImage&> (imageRef);
apGrayImage& downcast3  = dynamic_cast<apGrayImage&>  (imageRef);
```

In both of these cases, a run-time check determines that the conversion cannot be made. The exception, **std::bad_cast()**, is thrown when this error is detected. Use a **try** block to catch this error. On some compilers, like Microsoft Visual C++, run-time type identification must be enabled for this exception to be thrown. If this is not enabled, any attempt to use **dynamic_cast<>** at run time will throw an error. You are also free to use **static_cast<>** instead of **dynamic_cast<>**, but no run-time checks are made. In general, we do not recommend using **static_cast<>** for performing a down cast, because the small penalty of using **dynamic_cast<>** is negligible.

❖ RUN-TIME PERFORMANCE ISSUES

When you design your application, you need to think about how certain constructs affect performance at run time. For example, the use of inheritance can help turn an incredibly complex problem into a number of smaller, easier problems. Let's take a look at virtual functions.

When a compiler handles virtual functions, it creates virtual tables that are used at run time to determine which function pointer gets used. This additional level of indirection incurs a small run-time penalty each time a virtual function is called. If your design is such that virtual functions are called frequently, then this overhead adds up to a measurable quantity.

Once the first virtual function is added to a class (and hence a virtual table is created), other virtual functions incur only a very small size penalty. This is true because the virtual table only needs to grow by the number of virtual functions added. Note that there is only one virtual table for each type of object. However, as the number of virtual function calls increases, so does the number of table lookups. For many applications, this overhead can be ignored. For example, a drawing application where users manipulate objects by means of a graphical user interface (GUI) is constrained by how often the user generates events, and is not likely to be affected by virtual functions.

At the other end of the spectrum are real-time embedded systems. We learned a valuable lesson from one of our early large-scale C++ efforts. Our design ignored the effects of virtual function overhead, and we used virtual functions liberally. After all, processors were fast and this was such a small effect, or so we thought. As a result, one part of the system was written completely in C++, with a very rich framework. When the first benchmark test was run, the product team was stunned. What used to take one millisecond in an older product now took 50 milliseconds to run. It turns out that about 48 milliseconds of this time was wasted in an overly complex design, thanks in part to too many virtual functions.

We can observe the effect of virtual functions by looking at an example.

```
class apSimple
{
public:
  apSimple () : sum_ (0) {}
  void sum (int value) { sum_+=value;}
  int value () const { return sum_;}
private:
  int sum_;
};
```

apSimple is a non-virtual class that sums the value of all integers passed to it. We will use **apSimple** as the baseline for our measurements as we break this into a more complex design.

```
class apVirtualBase
{
public:
  apVirtualBase () : sum_ (0) {}
  virtual void sum (int value) { sum_+=value;}
  int value () const { return sum_;}
protected:
  int sum_;
};

class apDerivedBase : public apVirtualBase
{
public:
  virtual void sum (int value) { sum_+=value;}
};
```

Our base class, **apVirtualBase**, is almost identical to **apSimple**, except that our **sum()** method is now virtual. **apDerivedBase** derives from **apVirtual** base and defines an identical definition for **sum()**. The compiler won't know this, so we can accurately measure any differences between calling **apDerivedBase::sum()** or **apVirtualBase::sum()**.

Our baseline is to measure how long it takes this snippet of code to run.

```
apSimple simple;
Simple* sp = &simple;
for (i=0; i<1000000; i++)
  sp->sum (i);
```

Our measurements were done using Microsoft Visual C++, and we used the
QueryPerformanceCounter() function to obtain access to the Windows high-resolution
counter. We used a pointer to call **sum()** so it would match our test.

```
apDerivedBase derivedbase;
apVirtualBase* vb = &derivedbase;
for (i=0; i<1000000; i++)
  vb->sum (i);
```

This piece of code will return the same result as the previous one, except that each call to
sum() is done by way of the virtual table. A million calls to this function may seem
excessive, but look at a hypothetical image processing function to compute the sum of pixels
in an image.

```
int sum = 0;
for (int y=0; y<image->height(); y++)
  for (int x=0; x<image->width(); x++)
    sum += image->getPixel (x, y);
```

If **image** is a pointer to an **apImage** derived object, our calls to **getPixel()** will
accumulate virtual function call overhead, just like our example. For a 1024 by 1024 image,
we are making just over one million calls to have a meaningful benchmark.

Our test platform is an Intel Pentium 4 microprocessor-based machine, running at 2.0
GHz. Our baseline loop took 1.1 milliseconds to execute, while our virtual function loop
took 8.6 milliseconds. Seven milliseconds may not seem like much, but it can represent the
difference between your application running properly or not. If times like this are too small
for you to worry about, then just ignore this section. Otherwise, you need to understand the
ramifications of making any function virtual, especially when the function is involved in
time-critical code.

To see one possible workaround, let's look at another timing loop.

```
apDerivedBase derivedbase;
for (i=0; i<1000000; i++)
  derivedbase.sum (i);
```

The difference from our previous loop is that we are calling the method directly in the
derived class, rather than by means of a pointer. In this case, there is no ambiguity about
what function should be called, and the compiler can avoid the virtual table. If we time this,
we see that this function takes the same amount of time as our baseline example. If we apply
this concept to our image processing example, we can add a new member function, **sum()**,
to compute the sum.

```
int apImage::sum ()
{
  int sum = 0;
  for (int y=0; y<image->height(); y++)
    for (int x=0; x<image->width(); x++)
      sum += getPixel (x, y);
  return sum;
}
```

The **getPixel()** call is no longer using the virtual table and we completely eliminate this overhead. When the user calls **image->sum()**, we incur a single virtual table lookup.

5.3.3 Template Specialization

Template specialization is one of the run-time and compile-time issues you should be aware of when dealing with templates. Using specialization, you can define specific implementations that differ from the default one. By taking into account the data type of the template argument, a specialization can be written to more efficient. Sometimes this can result in huge performance gains, but this gain is only for a specific data type. It is easy to forget that templates do not behave like regular classes, because one template instance can have a much different performance than another template instance. Let's start by looking at a simple template design for an image class.

```
template<class T>
class apImage
{
public:
  apImage (int w, int h) : width_ (w), height_ (h), data_ (0)
  { data_ = new T [width() * height()];
    memset (data_, 1, width() * height() * sizeof(T));
  }
  ~apImage () { delete [] data_;}
  int width  () const { return width_;}
  int height () const { return height_;}
  T* getAddr (int x, int y) { return data_ + y*width()+x;}
  T getPixel (int x, int y) { return *getAddr(x, y);}
  int sum ();
private:
  T* data_;
  int width_, height_;
};

template<class T> int apImage<T>::sum ()
{
  int sum = 0;
  for (int y=0; y<height(); y++)
    for (int x=0; x<width(); x++)
      sum += getPixel (x, y);
  return sum;
}
```

This example does not do anything we haven't seen before. When you construct an **apImage<>** object, it will allocate memory for its storage and allocate all the bytes to 1. We offer both **getAddr()**, to fetch the address of a pixel, and **getPixel()**, which fetches the pixel value itself. **sum()** computes the sum of all pixels in the image and does so by calling **getPixel()** on every pixel. We wrote **sum()** to take no advantage of the memory layout of the image, to keep the example simple. This would make more sense if **apImage<>** were actually two objects. If the base class defines **sum()** and the derived class allocates the memory, **sum()** could not make any assumptions about how to fetch pixel data, other than to call **getPixel()**.

Now let's implement a specialization for the data type **unsigned char**, which is a very common pixel type.

```
template<> int apImage<unsigned char>::sum ()
{
  int sum = 0;
  unsigned char* p = getAddr (0, 0);
  for (int y=0; y<height(); y++)
    for (int x=0; x<width(); x++)
      sum += *p++;
  return sum;
}
```

In this example, we do make assumptions about how memory is stored. Instead of using **getPixel()** to fetch every pixel, we call **getAddr()** once to get a pointer to the first pixel in the image. We then simply increment this pointer every time we want to access the next pixel.

There is a large performance difference between these two versions of **sum()**. For a 1024 by 1024 image, our generic template function took 105 milliseconds to run. Our specialized version for **unsigned char** took 2 milliseconds. This is an excellent use of specialization to improve the performance of commonly used types.

We caution you to document very clearly where improvements have been made to enhance performance. In a large image processing system, it is doubtful that every team member will have a good understanding of all aspects of the system. What will happen when a team member needs a different template type, and writes:

```
apImage<char> image(1024, 1024);
...
image.sum();
```

We already know what will happen. This will work fine, but will take 105 milliseconds to run because our specialization is only valid for **unsigned char**. The compiler will not remind you to make sure this is what you intended. Nothing will happen at run time either, unless your code monitors the execution time. In fact, if your unit tests or release tests do not find this discrepancy, it might very well be that one of your customers will find this issue. To help minimize this from happening, we suggest you do the following:

■   Provide well-written documentation regarding performance improvements made to specific data types. This can be placed in the code itself, but it should be duplicated in any developer documentation.

■   Add performance measurements to unit tests to make sure these optimized functions execute as expected. If the measured performance does not fit within a desired operating range (adjusted for processor speed), the test should fail.

■   During release testing, generate a list of all template arguments used by the application. Compare this list against the existing documentation and prepare a list of possible discrepancies. The development team should review this list to see if any new specializations are needed.

5.4 Coding for Internationalization

If you want your application to be used in other countries, you have to make provisions that allow you to translate your user interface into other languages. If your application processes textual data, you also have to make provisions to handle data in other languages. These provisions are called *internationalization.*

When building applications, most developers don't think about internationalization issues unless there are immediate business requirements that force them to do so. When the requirements show up later, they force the developers to remediate the code — a process that is often far more complex and expensive than planning for internationalization from the start.

Almost all significant business software ends up internationalized sooner or later, and the technical requirements posed by internationalization are becoming more complex. For example, People's Republic of China (PRC) now requires that all software sold in China must support the GB18030 character set — a very large and complex character set.

Many people only think about the user-interface component of internationalization, which includes translating such items as messages, menus, and labels. The translation process can be fairly straightforward, regardless of the target market. Straightforward, however, is not the same thing as trivial. You cannot simply replace the strings in the original language with translated strings and expect a working result. The problems with such an approach include:

- The translated strings no longer make sense grammatically.

- Monetary values are printed incorrectly.

- Dates are semantically incorrect due to differences in locales.

- The translated strings no longer fit into the GUI (or dialog boxes), which were designed for Latin characters running under the English or European versions of the operating system.

In addition to translation issues, there are issues related to handling text inside your application. Almost all applications read, write, parse, or otherwise process some text. Code that works with text can require very significant adaptation to handle multiple languages. This is especially true for those languages with large and complex character sets, such as Chinese, Japanese, and Korean. See [Lunde99]. All kinds of things can and will go wrong when your code encounters text in other character sets, including:

- Overflow errors occur in those variables that store string values.

- The database underlying the product, which worked fine for Latin characters, starts to produce errors.

- Third-party components start to produce errors when they encounter double-byte strings.

- The performance of the system noticeably degrades.

To avoid these and other problems, you need a little forward thinking to allow for handling international text, even if it is not required for your initial release. In this section, we touch on a few of the largest issues involved in making your code ready for internationalization. Getting on the right track from the beginning is the key to making this process work. Toward that goal, Figure 5.3 highlights some of the issues you should consider.

Internationalization Checklist

✔ **Use Unicode.**

✔ **Maintain a single code base.**

✔ **Design and use a resource manager for strings.**

✔ **Make sure that your database back ends are configured to support non-Western European languages.**

✔ **Recognize that internationalization is much bigger than simple translation.**

✔ **Get the help you need.**

Figure 5.3: Internationalization Checklist

5.4.1 Unicode

If your program processes any significant amount of text, the most important issue is to decide how to represent text in your code – what character encoding to use. A *character encoding* defines the mapping from a set of characters to binary values in your code. As soon as you look outside of Western Europe, you will discover that there are many character encodings other than ASCII and Latin-1, sometimes several for each language. For example, the Japanese language appears in four different encodings in common applications: Shift-JIS, EUC-JP, UTF-8, and ISO-2022-JP.

You can write your code to process text in one or more of the hundreds of defined encodings. However, if you do this, you are likely to encounter defects and complexity that must be debugged one language at a time. The alternative is to follow the example of Oracle, Microsoft Windows, and Java, and use *Unicode* as your internal representation for text.

Unicode is not a font, nor is it a software program. Unicode is a standard means of representing text in all of the world's languages in computer systems. It defines a very large set of characters, and then offers several encoding methods for representing these characters in memory. These encoding methods, UTF-8, UTF-16, and UTF-32, replace character encodings like ASCII or Shift-JIS.

Microsoft Windows supports UTF-16 as a native data type in C, C++, C#, and Visual Basic. Various UNIX systems and compilers support different Unicode encoding methods. You will almost certainly have to support data sources in the many *legacy encodings*, but by converting to Unicode for your internal processing, you can avoid the complexity of handling all of these encodings in the bulk of your code.

The Unicode Standard has been adopted by such industry leaders as Microsoft, Apple, Oracle, Sun, HP, IBM, Sybase, and many others. Unicode is required by such standards as Java, JavaScript, XML, LDAP, CORBA 3.0, and WML. In addition, Unicode is the official way to implement ISO/IEC 10646 and GB18030, which have important business ramifications.

You can add Unicode support to your application either directly or by using a third-party library, such as Basis Technology's Rosette Core Library for Unicode (`http://www.basistech.com`) or International Components for Unicode's (ICU) open source software package (`http://oss.software.ibm.com/icu/index.html`). For detailed information about Unicode and the Unicode Standard, visit the web site: `http://www.unicode.org`.

5.4.2 A Simple Resource Manager for Strings

Handling strings is more complicated than making a new code base for each language and translating the existing strings in place. There are a number of issues when dealing with strings in the scope of internationalization: the size of the buffers, their placement on the GUI, and their use within the code, to name a few.

There are differing approaches to what strings should be *localized* (or translated). For example, some people feel that all strings should be localized, including all error messages. We take a simpler approach and consider the intended audience when determining whether or not to localize a message. For example, the message **File not found** should be localized because the user can take some corrective action when this message is received. However, a string like **Fatal Error #1004. Stack Trace: ...** mostly contains information useful only to the developer. In this case, we would split the string into two parts. The **Fatal Error #1004** would be localized because this tells the user that something bad happened. However, any other detailed information, such as a stack trace or internal dump of the system, can be in the native language.

Designing the Resource Manager

In this section, we design a simple resource manager to handle all strings used within the application. The goal of our resource manager is to make it easy to replace strings with a different list of strings, depending upon the desired language. We create a repository for all displayed strings, with a mechanism for replacing that repository with an alternate version. The design is flexible because few assumptions are made regarding where this list of strings is stored. Our application refers to strings with a unique ID, which is the key to the design.

Our resource manager, **apResourceMgr**, has the following features:

- Returns a string given the ID of the string.

- Exports all managed strings to a file, which is usually done during development after all the strings have been defined. This file is then given to translators to produce a localized version for another language.

- Imports strings from a file. This is usually done when the application starts running to load a set of translated strings.

- Stores the string files in XML. This permits the file to be edited using an XML-aware editor, or even a generic text editor, as long as it can display **wchar_t** characters.

It is important to note that our resource manager does not address the myriad of GUI issues that arise (due to localization and the rendering issues specific to native operating systems). We only briefly address the issue of string length. The CD-ROM contains the full source code for the resource manager.

❖ STRING REPOSITORY

apResourceMgr keeps all strings in a **std::map** object, which also does most of the work.

```
struct apStringData
{
  std::wstring str;      // Current string value
  std::wstring notes;    // Optional notes describing value
};

typedef std::map<unsigned int, apStringData>     stringmap;
```

❖ RETRIEVING A STRING

apResourceMgr controls an instance of **stringmap** called **strings_**. Regardless of what interface is used to access a string, a member function **fetchString()** is called. This function returns either the string associated with the **id** passed to it, or it returns a null string, as shown.

```
std::wstring apResourceMgr::fetchString (unsigned long id)
{
  stringmap::iterator i = strings_.find (id);
  if (i == strings_.end())
    return L"";

  return (*i).second.str;
}
```

❖ ADDING A STRING

Inserting a string into our **map** is only a little more complicated, as shown here.

```
unsigned int apResourceMgr::addString (const std::wstring& str,
                                       const std::wstring& notes,
                                       unsigned long id,
                                       bool overlay)
{
  if (id == 0)
    id = hash (str);    // Get a hash value
```

```
  if (id == 0)
    return id;   // null string. These can be safely ignored.

  // Ignore the string if overlay is false
  // and the string already exists
  if (!overlay) {
    stringmap::iterator i = strings_.find (id);
    if (i != strings_.end ()) {
      return id;
    }
  }

  apStringData data;
  data.str   = str;
  data.notes = notes;
  strings_[id] = data;

  return id;
}
```

Only the first argument of **addString()** is required. The **notes** field is optional and is needed only when you want to keep track of any requirements or translation notes. If **id** is not specified, a function **hash()** is called to compute an **id** based on the string itself. It is usually considered an error if the **id** is already found in our map. Some may consider this a bit harsh, so the **overlay** argument can be set to **true** to allow duplicate strings to replace any existing definition.

Using the Resource Manager

Our resource manager can be used, depending upon the style of the developer, in the following ways:

■ Accessing strings using IDs

■ Accessing strings using names

❖ ACCESSING STRINGS USING IDS

We have found it cumbersome to refer to strings by an ID value, because these IDs must be unique to the application. However, for developers that are comfortable with this method of localizing strings, our implementation supports it, as shown in the following example:

```
std::wstring msg = apResourceMgr::gOnly().fetchString (0x12345);
std::wcout << msg << std::endl;
```

In production code, using symbolic constants will help improve readability:

```
#define STRING_R 0x12345
std::wstring msg = apResourceMgr::gOnly().fetchString (STRING_R);
```

A Singleton object, **apResourceMgr**, is used to access a string value, given its **id** (**unsigned int**). The returned string is then used for display or other purposes. Notice that we are using a **std::wstring** object, and not a **std::string** object. **std::wstring** is a string of 16-bit characters (or 32-bit on some platforms), while a **std::string** is a string of 8-bit characters. We designed **apResourceMgr** to manage strings of 16-bit Unicode characters (UTF-16), as opposed to strings of multibyte characters (MBCS). Working with

wchar_t characters instead of **char** is not difficult, but it does require some changes in coding style, as follows:

```
std::wstring message = L"Hello World";
wchar_t* p = message.c_str();
```

If your compiler does not have reasonable wide-character or Unicode support, you can convert our resource manager to a multibyte (MBCS) manager without too much difficulty. GNU's gcc compiler lacks support for wide characters prior to version 3. Earlier GNU versions, like 2.95, are still very popular, so you should check on your requirements. Compiling and running this simple example is an adequate test of a compiler's support:

```
#include <string>
#include <iostream>

int main()
{
  std::string astr = "Hello World";
  std::wstring wstr = L"Hello World";
  std::cout << astr << std::endl;
  std::wcout << wstr << std::endl;
  return 0;
}
```

❖ ACCESSING STRINGS USING NAMES

The second way you can use **apResourceMgr** is to encapsulate all your strings inside another object, **apStringResource**. You can choose either to define these objects in each source file, or you can define them all in a single resource file. One nice feature of **apStringResource** is that you do not have to worry about string **id**s. You access the string using the variable name you created. Another advantage of using **apResourceMgr** is that your code contains a default string to display. If no translation is available for a particular string, the default string is shown.

▶ **EXAMPLE** ──

Let's look at a simple example:

```
apStringResource r1 (L"Hello World", L"Misc. Notes");

int main()
{
  std::wcout << r1.string() << std::endl;
}
```

In this example, a global instance of **apStringResource**, **r1**, is defined. It has an initial value of **L"Hello World"**, and this is what is displayed on the console. The second parameter contains optional notes you can add. These notes are never displayed to the user, but they are seen by whoever translates the strings. For instance, you can specify how long the translated string can be before it adversely affects the user interface.

The definition for **apStringResource** is shown here.

```
class apStringResource
{
public:
  static std::wstring sNullWString;

  apStringResource (const std::wstring& str,
                    const std::wstring& notes=sNullWString,
                    unsigned int id=0);

  std::wstring string () const;
  operator std::wstring () const { return string ();}

  unsigned int id () const { return id_;}
private:
  unsigned int id_;           // Id of this string

  apStringResource (const apStringResource&) {}
  apStringResource& operator= (const apStringResource&) {}
};
```

As you can see, **apStringResource** is a very simple object. When you construct an instance of **apStringResource**, the string is actually stored in **apResourceMgr**. When **string()** or the conversion operator accesses the string, the string is fetched from **apResourceMgr**. There is a optional third argument to the **apStringResource** constructor. If no **id** is specified, a hash function is run on the string to compute a unique ID. In this case, you should not change the text of the default string, which was used to compute the **id**. This is especially true once the strings have been localized.

5.4.3 Saving and Restoring Strings from Files

The other important part of our implementation is saving and restoring strings from a file as shown here.

```
        bool exportStrings (const std::string& file);
        bool importStrings (const std::string& file);
```

Instead of choosing a binary format, we chose XML because it means we don't have to write any special tools to allow a translator to edit these files; any text or XML editor will do

To keep this subject brief we will not go into every aspect of the XML tools we use. We wrote a simple XML parser because we support a limited number of tags and do not require a comprehensive package. There are many XML parsers available, including the open source **Expat** library (see **http://www.jclark.com/xml/expat.html**). These are somewhat large packages and we simply did not need all this functionality. However, if your application uses XML for other purposes, we encourage you to write your own version of **exportStrings()** and **importStrings()** to take advantage of the parser you already use.

► **EXAMPLE**

Our use of XML can best be seen from example:

```
apStringResource r1 (L"This is string 1", L"Notes");
apStringResource r2 (L"This is string 2", L"Notes 2");
apResourceMgr::gOnly().exportStrings ("test.xml");
```

The file, **test.xml**, contains the following data:

```
<?xml version="1.0" encoding="UTF-16" ?>
<resources>
<phrase>
<id>324936760</id>
<string>This is string 1</string>
<notes>Notes</notes>
</phrase>
<phrase>
<id>324936761</id>
<string>This is string 2</string>
<notes>Notes 2</notes>
</phrase>
</resources>
```

For more information on XML, refer to **http://www.xml.com**. In our example, this file is written using **wchar_t** characters and many text editors will be unable to display it because most editors are only able to display 8-bit characters. We recommend that you use Microsoft's Internet Explorer to view the XML file.

The first line of the file, **<?xml version="1.0" encoding="UTF-16" ?>**, describes the data to be XML using UTF-16 format. What is not shown is that two bytes precede the first printed data. This data is called the BOM, or byte-order mark. Because machines store data in either little-endian or big-endian order, the BOM specifies which order is used in the file. This permits your localized string files to be used on any machine, regardless of whether the endian order of the file matches that of the machine.

Use the tag, **<resources>...</resources>**, once per file. This must surround all other elements in the file.

The tag, **<phrase>...</phrase>**, contains information for a single string. It relates an **id** with a **string** and a **notes** field. A phrase contains two or three nested elements (the **notes** field is optional), as shown here.

```
<id>id</id>
<string>string</string>
<notes>notes</notes>
```

Our simple parser can also accept comments, but these are removed when the file is read. A comment looks like this:

```
<!-- This is a comment -->
```

That's it! Our XML parsing uses the search capability of **std::wstring**. The entire XML document is stored here when it is read from the file. Comments and other XML declarations are removed and the BOM is compared with the endian order of the system to see if the bytes must be swapped before parsing. The **find()** method is used to find the next element, or skip forward to the end of an existing element. Because our XML is so simple, we do not have to worry about any complicated nesting of elements. We have also defined a Singleton object, **apWideTools**, to encapsulate endian detection and byte swapping. The XML functionality is kept inside an object, **apXMLTools**. You can use this for other simple parsing needs, or you can substitute it with a comprehensive XML parser.

5.4.4 An Alternate Approach to Handling Strings

There is a package that works in a similar way to our resource manager. The **gettext** package was originally released on UNIX systems but is now available on most platforms. This package includes:

- API to retrieve messages from a file. Macros are used to replace the user string with a version that will look up, and return, a translated string.

- Programs to extract existing strings from your code base.

- Programs to edit and manipulate lists of translated string.

You can find its full documentation by going to **http://www.gnu.org/manual/gettext**.

5.4.5 Locales

You can't discuss internationalization in the context of C++ without mentioning locales. Although we don't recommend using locales for managing large-scale commercial internationalization efforts, we provide a very brief overview here. For an extensive discussion, see [Stroustrup00] or [Langer00].

The standard library includes a complicated package called locales. Although it is easy to understand the intention of **std::locale**, its difficulty lies in its extensibility. **std::locale** was intended to be used by the stream classes, although it is a general purpose object. You can think of a locale as a collection of preferences, usually with regard to how something is displayed.

A locale is a collection of these preferences and a single preference is called a facet. Examples of locales include not only English, French, and Japanese, but also more specific ones, like US English or French Canadian. Facets are provided for date and time display, monetary values, and numeric quantities.

For example, time and date formatting depends upon standards that vary around the world. The date December 31st, 2002 would be represented as follows:

- In the US: 12/31/2002
- In Europe: 31/12/2002

- In Japan: 2002/12/31
- ISO specification: 20021231

Fortunately, when an application runs, these preferences are typically specified by the user.

C++ allows facets to be reused by different locales, and you can take an existing locale and change one or more facets. Delving deeper into locales and facets is beyond the scope of this book. However, we do recommend the following:

- Even if you do not use locales directly, the underlying stream package and many run-time library functions do. When you write locale-type data to a buffer (for example, `strftime` to format a time string), be generous about the size of any temporary buffers you allocate. If you use a fixed size buffer and the function asks for a maximum buffer size, you should use `sizeof()` instead of a hard-coded value.

- If you display any string whose length might be affected by a locale, you should verify that the string will fit before displaying it.

5.5 Summary

In this chapter, we explore multithreaded and multiprocess designs. We introduced the concepts of locking objects and defined an object to manage the lock. We also contrast the UNIX and Win32 implementations of threads and process, and provide practical techniques for avoiding deadlocks.

We also discuss exception handling, and provide specific recommendations for top-level catch handlers, as well as detailed guidelines for creating your own exception handling framework. Smaller topics, such as catching specific types of exceptions like memory allocation errors, and exception specifications are also covered. See Figure 5.1 for a checklist of rules for handling exceptions. See Figure 5.2 for a checklist of guidelines for using assertions.

It is important to understand the effects of these constructs in both compile-time and run-time environments. The subsequent sections discuss a myriad of common compilers and their specific issues in handling constructs, such as dynamic casting, templates, and template specialization.

Finally, we provide a discussion of building an application such that it is ready for internationalization, should the business requirements require it. This section presents the high-level strategy and background to make the appropriate design decisions, while also providing a resource manager object for handling strings, and which uses XML to save and restore strings to files. We also present an alternative approach to managing strings using a gnu utility, `gettext`.

In Chapter 6, we use everything we have considered in the past chapters to finalize the design and implementation strategy for the image framework. In addition, we demonstrate how to integrate third-party libraries to further extend the framework's functionality and improve the performance of some image processing functions.

6

Implementation Considerations

In this chapter, we apply what we have learned through prototyping and examples to finalize the design for the image framework. The components of the framework are shown in Figure 6.1.

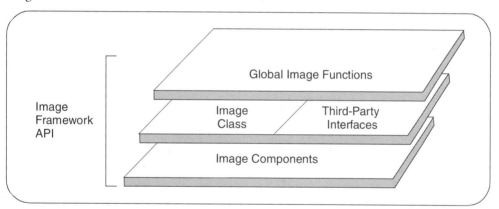

Figure 6.1: Image Framework Components

Our design has had many iterations, using a variety of C++ techniques. We started by using inheritance to create a framework that could handle numerous image types. It quickly became apparent in our subsequent prototype that templates both improved and simplified the design by eliminating most of the object hierarchy. However, we were still including image storage as a component of the image class, instead of separating it as an image component. We also explored using handles, but found they did nothing to improve the design. Once we prototyped a solution that separated storage from the image class, we knew that the final design was close at hand.

Each prototype was incomplete, but collectively they allowed us to test different design principles. We used a single, trivial, image processing function (computing thumbnail images) to observe the merits of each design. And, we wrote a unit test for each prototype to verify the correctness and the behavior of memory allocation, and to verify how pixels are accessed.

Often, the final design grows out of one or more prototypes. Sometimes it is obvious that you have hit on the right design, and other times it becomes an iterative process. From our prototypes, we applied the following ideas:

- Image storage should be separate from the image processing functions. The image storage classes are independent of the image processing functions (but not vice versa).

- Templates should be used for a more efficient design, allowing us to: produce a single version of code that works with any pixel type; optimize performance where needed by using specialization; and adapt our image storage component to use other memory allocators.

6.1   Finalizing the Image Components

Overall, the time we spent prototyping was very productive. This section describes the final design for the image components within the framework, including:

- Image coordinates

- Image storage

- Pixel types

6.1.1 Image Coordinates

In Section 1.1 on page 4 we discussed image coordinates by saying that the image origin (0,0) is located at the top left corner of the image. Doing so makes the mapping easier from a pixel coordinate to a physical memory location. This convention is widely used in image processing. We will take this definition one step further and relax the restriction that (0,0) is the top left corner. This allows us to deal with image windows, where a window is a portion of another image.

User-defined image coordinates are not discussed in this book. With user-defined coordinates, the user can access images using coordinates that make sense for a particular application. This can be something as simple as redefining the coordinate system, such that (0,0) is located at the lower left corner of the image. Or, it can be as complicated as specifying coordinates in terms of real units, like millimeters. We don't deny that this is a useful feature, but it is also very application-specific. If you need to define your own coordinate system, you can encapsulate this in your own code and transform it to our native coordinates.

In the final version of our framework, an image has three properties:

- origin — the x and y coordinates of the upper left corner

- width — the width (x-axis) of the image in pixels
- height — the height (y-axis) of the image in pixels

When an image is created, all three values are specified, with the origin typically being (0,0).

To make working with coordinates easier, we create two generic objects to handle points and rectangles.

❖ POINT

A *point* is an (x,y) pair that specifies the integer coordinates of a pixel. Our **apPoint** object is shown here.

```
class apPoint
{
public:
  apPoint () : x_ (0), y_ (0) {}
  apPoint (std::pair<int, int p)
    : x_ (p.first), y_ (p.second) {}
  apPoint (int x, int y) : x_ (x), y_ (y) {}

  int x () const { return x_;}
  int y () const { return y_;}
  std::pair<int, int> point () const
  { return std::pair<int, int>(x_, y_);}

  bool  operator == (const apPoint& p) const
  { return x() == p.x() && y() == p.y();}

  apPoint& operator += (const apPoint& p)
  { x_ += p.x(); y_ += p.y(); return *this;}

  // Default copy constructor and assignment operators ok.
private:
  int x_, y_;
};
```

We considered using the standard library object, **std::pair<>**, to represent a pair of coordinates, but we implemented our own point class instead so that we can add exactly what functionality we need. Coordinate information is stored as an **int**, permitting signed coordinate values. Our application uses **apPoint** frequently, so we define stream operators for our **apBString** class, as shown.

```
apBString& operator<< (apBString& stream, const apPoint& point);
apBString& operator>> (apBString& stream, apPoint& point);
```

For information on **apBString**, refer to our earlier discussion on page 88. By defining insertion and extraction operators for our common objects, we can later use them as a persistence mechanism. These functions are very simple, as we can see by looking at the insertion operator:

```
apBString& operator<< (apBString& stream, const apPoint& point)
{
  apBString bstr;
  bstr << point.x() << point.y();
```

```
      stream << bstr;
      return stream;
   }
```

This function writes a single value, another **apBString**, instead of writing two separate values to **stream**. By encapsulating the x and y coordinates inside **apBString**, we adhere to our standard of writing a single element for each object or datatype.

❖ RECTANGLE

A *rectangle* describes a point with a width and height. We use this to define the boundary of an image. The **width_** and **height_** parameters are **unsigned int**, since they can only take on positive values. A rectangle with an origin at **(0,0)**, and **width_** of 10, and **height_** of 10, describes a region with corners **(0,0)** and **(9,9)** because the coordinates are zero-based. A *null rectangle*, a degenerate case where the rectangle is nothing more than a point, occurs when **width_** or **height_** is zero.

Our rectangle object, including inline functions, is shown here.

```
class apRect
{
public:
  apRect ();
  apRect (apPoint ul, unsigned int width, unsigned int height);
  apRect (apPoint ul, apPoint lr);
  apRect (int x0, int y0, unsigned int width, unsigned int height);

  const apPoint& ul () const { return ul_;}
  apPoint        lr () const;

  int   x0      () const { return ul_.x();}
  int   y0      () const { return ul_.y();}
  int   x1      () const { return lr().x();}
  int   y1      () const { return lr().y();}

  unsigned int  width  () const { return width_;}
  unsigned int  height () const { return height_;}

  bool  isNull () const { return width_== 0 || height_==0;}

  bool  operator == (const apRect& r) const;
  bool  operator != (const apRect& r) const
  { return !operator== (r);}

  bool  within (const apPoint& p) const;

  apRect intersect (const apRect& r) const;

  void expand (int x, int y);

  // Default copy constructor and assignment operators ok.
private:
  apPoint ul_;            // Upper-left-hand coordinates
  unsigned int width_;    // Image width
  unsigned int height_;   // Image height
};
```

Let's discuss a few of the methods in our rectangle object.

❖ INTERSECT()

The **intersect()** method computes the intersection of two rectangles, producing an output rectangle, or a null rectangle if there is no intersection. This method handles a number of conditions, including partial and complete overlap, as illustrated in Figure 6.2.

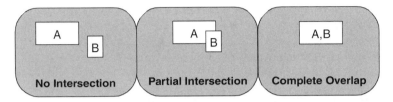

Figure 6.2: Intersection Conditions

The implementation of the **intersect()** method is shown here.

```
template <class T> const T& apMin (const T& a, const T& b)
{ return (a<b) ? a : b;}

template <class T> const T& apMax (const T& a, const T& b)
{ return (a>b) ? a : b;}

apRect apRect::intersect (const apRect& r) const
{
  // Get the corner points.
  const apPoint& ul1 = ul ();
  const apPoint& ul2 = r.ul ();
  int x = apMax (ul1.x(), ul2.x());
  int y = apMax (ul1.y(), ul2.y());
  int w = apMin (ul1.x()+width(),  ul2.x()+r.width()) - x;
  int h = apMin (ul1.y()+height(), ul2.y()+r.height()) - y;
  if (w < 0 || h < 0) {
    // No intersection
    return apRect ();
  }

  return apRect (x, y, w, h);
}
```

❖ WITHIN()

The **within()** method tests whether or not a point is inside the rectangle. It returns **true** if the point is inside or on the border. The implementation of **within()** is shown here.

```
bool apRect::within (const apPoint& p) const
{
  apPoint lr (ul_.x() + width_, ul_.y()+height_);
  return (ul_.x() <= p.x()) && (lr.x() > p.x()) &&
         (ul_.y() <= p.y()) && (lr.y() > p.y());
}
```

❖ EXPAND()

The **expand()** method increases the size of the rectangle by adding a specific quantity to its dimensions. This method is very useful when performing image processing operations that create output images larger than the original image. Note that you can also pass in negative values to shrink the rectangle. The implementation of **expand()** is shown here.

```
void apRect::expand (int x, int y)
{
  if (!isNull()) {
    ul_      += apPoint (-x, -y);
    width_   += 2*x;
    height_  += 2*y;
  }
}
```

6.1.2 Image Storage

Our third prototype (Section 3.2.6 on page 60) contributed the concept of separating image storage from the image class. After working with many examples, we realized that this prototype was still lacking the ability to handle certain details. The details that we now address in the final design include:

■ **Handles and rep objects**. The bottom line is that they do not fit in the design. We still use reference counting by means of **apAlloc<>**, but having another layer of abstraction is not necessary. Our final image storage object encapsulates an **apAlloc<>** object along with other storage parameters. Because we aren't using handles, these storage objects get copied as they are passed. Fortunately, the copy constructor and assignment operators are very fast, so performance is not an issue because the pixel data itself is reference counted. The complexity of the additional layer of abstraction didn't provide enough of a benefit to make it into the final design.

■ **Memory alignment**. The alignment issues we introduced during the discussion of **apAlloc<>** (Section 3.1.5 on page 31) require more refinement. **apAlloc<>** supports the alignment of memory on a user-specified pixel boundary. Proper alignment can be critical for efficient performance of many image processing functions. As it turns out, it is not sufficient to align the first pixel in the image as **apAlloc<>** does. Most image processing routines process one line at a time. By forcing the first pixel in each line   to have a certain alignment, many operations become more efficient. For generic algorithms, this savings can be modest or small because the compiler may not be able to take advantage of the alignment. However, specially tuned functions can be written to take advantage of particular memory alignments. Many third-party libraries contain carefully written assembly language routines that can yield impressive savings on aligned data. Our final design has been extended to better address memory alignment.

■ **Image shape**. We refer to the graphical properties of the storage as *image shape*. For example, almost all images used by image processing packages are rectangular; that is, they describe pixels that are stored in a series of rows. Our prototypes and test application described rectangular images. In our final design, we explicitly support rectangular images so that we can optimize the storage of such images, but we also allow the future implementation of non-rectangular images. For example, you might have valid image information for a large, circular region. If we store this information as a rectangle, many bytes are wasted because we have to allocate space for pixels that do not contain any useful information. A more memory-efficient method for storing non-rectangular pixel data is to use *run-length encoding*. With run-length encoding, you store the pixel data along with the (x,y) coordinates and length of the row. This allows you to store only those pixels that contain valid information. The disadvantage of run-length encoding is the difficulty of writing image processing routines that operate on one or more run-length encoded images.

Final Design

The final design partitions image storage into three pieces, as illustrated in Figure 6.3.

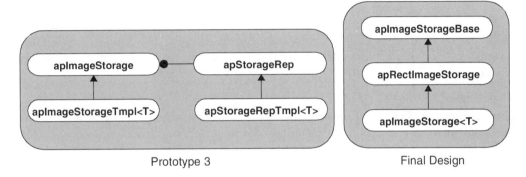

Figure 6.3: Image Storage Final Design

apImageStorageBase is the base class that describes the rectangular boundary of any storage object. For rectangular images, it describes the valid coordinates for pixels in the image. If you extend the framework to implement non-rectangular images, you would describe the minimum enclosing rectangle surrounding the region. **apRectImageStorage** extends **apImageStorageBase** to manage the storage for rectangular images. **apRectImageStorage** is not a template class; instead, it allocates storage based on the number of bytes of storage per pixel and a desired memory alignment for each row in the image. By making this a generic definition, **apRectImageStorage** can handle all aspects of image storage. **apImageStorage<T>**, however, is a template class that defines image storage for a particular data type. Most **apImageStorage<>** methods act as wrapper functions by calling methods inside **apRectImageStorage** and applying a cast. Let's look at these components in more detail in the following sections.

❖ APIMAGESTORAGEBASE

We start by looking at **apImageStorageBase**. This base class only has an understanding of the boundary surrounding the image storage.

```
class apImageStorageBase
{
public:
  apImageStorageBase ();
  apImageStorageBase (const apRect& boundary);

  virtual ~apImageStorageBase ();
```

```
    const apRect& boundary () const { return boundary_;}

    int  x0           () const { return boundary_.x0();}
    int  y0           () const { return boundary_.y0();}
    int  x1           () const { return boundary_.x1();}
    int  y1           () const { return boundary_.y1();}
    unsigned int width  () const { return boundary_.width();}
    unsigned int height () const { return boundary_.height();}

    // Default copy constructor and assignment operators ok.
  protected:
    apRect boundary_;
};
```

Once the rectangular boundary is specified in the constructor, the object is immutable and cannot be changed. It is designed this way because changing the boundary coordinate information would affect how this object interacts with other images that are already defined.

❖ APRECTIMAGESTORAGE

apRectImageStorage is the most complicated object in our hierarchy. It handles all aspects of memory management, including allocation, locking, and windowing. In this section, we describe in detail how this object works. (The full source code is found on the CD-ROM.) Reviewing the protected member data of **apRectImageStorage** shows us the details of the implementation:

```
    protected:
      mutable apLock lock_;          // Access control
      apAlloc<Pel8>  storage_;       // Pixel storage
      Pel8*          begin_;         // Pointer to first row
      Pel8*          end_;           // Pointer past last row
      eAlignment     align_;         // Alignment
      unsigned int   yoffset_;       // Row offset to first row
      unsigned int   xoffset_;       // Pixel offset in first row
      unsigned int   bytesPerPixel_; // Bytes per pixel
      unsigned int   rowSpacing_;    // Number of bytes between rows
```

storage_ contains the actual pixel storage as an array of bytes. **apAlloc<>** allows a number of objects to share the same storage, but the storage itself is fixed in memory. This allows us to create *image windows*. An image window is an image that reuses the storage of another image. In other words, we can have multiple **apRectImageStorage** objects that use identical storage, but possibly only a portion of it. To improve the efficiency of accessing pixels in the image, the object maintains **begin_** and **end_** to point to the first pixel used by the object and just past the end, respectively. Derived objects use these pointers to construct iterator objects, similar to how the standard C++ library uses them. **bytesPerPixel_** and **align_** store the pixel size and alignment information passed during object construction. Instead of directly specifying the numeric alignment value, **eAlignment** provides a clean way to specify alignment, as shown.

```
    enum eAlignment {eNoAlign=0, eWordAlign=2, eDoubleWordAlign=4,
                     eQuadWordAlign=8, e2ByteAlign=2, e4ByteAlign=4,
                     e8ByteAlign=8, e16ByteAlign=16};
```

eAlignment has entries using two different naming conventions, giving the user the flexibility of choosing from two popular ones. **rowSpacing_** contains the number of bytes from one row to the next. This is often different than the width of the image because of alignment issues. By adding **rowSpacing_** to any pixel pointer, you can quickly advance to the same pixel in the next row of the image.

xoffset_ and **yoffset_** are necessary for image windows. Just because two images share the same **storage_** does not mean they access the same pixels. Image windowing lets an image contain a rectangular portion of another image. **xoffset_** and **yoffset_** are the pixel offsets from the first pixel in **storage_** to the first pixel in the image. If there is no image window, both of these offsets are zero.

The only remaining protected data member that we haven't described is **lock_**. **lock_** handles synchronization to the rest of the image storage variables, with the exception of **storage_** (because it uses **apAlloc<>**, which has its own independent locking mechanism).

The constructor of **apRectImageStorage** is as follows:

```
class apRectImageStorage : public apImageStorageBase
{
public:
  apRectImageStorage ();
  apRectImageStorage (const apRect& boundary,
                      unsigned int bytesPerPixel, eAlignment align);
```

Constructing the storage for an image requires the size and location of the image, the pixel depth (i.e., the number of bytes per pixel), and alignment requirements. For example:

```
struct RGB { char r, char g, char b };
apRect rect (0, 0, 2, 3);
apRectImageStorage storage (rect, sizeof (RGB), eDoubleWordAlign);
```

creates a **2x3** image, with an origin at (**0,0**). Each pixel requires 3 bytes, and the start of each line will have double-word (i.e., 4-byte) alignment, as shown in Figure 6.4.

Memory Locations →	0	1	2	3	4	5	6	7
	pixel(0,0)			pixel(1,0)			free	free
	pixel(0,1)			pixel(1,1)			free	free
	pixel(0,2)			pixel(1,2)			free	free

Figure 6.4: Image Storage Alignment

Each line in the image requires 8 bytes of storage, although only 6 bytes contain pixel data. The first three bytes hold the storage for the first pixel in the line, and are followed by three more bytes to hold the next pixel. In order to begin the next row with double-word alignment, we must skip 2 bytes before storing the pixels for the next line. We dealt with memory alignment when we introduced **apAlloc<>**. The arithmetic is the same, except we must apply it to each line, as shown in the implementation of **apRectImageStorage()**:

```
apRectImageStorage::apRectImageStorage (const apRect& boundary,
                                        unsigned int bytesPerPixel,
                                        eAlignment align)
: apImageStorageBase (boundary), begin_ (0), end_ (0),
  xoffset_ (0), yoffset_ (0), bytesPerPixel_ (bytesPerPixel),
  rowSpacing_ (0), align_ (align)
{
  // Round up our row size for alignment purposes. The
  // enumeration values match our alignment values so we can
  // cast it and do some bit manipulation.
  rowSpacing_ = width () * bytesPerPixel_;
  if (align_ != eNoAlign) {
    int alignment = static_cast<int>(align_) - 1;
    rowSpacing_ = (rowSpacing_ + alignment) & (~alignment);
  }

  // Allocate our memory. Force our base address to start at a
  // 8-byte aligned boundary.
  storage_ = apAlloc<Pel8> (rowSpacing_ * boundary.height (), 8);
  begin_ = rowAddress_ (y0());
  end_   = begin_ + height() * rowSpacing_;
}
```

We also use a number of locking functions to synchronize access to both the image storage parameters and the image storage itself, as shown.

```
bool lockState      () const { return lock_.lock();}
bool unlockState    () const { return lock_.unlock();}
// Lock/unlock our image state, but not the storage

bool lockStorage    () const { return storage_.lockStorage ();}
bool unlockStorage () const { return storage_.unlockStorage ();}
// Lock/unlock our image storage

bool lock   () const { return lockState() && lockStorage();}
bool unlock () const { return unlockState() && unlockStorage();}
// Lock/unlock our image state and storage
```

Locking is not a difficult feature to add to an object, but it is important to consider where to use it effectively. In our design, for example, several instances of **apRectImageStorage** can use the same underlying pixel storage. There is no need to lock access to this storage if we are only manipulating other member variables of **apRectImageStorage**. **lockState()** is best used when the state of **apRectImageStorage** changes. **lockStorage()** is used when the actual pixel data is accessed. **lock()** is a combination of the two, and is useful when all aspects of the image storage are affected. These functions are used by derived objects and non-member functions, since locking is a highly application-specific issue.

 When adding synchronization to a class, consider how clients will usually access your object.

Using image windows is a powerful technique that lets you change which pixels an instance of **apRectImageStorage** can access, as shown.

```
bool window (const apRect& window);
```

window() modifies an instance of **apRectImageStorage** by computing the intersection of the specified rectangle with the rectangle that defines which pixels are managed. This function is not as complicated as it sounds, because the **intersect()** method of **apRect** computes the overlap between the window and the original image. Once this is computed, the other variables can be updated, as shown.

```
bool apRectImageStorage::window (const apRect& window)
{
  lockState ();

  apRect intersect = boundary().intersect (window);
  if (intersect.isNull()) {
    // No intersection so make this a null image
    init ();
    unlockState ();
    return false;
  }

  // Adjust our boundary and compute the new offset to our
  // first pixel.
  xoffset_  += intersect.x0() - x0();
  yoffset_  += intersect.y0() - y0();
  boundary_  = intersect;
  begin_     = rowAddress_ (y0());
  end_       = begin_ + height() * rowSpacing_;

  unlockState ();
  return true;
}
```

If the intersection is null, that is, there is no overlap between the rectangles, **init()** resets the object to a null state. The remainder of the member variables are then updated to reflect the intersection. The **window()** function only affects local variables, so we call **lockState()** to lock access to member variables, because we do not also have to lock the underlying image storage.

Basic access to pixel data is provided by functions we have seen before:

```
    const Pel8* rowAddress_ (int y) const;
    Pel8*       rowAddress_ (int y);
  protected:
    const Pel8* getPixel (int x, int y) const;
    void        setPixel (int x, int y, const Pel8* pixel);
```

rowAddress_() is used by derived classes to return the address of the first pixel in a specific row. Derived objects will cast these pointers to their proper type. You use **getPixel()** and **setPixel()** in a similar manner. We use the underscore, _, as a suffix in **rowAddress_()** to indicate that it is primarily an internal function.

❖ apRowIterator<>

Before we introduce the actual storage objects, we need to introduce an iterator that can be used to simplify image processing functions. Like iterators defined by the standard C++ library, our **apRowIterator<>** object allows each row in the image to be accessed, as shown.

```
template<class T> class apRowIterator
{
public:
  struct current
  {
    T*   p;      // Pointer to start of row y
    int x;       // x coordinate of start of row
    int y;       // y coordinate of current row
    int bytes;   // Number of bytes to offset to next row
  };

  apRowIterator ()
  { cur_.p = 0; cur_.x = 0; cur_.y = 0; cur_.bytes = 0;}
  apRowIterator (T* p, long bytes, long x, long y)
  { cur_.p = p; cur_.bytes = bytes; cur_.x = x; cur_.y = y;}

  current*       operator->()        { return &cur_;}
  const current* operator->() const { return &cur_;}
  current&       operator* ()        { return cur_;}
  const current& operator* () const { return cur_;}

  apRowIterator& operator++ ();
  apRowIterator  operator++ (int);

  apRowIterator& operator-- ();
  apRowIterator  operator-- (int);

  apRowIterator& operator+= (int s);
  apRowIterator& operator-= (int s);

  bool operator== (const apRowIterator& i) const
  { return (cur_.p == i.cur_.p);}
  bool operator!= (const apRowIterator& i) const
  { return (cur_.p != i.cur_.p);}
private:
  current cur_;
};
```

Once you obtain an **apRowIterator** object from an **apImageStorage<>** object (presented in the next section), you can use it to access each row in the image, as follows:

```
apRowIterator i;
for (i=image.begin(); i != image.end(); i++) {
  // i->p points to the next pixel to process
  ...
}
```

Iterators don't really save us much typing, but they do hide the operation of fetching the address of each line. If we did not have an iterator, we would write something like the following, where **T** represents the pixel type:

✗ ```
for (int y=0; y<image.height(); y++) {
  T* p = image.rowAddress (y); // Address of first pel of line
  ...
```
```

❖ apPixelIterator

We also create an iterator suitable for accessing every pixel in an image. **apPixelIterator**
is similar in design to **apRowIterator**, but it is implemented using the standard STL
iterator traits. See [Stroustrup00]. This makes the iterator usable by the generic STL
algorithms, as shown.

```
template<class T> class apPixelIterator
{
public:
  // Standard iteration typedef's
  typedef std::forward_iterator_tag iterator_category;
  typedef T value_type;
  typedef ptrdiff_t difference_type;
  typedef T* pointer;
  typedef T& reference;

  struct current
  {
    T*   p;       // Current pointer to pixel
    int x, y;     // Current pixel coordinates

    T*   end;     // Pointer past last pixel in current row
    int x0;       // x coordinate of start of row
    int width;    // Width of row
    int bytes;    // Number of bytes to offset to next row
  };

  apPixelIterator ();
  apPixelIterator (T* p, int bytes, int x, int y, int width);

  T*        operator->()         { return cur_.p;}
  const T* operator->() const { return cur_.p;}
  T&        operator* ()         { return *cur_.p;}
  const T& operator* () const { return *cur_.p;}

  apPixelIterator& operator++ ();
  apPixelIterator  operator++ (int);

  bool operator== (const apPixelIterator& i) const
  { return (cur_.p == i.cur_.p);}
  bool operator!= (const apPixelIterator& i) const
  { return (cur_.p != i.cur_.p);}

private:
  current cur_;
};
```

❖ apImageStorage<>

apImageStorage<> is a template object, derived from **apRectImageStorage**, that defines
image storage for arbitrary datatypes. Its definition is shown here.

```
template<class T>
class apImageStorage : public apRectImageStorage
{
public:
  typedef apRowIterator<T>   row_iterator;
  typedef apPixelIterator<T> iterator;

  apImageStorage () {}
  apImageStorage (const apRect& boundary,
```

```
                    eAlignment align = eNoAlign)
    : apRectImageStorage (boundary, sizeof (T), align) {}

    const T* rowAddress (long y) const;
    T* rowAddress (long y);
    // Returns a pointer to the first pixel in the specified row
    // Not thread-safe. Clients need to lock storage
    // Throws apBoundsException if the argument is not in range

    const T& getPixel (int x, int y) const;
    const T& getPixel (const apPoint& point) const;
    void     setPixel (int x, int y, const T& pixel);
    void     setPixel (const apPoint& point, const T& pixel);
    // Gets or sets the specified pixel. Thread-safe.

    virtual ~apImageStorage () {}

    // row iterators. Not thread-safe. Clients need to lock storage
    row_iterator       row_begin ();
    const row_iterator row_begin () const;

    row_iterator       row_end ();
    const row_iterator row_end () const;

    // pixel iterators. Not thread-safe. Clients need to lock storage
    iterator        begin ();
    const iterator begin () const;

    iterator        end ();
    const iterator end () const;
};
```

This object builds upon its base class. You can continue to access pixel data using **getPixel()** and **setPixel()**, but you can also access a row of data by using **rowAddress()**, or a row or pixel iterator. Our **row_begin()** and **row_end()** iterators use a **typedef** called **row_iterator** to hide direct references to **apRowIterator<>**. Likewise, our **begin()** and **end()** iterators use a typedef called **iterator** to hide direct references to **apPixelIterator<>**.

 Use iterators to access all of the pixels in the image.

Although the full comments are in the source code, we left a few critical ones in the code snippet to indicate those member functions that synchronize access to the image data and those that do not. Our decision about what functions should lock is based upon efficiency.

getPixel() and **setPixel()** lock both the object and the memory because these functions are fairly inefficient to begin with. No locking is built into the other functions, and you are responsible for determining the appropriate locking. Proper locking also requires us to catch any exceptions that are thrown, as we do in our definition of **getPixel()**:

```
template<class T>
const T& apImageStorage<T>::getPixel (int x, int y) const
```

```
{
  static T pixel;

  lock ();
  try {
    const Pel8* p = apRectImageStorage::getPixel (x, y);
    memcpy (&pixel, p, sizeof (T));
  }
  catch (...) {
    unlock ();
    throw;
  }

  unlock ();
  return pixel;
}
```

On page 188, we will see how to dramatically simplify **getPixel()** by using an exception-safe locking object.

▶ **EXAMPLE** ───

Let's write a few different versions of a **set()** function to set all of the pixels in the image to a fixed value. These versions demonstrate how to use row iterators, pixel iterators, and generic algorithms from the STL, as follows:

```
template<class T>
void row_set (apImageStorage<T> image, T value)
{
  typename apImageStorage<T>::row_iterator i;
  unsigned int width = image.width ();
  for (i=image.row_begin(); i != image.row_end(); i++) {
    T* p = i->p;
    for (unsigned int x=0; x<width; x++)
      *p++ = value;
  }
}

template<class T>
void pixel_set (apImageStorage<T> image, T value)
{
  typename apImageStorage<T>::iterator i;
  for (i=image.begin(); i != image.end(); i++)
    *i = value;
}

template<class T>
void stl_set (apImageStorage<T> image, T value)
{
  std::fill (image.begin(), image.end(), value);
}
```

There are more efficient ways to write these for basic data types, but these versions have the advantage of working with any data type you might define. There is no **try/catch** block defined because none is necessary. As long as we write a loop using **begin()** and **end()** as shown, we will never access an invalid row.

◀

❖ EXCEPTION-SAFE LOCKING

Most functions that operate on **apImageStorage<>** objects will require some form of record locking. This is true for functions that modify both the state of the object and the underlying pixels. Writing a function that calls **lock()** and **unlock()** is not difficult, but you need to consider how exceptions influence the design; otherwise, it is quite possible that when an exception is thrown, the lock will not be cleared because the function does not terminate properly. One solution is to add a **try** block to each routine to catch all errors, so that the object can be unlocked before the exception is re-thrown. An easier approach is to construct an object that uses the same RAII technique we describe on page 136, as shown.

```
template<class T> class apImageStorageLocker
{
public:
  apImageStorageLocker (const apImageStorage<T>& image) :
                        image_ (image) { image_.lock();}
  ~apImageStorageLocker () { image_.unlock();}
private:
  const apImageStorage<T>& image_;

  // No copy or assignment is allowed
  apImageStorageLocker (const apImageStorageLocker&);
  apImageStorageLocker& operator= (const apImageStorageLocker&);
};
```

Our **apImageStorageLocker<>** implementation locks only **apImageStorage<>** objects, although it wouldn't be hard to create a generic version. Here is how it works. When an **apImageStorageLocker<>** object is created, a reference to an **apImageStorage<>** object is stored and the object is locked. When the **apImageStorageLocker<>** object is destroyed, the lock on **apImageStorage<>** is released. You can see how powerful this simple technique is when it is used within another function.

For example, **getPixel()** explicitly handles the locking and unlocking in its implementation. This function can be greatly simplified with the use of **apImageStorageLocker<>**, as shown.

```
template<class T>
const T& apImageStorage<T>::getPixel (int x, int y) const
{
  static T pixel;

  apImageStorageLocker<T> locker (*this); // Exception-safe locking

  const Pel8* p = apRectImageStorage::getPixel (x, y);
  memcpy (&pixel, p, sizeof (T));

  return pixel;
}
```

As you can see, we create a temporary instance of **apImageStorageLocker<>** on the stack. When **getPixel()** goes out of scope, either because of normal completion or during stack unwinding of an exception, the lock is guaranteed to be released.

❖ COPYING IMAGE STORAGE

In the source code, we provide two generic functions: **copy()** and **duplicate()**. **copy()** moves pixels between two images, while **duplicate()** generates an identical copy of an **apImageStorage<>** object. Because we are dealing with template objects, our **copy()** function copies image pixels from one data type to another, as shown.

```
void copy (const apImageStorage<T1>& src, apImageStorage<T2>& dst,
          bool fastCopy = true)
```

Our design of **copy()** has the following interesting features:

- The output storage must have the same dimensions as the input image. If not, a new **apImageStorage<T2>** object is returned. This is a low-level copy function and we do not want to worry about image boundaries that do not match. It would be better to handle this at a higher level in the code.

- If **T1** and **T2** are identical, **memcpy()** is used to duplicate pixels. This technique doesn't work for complex data types, so an optional argument, **fastCopy**, has been added.

- If **T1** and **T2** are not identical, or if **fastCopy** is **false**, a pixel-by-pixel copy occurs.

The **copy()** implementation is shown here.

```
template <class T1, class T2>
void copy (const apImageStorage<T1>& src, apImageStorage<T2>& dst,
          bool fastCopy = true)
{
  if (src == dst)
    return;

  // Exception-safe locking
  apImageStorageLocker<T1> srcLocker (src);
  apImageStorageLocker<T1> srcLocker (dst);

  if (src.boundary() != dst.boundary())
    dst = apImageStorage<T2> (src.boundary(), src.alignment());

  typename apImageStorage<T1>::row_iterator i1;
  typename apImageStorage<T2>::row_iterator i2;
  unsigned int w = src.width ();
  int bytes = w * src.bytesPerPixel ();

  const T1* p1;
  T2* p2;

  if (typeid(T1) == typeid(T2) && fastCopy) {
    // We're copying like datatypes so use memcpy for speed
    for (i1=src.row_begin(), i2=dst.row_begin(); i1 != src.row_end();
         i1++, i2++) {
      p1 = i1->p;
      p2 = i2->p;
      memcpy (p2, p1, bytes);
    }
  }
  else {
    // We have to do a pixel by pixel copy
    for (i1=src.row_begin(), i2=dst.row_begin(); i1 != src.row_end();
         i1++, i2++) {
```

```
        p1 = i1->p;
        p2 = i2->p;
        for (unsigned int x=0; x<w; x++)
          *p2++ = static_cast<T2>(*p1++);
    }
  }
}
```

When using synchronization objects, unlock objects in the reverse order from how they were locked. Using a technique to automatically handle locking issues will improve the readability and robustness of your code.

6.1.3 Pixel Types

In addition to the standard C data types that are used in image processing applications, a robust image processing framework must also handle the following complexities:

- Support for basic data types such that they can be manipulated (i.e., added, subtracted, and so on) in the standard ways

- An RGB data type that allows a generic image processing routine to handle color pixels

- A clamping (i.e., saturation) object that is used like other data types and eliminates the undesirable pixel-wrapping behavior arising from overflow issues

Basic Data Types

In our image framework, the pixel type is specified as a template parameter. In reality, there are only a few common data types that most image processing applications need. Here are the basic types used in image processing:

```
typedef unsigned char  Pel8;    // 1-byte
typedef unsigned short Pel16;   // 2-bytes
typedef unsigned int   Pel32;   // 4-bytes  (Unsigned)
typedef int            Pel32s;  // 4-bytes  (Signed)
```

These names are very descriptive since they refer to pels (picture elements, or pixels) and there is no confusion when used in image processing applications. Most images captured from monochrome sensors are represented using the **Pel8** data type. Some sensors have more sensitivity and output 10 or 12 bits of information. In that case, we would use a **Pel16** to store the image.

RGB Data Type

Pixels in color images are usually represented by RGB triplets. We showed a simple implementation of an RGB triplet during the prototyping stage.

The following simple structure is not sufficient for our final design:

✗
```
template<class T> class apRGBTmpl
{
public:
  T red;
  T green;
  T blue;
};
```

We need to have the ability to write statements like the following:

```
apRGBTmpl<Pel8> rgb1, rgb2, rgb3;
...
rgb3 = rgb1 + rgb2;
```

Instead of defining a separate structure for each type of RGB image, we define **apRGBTmpl<>**, where the template parameter is the data size of the red, green, and blue component. In **apRGBTmpl<>** we add basic operators, as well as conversion functions between a color and monochrome pixel, as shown.

```
template<class T> class apRGBTmpl
{
public:
  T red;
  T green;
  T blue;

  apRGBTmpl ()               : red(0), green(0), blue(0) {}
  explicit apRGBTmpl (T v)   : red(v), green(v), blue(v) {}
  apRGBTmpl (T r, T g, T b)  : red(r), green(g), blue(b) {}

  apRGBTmpl (const apRGBTmpl& s);
  apRGBTmpl<T>& operator= (const apRGBTmpl& src);

  template<class T1> apRGBTmpl (const apRGBTmpl<T1>& s);
  template<class T1> apRGBTmpl<T>& operator= (const apRGBTmpl<T1>& src);

  apRGBTmpl& operator= (const T& c)

  operator T () const
  // Conversion to monochrome

  apRGBTmpl<T>& operator+= (const apRGBTmpl<T>& s);
  apRGBTmpl<T>& operator-= (const apRGBTmpl<T>& s);
  apRGBTmpl<T>& operator*= (const apRGBTmpl<T>& s);
  apRGBTmpl<T>& operator/= (const apRGBTmpl<T>& s);

  apRGBTmpl<T>& operator+= (const T& s);
  apRGBTmpl<T>& operator-= (const T& s);
  apRGBTmpl<T>& operator*= (const T& s);
  apRGBTmpl<T>& operator/= (const T& s);

};
```

The complete implementation can be found in **imageTypes.h** on the CD-ROM. You will notice that we added functions, such as **operator apRGBTmpl<T2>**, to make it easy to convert between different RGB types.

Clamping Object for Overflow

Overflow is usually not an issue when an application uses mostly **int** and **double** data types. However, when you use the smaller data types, like **unsigned char**, you have to be very aware of overflows. What happens to the pixels that overflow the storage? What usually happens is that the output will wrap, just like any mathematical operation on the computer.

This behavior has never seemed correct when dealing with image processing functions. After all, if a value of 0 is black and 255 is white, 255+1 should be stored as 255 and not 0. This *clamping* behavior is also called *saturation*.

► EXAMPLE

8-bit images are still very popular. If you are using 8-bit images and you write something like the following:

```
apImage<Pel8> image1, image2;
set (image1, 255);
set (image2, 1);
image2 += image1;
```

every pixel in **image2** will be **0** (or black). This demonstrates that wrapping really isn't the behavior we want.

We think a better design for image processing is to use clamping as the default, while also keeping the original wrapping behavior available if desired. Keep in mind that there is an execution cost associated with clamping, and this may not always be tolerable. The clamping operation is applied to every pixel that is processed, so the cost increases as the size of the image increases.

For example, to detect and correct an overflow condition in a variable **value** larger than a **Pel8** looks like this:

```
Pel8 b = value > 255 ? : 255 : static_cast<Pel8>(value);
```

In order for our design to handle the overflow issue, our code must partition this functionality so that it can be integrated into image processing functions. If you are not careful, this can get very difficult, because the overflow check must be made prior to the conversion to the final pixel type. If you allow the compiler to make an implicit conversion before any overflow checks are made, you will not be able to clamp the output values at their limits, and your checks will be wasted.

► EXAMPLE

Let's look at an example to clarify the handling of overflow issues:

```
Pel32 l;
... some computation that sets l
Pel8 b = static_cast<Pel8>(l);
b = b > 255 ? : 255 : static_cast<Pel8>(b);
```

Clearly, the last line of this example does nothing, because **b** is already defined as a **Pel8**. This demonstrates the problem, though, of trying to add clamping as a separate step.

In order to get the behavior that you want, clamping must be designed into the image processing routines. The hard way to solve this problem is to have two versions of every routine: one that clamps the output data, and one that wraps.

The easier way is to use templates to define new pixel types that not only define the size of each pixel, but also specify the clamping behavior. You want to be able to use an **apImage<Pel8>** that defines an image using byte storage with the usual overflow behavior (wrapping). You also want an **apImage<apClampedPel8>** that defines an image using byte storage, but employs clamping. This solution requires three pieces:

- Functions to convert and clamp a numeric quantity from one data type to another. In addition to basic data types, our solution must also work for RGB and other complex data types.

- A new object, **apClampedTmpl<>**, that is similar to a basic data type, but has clamping behavior.

- Operators and functions that define the basic mathematical operations needed for image processing functions.

Clamping Functions

To clamp a value at the limits of a data type, we must know the limits. With C, we used **#include <limits.h>** to get this functionality. With C++, we can use **#include <limit>**. The **std::numeric_limits** class gives us everything we need. We can easily determine the minimum and maximum values for a data type by querying the static functions of this object, as shown:

```
Pel8 minvalue = std::numeric_limits<Pel8>::min();
Pel8 maxvalue = std::numeric_limits<Pel8>::max();
```

We do not use these limits directly; rather, we encapsulate them in one of our own objects, **apLimitInfo<>**. We are doing this because some of our data types, such as **apRGB**, have no **std::numeric_limits** defined. Instead of defining 30 or so constants and static methods, we decided it was easier to define only what we need. If you insist on using **std::numeric_limits**, you can define your own implementation for any new types, and then replace our references to **apLimitInfo<>**. The **apLimitInfo<>** definition is as shown.

```
template<class T> class apLimitInfo
{
public:
   static apLimitInfo<T> sType;

   T minValue;
   T maxValue;

private:
   apLimitInfo (T min, T max) : minValue (min), maxValue (max) {}
};
```

`apLimitInfo<>` gives us a common place to define limit information for any data type. The definitions for a few of the data types are shown here.

```
template<> apLimitInfo<Pel8>
apLimitInfo<Pel8>::sType (std::numeric_limits<Pel8>::min(),
                          std::numeric_limits<Pel8>::max());


template<> apLimitInfo<apRGB>
apLimitInfo<apRGB>::sType (
  apRGB(std::numeric_limits<Pel8>::min(),
        std::numeric_limits<Pel8>::min(),
        std::numeric_limits<Pel8>::min()),
  apRGB(std::numeric_limits<Pel8>::max(),
        std::numeric_limits<Pel8>::max(),
        std::numeric_limits<Pel8>::max())));
```

These may look long, but they are just a machine-independent way of saying:

```
template<> apLimitInfo<Pel8>  apLimitInfo<Pel8>::sType (0, 255);

template<> apLimitInfo<apRGB> apLimitInfo<apRGB>::sType
  (apRGB(0, 0, 0), apRGB(255, 255, 255));
```

❖ CLAMPING FUNCTION

We can now construct a simple clamping function to test and clamp the output to its minimum and maximum value.

```
template<class D, class S> D apLimit (const S& src)
{
  return src < apLimitInfo<D>::sType.minValue ?
    apLimitInfo<D>::sType.minValue :
      (src > apLimitInfo<D>::sType.maxValue ?
        apLimitInfo<D>::sType.maxValue : static_cast<D>(src));
}
```

You can use these functions as follows:

```
Pel32 l = 256;
Pel8 b = apLimit<Pel8> (1);    // b = 255
```

With this syntax, you explicitly define the type of clamping you desire. In this particular example, the benefits are well worth the added bit of typing. The compiler will generate an error if you neglect to specify the clamping data type.

Clamping Object

We define an `apClampedTmpl<>` object to add our clamping behavior. `apClampedTmpl<>` can be used in place of the `Pel8`, `Pel16`, `Pel32`, and other data types to add our clamping behavior whenever a numeric quantity is used. The `apClampedTmpl<>` definition is shown here.

```
template<class T> class apClampedTmpl
{
public:
  T val;
```

```
    apClampedTmpl ()     : val(0) {}
    apClampedTmpl (T v) : val(v) {}

    operator T () const { return val;}

    apClampedTmpl (const apClampedTmpl& src)
    { val = apLimit<T> (src.val);}

    template<class T1>
    apClampedTmpl (const apClampedTmpl<T1>& src)
    { val = apLimit<T> (src.val);}

    apClampedTmpl<T>& operator= (const apClampedTmpl& src);

    apClampedTmpl<T>& operator+= (const apClampedTmpl<T>& s);
    apClampedTmpl<T>& operator-= (const apClampedTmpl<T>& s);
    apClampedTmpl<T>& operator*= (const apClampedTmpl<T>& s);
    apClampedTmpl<T>& operator/= (const apClampedTmpl<T>& s);

    template <class T2>
    apClampedTmpl<T> operator+ (const apClampedTmpl<T2>& s2);
};
```

We have included conversions between **apClampedTmpl<>** and our template parameter, **T**, to make **apClampedTmpl<>** easier to work with. By providing these operators, the compiler can make whatever implicit conversions are necessary.

One last step is to make **apClampedTmpl<>** look more like a data type by using **typedef**s, as shown.

```
    typedef apClampedTmpl<Pel8>   apClampedPel8;
    typedef apClampedTmpl<Pel16>  apClampedPel16;
    typedef apClampedTmpl<Pel32>  apClampedPel32;
    typedef apClampedTmpl<Pel32s> apClampedPel32s;    // This is signed!!
```

Operators and Mathematical Functions

We also need to define a number of other global operators and functions that image processing routines will need.

❖ OPERATOR-

An example of the subtraction operator, which subtracts a constant value from **apClampTmpl<>**, is as follows:

```
    template<class T1, class T2>
    apClampedTmpl<T1> operator- (const apClampedTmpl<T1>& s1,
                                 const T2& s2)
    {
      apClampedTmpl<T1> dst;
      dst.val = apLimit<T1> (s1.val - s2);
      return dst;
    }
```

Notice that **apLimit** is used to apply clamping before the result is assigned to the destination pixel type. This gives us the ability to write such code as this:

```
    Pel32 longpel = 12345;
    apClampedTmpl<Pel8> bytepel = 128;
    bytepel = bytepel - longpel;
```

We now add a few more arithmetic operations that our image processing functions require.

❖ ADD2()

We implement two versions of image addition: one version that operates on a generic type, and one version that employs clamping. These are as shown here.

```
template<class D, class S1, class S2>
D add2 (const S1& s1, const S2& s2)
{
  return static_cast<D>(s1) + s2;
}

template<class D, class S1, class S2>
D add2 (const apClampedTmpl<S1>& s1, const apClampedTmpl<S2>& s2)
{
  return apLimit<D> (s1.val + s2.val);    // d = s1 + s2;
}
```

We do the same thing for **sub2**, **mul2**, and **div2**. The C++ standard is very specific regarding which template to instantiate. The generic implementation of **add2<>** shown here is too similar to the versions that use **apClampedTmpl<>** objects, causing errors to be generated by the compiler. Instead, we define explicit versions to handle the cases we need and turn the generic version of **add2<>** into a comment. For example, a version of **add2<>** that works with 32-bit pixel types is shown here.

```
template<class D> D add2 (Pel32s s1, Pel32s s2)
{ return static_cast<D>(s1 + s2);}
```

❖ SCALE()

scale() does a simple scaling of the source argument by a floating parameter, as shown here.

```
template<class D, class S>
D scale (S& s1, float scaling)
{
  return static_cast<D> (scaling * s1);
}
```

We also apply these operations to our RGB data type. Since RGB images require more processing than monochrome images, we built clamping into the RGB image, instead of defining another type. We can see that by looking at the definition shown here.

```
template<class T> class apRGBTmpl
{
public:
  ...
  apRGBTmpl<T>& operator+= (const apRGBTmpl<T>& s)
  {
    red   = apLimit (red   + s.red);
    green = apLimit (green + s.green);
    blue  = apLimit (blue  + s.blue);
    return *this;
  }

  apRGBTmpl<T>& operator+= (const T& s)
  {
```

```
      red   = apLimit (red   + s);
      green = apLimit (green + s);
      blue  = apLimit (blue  + s);
      return *this;
   }
};

template<class D, class S1, class S2>
apRGBTmpl<D> add2 (const apRGBTmpl<S1>&s1, const apRGBTmpl<S2>&s2)
{
   apRGBTmpl<D> d;
   d.red   = apLimit<D> (s1.red   + s2.red);
   d.green = apLimit<D> (s1.green + s2.green);
   d.blue  = apLimit<D> (s1.blue  + s2.blue);
   return d;
}
```

During the development of generic image processing routines, you should use these functions at every opportunity.

What's So Important About Clamping?

It may seem like we have gone through great lengths for little benefit. After all, we have mandated that image processing functions do this:

```
dst = add2<T> (s1, s2);
```

instead of this:

✗ `dst = s1 + s2;`

The latter is more intuitive, but it is also more prone to error. If we are careful, we can construct **operator+** and **operator=** for the various data types to give the desired behavior. The problem is that the compiler can do almost too good a job at finding a way to compile this line by applying suitable conversions. Because we are dealing with basic data types, like **unsigned char**, the compiler often has many ways to convert from one data type to another. This makes it easy to write code that does not perform as you expect. If this happens, there is a possibility that the error may not be caught until your testing phase.

6.2   Finalizing the Image Class

Instead of thinking of **apImage<>** as an object, you should think of it in terms of an API or toolbox. There are lots of possible image processing functions, and very few are part of the **apImage<>** class definition itself. Most are global functions, making it very easy to add new functionality without weighing down the object itself.

A common mistake when designing C++ classes is to make everything a member function of the underlying class. As disparate functionality is added to an object, understanding what the object does become more difficult. A simple class can grow to over 100 member functions with little effort if you add new functionality at every opportunity. If these methods consist of 20 to 30 different pieces of functionality with similar, but different, interfaces, the object is still of manageable size. The **std::string** class is a good example of this type of object. There are a lot of member functions, but the functionality can be divided into one of about 25 families of functions. Our image class, on the other hand, can have a large number of different routines, so instead most are implemented as functions.

apImageStorage<> contains most of the actual functionality exposed by **apImage<>**, but does not handle some of the special conditions we expect to encounter. For example, **apImageStorage<>** knows very little about image windows, other than how to create one. The image processing functions that we write will use image windows to determine which pixels to process. This will become especially important for image processing functions that take more than one image as an argument.

There are two consumers of our image class: imaging applications and application-specific frameworks:

- For real applications, our API must be sufficiently broad so that images can be manipulated. This includes image filtering, transformation, and arithmetic operations.

- For application-specific frameworks, **apImage<>** must be a generic collection of tools that can be extended to create a new API with a different set of capabilities.

Once we discuss the final design of **apImage<>**, we will apply that design to enhance the framework, so that it works with a number of image types that offer enhanced performance on some platforms.

6.2.1 Image Object

Our final image object, **apImage<>**, is rather modest. Besides exposing the features of the underlying storage object, only the most basic image processing methods are included. To keep this object generic, we modified the design from Prototype 3 to remove one template parameter (Section 3.2.6 on page 60), and we replaced it with another template parameter, as shown in Figure 6.5.

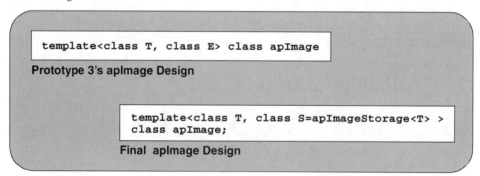

```
template<class T, class E> class apImage
```
Prototype 3's apImage Design

```
template<class T, class S=apImageStorage<T> >
class apImage;
```
Final apImage Design

Figure 6.5: Evolution of apImage Design

In the final design, we kept the **class T** template parameter, but moved the **class E** template parameter, which is the internal pixel type used during computations, to the global image functions. Then we added an additional template parameter, **class S**, to make the declaration, as follows:

```
template<class T, class S=apImageStorage<T> > class apImage;
```

> **class T**   The pixel type. This parameter has the same meaning as in earlier classes.
>
> **class S**   The underlying image storage object. The default parameter, **apImageStorage<T>**, which uses **apAlloc<>** to allocate memory, is applicable for most applications. If you want to use another object to handle memory allocation, then specify it here. This object also contains the iterators necessary to process the image on a row or pixel basis.

Most applications can think of the image class as **apImage<T>**, rather than **apImage<T,S>**. This is certainly desirable, because everything is more readable and it makes the class look less onerous. When using **apImage<>** to write new image processing functions, you will still need to deal with both parameters, but this is usually nothing more than a bookkeeping task, and the compiler always reminds you if you made a mistake.

The **apImage<T,S>** class is shown here.

```
template<class T, class S=apImageStorage<T> >
class apImage
{
public:
  typedef typename S::row_iterator row_iterator;
  typedef typename S::iterator iterator;

  static apImage sNull;

  apImage () {}
  apImage (const apRect& boundary,
           apRectImageStorage::eAlignment align =
           apRectImageStorage::eNoAlign)
    : storage_ (boundary, align)
  {}
  apImage (S storage) : storage_ (storage) {}
  virtual ~apImage () {}

  apImage             (const apImage& src);
  apImage& operator=  (const apImage& src);

  bool lockImage    () const { return storage_.lock ();}
  bool unlockImage  () const { return storage_.unlock ();}
  bool lockState    () const { return storage_.lockState ();}
  bool unlockState  () const { return storage_.unlockState ();}
  bool isNull       () const { return storage_.isNull();}
  int  ref          () const { return storage_.ref();}
  int  xoffset      () const { return storage_.xoffset();}
  int  yoffset      () const { return storage_.yoffset();}
  unsigned int bytesPerPixel () const
    { return storage_.bytesPerPixel();}
  unsigned int rowSpacing    () const
    { return storage_.rowSpacing();}
```

```
apRectImageStorage::eAlignment alignment () const
{ return storage_.alignment();}

S storage () { return storage_;}

const apRect& boundary () const { return storage_.boundary();}
int           x0        () const { return storage_.x0();}
int           y0        () const { return storage_.y0();}
int           x1        () const { return storage_.x1();}
int           y1        () const { return storage_.y1();}
unsigned int  width     () const { return storage_.width();}
unsigned int  height    () const { return storage_.height();}

const T* base      ()          const;
const T* rowAddress (int y) const ;
T*       rowAddress (int y);

const T& getPixel (int x, int y) const;
const T& getPixel (const apPoint& point) const;
void     setPixel (int x, int y, const T& pixel);
void     setPixel (const apPoint& point, const T& pixel);

void setRow (int y, const T& pixel);
void setCol (int x, const T& pixel);

// iterators
row_iterator       row_begin () { return storage_.row_begin();}
const row_iterator row_begin () const
                                { return storage_.row_begin();}
row_iterator       row_end   () { return storage_.row_end();}
const row_iterator row_end   () const
                                { return storage_.row_end();}
iterator       begin ()        { return storage_.begin();}
const iterator begin () const { return storage_.begin();}
iterator       end   ()        { return storage_.end();}
const iterator end   () const { return storage_.end();}

// Image memory operations
bool window (const apRect& window)
{ return storage_.window (window);}

void trim ();
// Duplicate the image data, if it is shared, to use the
// minimum amount of memory possible. Use this function to
// duplicate the underlying image data. Thread-safe.

apRectImageStorage::eAlignment bestAlignment () const;
// Return best alignment of this image. This is a measured
// quantity so it will work with all images.

apImage<T,S> align   (apRectImageStorage::eAlignment align =
                      apRectImageStorage::eNoAlign);
// Return an image that has the specified alignment. This
// may return a new image

apImage<T,S> duplicate   (apRectImageStorage::eAlignment align =
                          apRectImageStorage::eNoAlign) const;
// Duplicate the image data such that it has the specified
// alignment. The image data is always duplicated, unlike align()

// Image operations with constants. Thread-safe
void set (const T& value);
void add (const T& value);
void sub (const T& value);
void mul (const T& value);
void div (const T& value);
void scale (float scaling);
```

```
    // Conditionals
    bool isIdentical (const apImage& src) const;
    // Checks for same boundary and identical image storage only

    bool operator== (const apImage& src) const;
    bool operator!= (const apImage& src) const;
protected:
    S         storage_;   // Image storage
};
```

Over half of this class is nothing more than a wrapper around the storage object. Although we allow complete access to the storage object by means of the **storage()** method, we still try to make direct access to the individual members as easy as possible. The remaining methods belong to two categories: image operations and image storage operations.

❖ IMAGE OPERATIONS

Most image operations alter the image with a constant value. The **set()**, **add()**, **sub()**, **mul()**, and **div()** functions modify each pixel value with a constant value. **scale()** is similar to **mul()**, except that a floating point scaling parameter is specified. These functions are very intuitive to use:

```
apImage<Pel8> image;
image.set (0);    // Set each pixel to 0
image.add (1);    // Each pixel is now 1
image.mul (2);    // Each pixel is now 2
image.scale (.5); // Each pixel is now 1
```

❖ IMAGE STORAGE OPERATIONS

Image storage operations manipulate how an image is stored in memory. We spent a lot of time in earlier sections describing how important image alignment is, especially when it comes to performance on many platforms. Many image processing routines allocate and return new images that may not have the desired alignment. Another need to adjust alignment arises when **window()** is used to return a window of an image. The alignment of the image window will depend on the size and location of the window itself. If you need to perform a number of operations, and do not need to modify the parent image data, you should work with an aligned image. **align()** returns an image that has the desired alignment for each row in the image. If the image already has this alignment, the original image is returned; otherwise, a new image is returned that contains the same pixel values as the original image.

```
apRect boundary (0, 0, 16, 16);
apImage<Pel8> image1 (boundary);
image.set (0);
apImage<Pel8> image2
    = image1.align (apRectImageStorage::eDoubleWordAlign);
```

In this example, it isn't clear if **image2** refers to the same memory as **image1**, because **image1** was created with no specified image alignment. If you need to know in advance whether an operation will create a new image, use the **bestAlignment()** method to measure the alignment of the image storage.

► EXAMPLE ————————————————————————————

We now have enough functionality to write a simple application. Let's create an image and use an image window to demonstrate a useful feature of windows.

```
int main()
{
  apRect boundary (0, 0, 16, 16);
  apImage<Pel8> image1 (boundary);
  image1.set (0);

  apRect window (6, 6, 4, 4);
  apImage<Pel8> image2 = image1;
  image2.window (window);
  image2.set (1);

  apImage<Pel8>::row_iterator i;
  for (i=image1.row_begin(); i != image1.row_end(); i++) {
    Pel8* p = i->p;
    for (unsigned int x=0; x<image1.width(); x++)
      std::cout << static_cast<int>(*p++);
    std::cout << std::endl;
  }

  return 0;
}
```

This application sets each pixel in a 16x16 image to **0**. A 4x4 image window, **image2**, is created, and these values are set to **1**. Finally, the pixels from the initial image are displayed. The following display demonstrates that no pixels were copied when the image window is created. **image2** is pointing to the same pixels as those of **image1**.

```
0000000000000000
0000000000000000
0000000000000000
0000000000000000
0000000000000000
0000000000000000
0000001111000000
0000001111000000
0000001111000000
0000001111000000
0000000000000000
0000000000000000
0000000000000000
0000000000000000
0000000000000000
0000000000000000
```

The **static_cast<>** reference in the example is just a simple cast, because we want to display the image pixel as a number and not as a character. Most stream packages will display a **Pel8** (i.e., **unsigned char**) as a character.

❖ ADD()

Let's look at the implementation of **add()**. It bears a close resemblance to the code that displayed the image to the console in the previous example.

```
template<class T, class S>
void apImage<T,S>::add (const T& value)
{
  apImageLocker<T,S> locking (*this); // Lock image

  typename apImage<T,S>::row_iterator i;
  unsigned int w = width ();
  T* p;
  for (i=row_begin(); i != row_end(); i++) {
    p = i->p;
    for (unsigned int x=0; x<w; x++)
      *p++ += value;
  }
}
```

There are a few differences between **add()** and the display code:

■ **add()** locks and unlocks the image to prevent other threads from accessing the image data or changing the state of the image until the function is finished.

■ **add()** includes performance enhancements. It defines a width variable, **w**, and a pointer variable **p**, outside of the loop to ensure that the compiler generates efficient code. Assigning **width()** to variable **w** once prevents **width()** from running each iteration. Moving **p** outside the loop ensures that the compiler does not attempt to reallocate the variable during each iteration. Our example code did not worry about this.

6.3 Adding Global Image Functions

You have probably noticed that our **apImage<>** class does not include the image processing functions. We decided that the image class should only contain the absolute essentials. At first we were only going to offer **set()** and make the operations, such as **add()**, be functions rather than methods. However, **set()** and **add()** are so similar in appearance that we decided to keep them in the class interface.

When creating a minimalistic class design, do not split similar functionality between members and functions.

For example, how do we go about copying an image? Is it possible to copy just a section of the image? To answer these questions, we need to analyze what copying an image really entails. We will take the lessons we learn from copying images and apply them to almost all of our image processing functions. Our generic interpretation means that these functions become more difficult to write, but they also become much more powerful to use.

6.3.1 Copying an Image

There are three ways that images can be copied:

- Method 1: The source image is specified and the copy function creates the destination image.

```
apImage<Pel8> image1;
...
apImage<Pel8> image2 = copy (image1);
```

- Method 2: The source image and destination image are specified. The pixel types are the same.

```
apImage<Pel8> image1;
...
apImage<Pel8> image2;
copy (image1, image2);
```

- Method 3: The source image and destination image are specified. The pixel types are different.

```
apImage<Pel8> image1;
...
apImage<Pel32> image2;
copy (image1, image2);
```

▶ **EXAMPLE** ──

This example shows how not to copy an image:

```
✗ apImage<Pel8> image1;
  ...
  apImage<Pel8> image2 = image1;
```

image2 and **image1** share the same underlying pixel data. While this is an efficient way to share memory between images, it is not what you want to do, especially when you want to modify a copy of the image and keep the original image intact.

── ◀

You might be tempted to implement a different version of **copy()** for each method. The semantics of method 1 differs from methods 2 and 3, but if we can design a solution for method 3, we can use it to solve method 1 as well. We have already seen that in method 3, the source and destination images do not have to be the same pixel type. This is a very desirable feature because certain image conversions are very common operations. For example, look at the conversion from a color image to a monochrome image:

```
apImage<apRGB> image1;
...
apImage<Pel8> image2;
copy (image1, image2);
```

There is a more complicated case we need to consider. What happens if the destination image is not null? In other words, what should the behavior of **copy()** be if both the source and destination images are valid? Most imaging software packages will probably discard whatever is stored in the destination image and replace it with a copy of the source image.

Doing so makes the implementation of **copy()** easier, but it does not address what the user is asking for. Our interpretation of the problem is quite different:

- If the source image is null, the destination image is also null.

- If no destination image is specified, create an image with the same boundary and alignment as the source image.

- If a destination image is specified, the copy operation is restricted to those pixels in common between the source and destination image. If there is no overlap in pixels, the destination image is set to null.

You might wonder if all this is really necessary for a **copy()** function. The answer is yes, because we want to offer this type of functionality for any image processing function that looks like:

```
template<class T1, class S1, class T2, class S2>
void func (const apImage<T1,S1>& src, apImage<T2,S2>& dst);
```

If we offer this functionality for some arbitrary function **func()**, we should have the same functionality for **copy()**, since it takes the identical form.

Computing the overlap between two images is easy. Mathematically, we want to compute the intersection between the source image boundary and the destination image boundary. The result is an **apRect** that specifies which pixels should be processed. **apRect** has an **intersect()** method that will compute the overlap for us:

```
template<class T1, class S1, class T2, class S2>
void func (const apImage<T1,S1>& src, apImage<T2,S2>& dst)
{
    ...
    apRect overlap = src.boundary().intersect (dst.boundary());
    if (overlap.isNull()) return;

    // Restrict processing to this region
    apImage roi1 = src;
    roi1.window (overlap);
    apImage roi2 = dst;
    roi2.window (overlap);

    // Run our function on the pixels in roi1 and roi2
    ...
}
```

As you can see, we determine the pixels that need to be processed by computing the image windows (**roi1** and **roi2**) that contain the intersection of the two images. Although this code is fairly simple, we do not want to duplicate it in every image processing function. Instead, we create a small framework to off-load most of the work, so new image processing functions can be added without having to worry about all the math. This framework also provides a consistent interface for each function. We are calling this a framework because we need more than one class to add this capability. Each class handles a specific type of image processing function, also referred to as an image filtering function. Usually this corresponds to the number of image arguments required by the function, but it can also include other parameters. We almost chose to use function objects, but decided in our own implementation to maximize code reuse between similar classes of image processing functions. For information on function objects, see [Stroustrup00].

6.3.2 Processing Single Source Images

Single source image processing operations take a single source image and produce a single destination image. We provide a number of single source image processing operations, including:

- **copy()**
- **operator+=**
- **operator-=**
- **duplicate()**

operator+= and **operator-=** might not look like single source operations, but these operators take a single image and add or subtract it to the destination image.

Single source image processing operations have the following form:

```
template<class T1, class S1, class T2, class S2>
void func (const apImage<T1,S1>& src, apImage<T2,S2>& dst);
```

❖ SINGLE SOURCE PROCESSING CLASS

We provide a general class, **apFunction_s1d1**, that you can use to easily add your own single source image processing functions. (Note that we have chosen to make this class name descriptive, rather than concise, because it is used internally by developers. We reuse this naming convention when we provide a similar class, named **apFunction_s1s2d1**, for two source image processing functions.)

apFunction_s1d1 lets us logically divide the processing operations, each as a separate method. We have made some of those methods virtual so that we can derive new classes from **apFunction_s1d1** to handle custom requirements.

In general, we cannot assume that the same intersection region is applied to both the source and destination images, so we keep these regions separate. We use the **apIntersectRects** structure, as shown:

```
struct apIntersectRects
{
  apRect src;    // Intersection region for source image(s)
  apRect dst;    // Intersection region for dest image(s)
};
```

The **apFunction_s1d1** class is shown here.

```
template<class R, class T1, class T2,
         class S1=apImageStorage<T1>, class S2=apImageStorage<T2> >
class apFunction_s1d1
{
public:
  apFunction_s1d1 () : function_ (0) {}
```

```
        typedef void(*Function) (const R&, const apImage<T1,S1>& src1,
                                 apImage<T2,S2>& dst1);
        apFunction_s1d1 (Function f) : function_ (f) {}

        virtual ~apFunction_s1d1 () {};

        void run (const apImage<T1,S1>& src1, apImage<T2,S2>& dst1)
        { return execute (src1, dst1);}
        // Executes the image processing function
    protected:
        Function          function_; // Our process function, if any
        apImage<T1,S1> roi1_;        // roi of src1 image
        apImage<T2,S2> roi2_;        // roi of dst1 image

        virtual apIntersectRects intersection
                                (const apImage<T1,S1>& src1,
                                 apImage<T2,S2>& dst1);
        { return intersect (src1.boundary(), dst1.boundary());}

        virtual void execute (const apImage<T1,S1>& src1,
                              apImage<T2,S2>& dst1);

        virtual void createDestination (const apImage<T1,S1>& src1,
                                        apImage<T2,S2>& dst1);

        virtual void process ();
    };
```

apFunction_s1d1 has five template parameters. Four of these parameters are present because there are two images, each requiring two parameters. We have reordered the template parameters because many have default values that applications can simply use. This means that there are really only three parameters we need to consider:

R	Pixel type for intermediate computations
T1	Pixel type for the source image
T2	Pixel type for the destination image

When **T1** pixels are manipulated by an image processing function to compute **T2** pixels, any temporary storage will use **R** as the pixel type. There is no default argument for **R** because this value is highly application-dependent. If you remember, it was our third prototype (separating the image class and image storage) that demonstrated the need for **R**. **R** is the first parameter because it must be explicitly defined.

apFunction_s1d1 can be used in two different ways, depending on how you want to specify the actual image processing operations. You can either override **process()** to define your processing function, or you can pass a function pointer to the constructor. We recommend that you pass a pointer because it means that there will be no changes to **apFunction_s1d1**, and no need to derive objects from it. It also encourages you to write stand-alone image processing operations that potentially have other uses in your application. You pass a function pointer to the constructor, as shown:

```
typedef void(*Function) (const R&, const apImage<T1,S1>& src1,
                         apImage<T2,S2>& dst1);
apFunction_s1d1 (Function f) : function_ (f) {}
```

Function looks a lot like the function that you will actually write (see our **func()** definition on page 206). The big difference is that the function you write can safely ignore issues, such as image overlap or constructing the destination image if none is specified. Our first argument is a placeholder for the data type for intermediate computations. We would have preferred to specify the first parameter using explicit template instantiation, but the compiler does not accept this.

❖ EXECUTE()

The **run()** method is the main entry point of **apFunction_s1d1**, but it only calls the virtual function, **execute()**. The **execute()** method constructs the intersection and performs the image processing operation. **execute()** is only overridden if the standard rules for computing the image windows changes. We will soon see how image processing operations, such as convolution, require a new definition for **execute()**. The definition for **execute()** is shown here.

```
virtual void execute (const apImage<T1,S1>& src1,
                      apImage<T2,S2>& dst1)
{
  // If a null image is passed, return a null image
  if (src1.isNull()) {
    dst1 = dst1.sNull;
    return;
  }

  // Exception-safe locking.
  apImageLocker<T1,S1> srcLocking (src1);

  // Create the destination if it was not specified. Create an
  // output image with the same alignment as the input.
  if (dst1.isNull())
    createDestination (src1, dst1);

  // Lock destination after it is created (if necessary)
  apImageLocker<T2,S2> dstLocking (dst1);

  // Compute the overlap between the images
  apIntersectRects overlap = intersection (src1, dst1);

  // Return a null image if there is no overlap
  if (overlap.dst.isNull()) {
    dstLocking.unlock(); // Unlock the object before assignment
    dst1 = dst1.sNull;
    return;
  }

  // Work only within the overlap area
  roi1_ = src1;
  roi2_ = dst1;
  roi1_.window (overlap.src);
```

```
    roi2_.window (overlap.dst);

    // Run the image processing routine.
    try {
      process ();
    }
    catch (...) {
      // Add any recovery code here.
      throw;
    }
  }
```

In broad terms, **execute()** does the following:

- Provides lock/unlock access to the image to prevent problems in multithreaded applications.

- Returns a null destination image if the source image is null. We can take advantage of the **sNull** definition available in every **apImage** object.

- Creates the destination image if none was specified. This is performed by the virtual function **createDestination()**. The default definition creates an image of the same size and alignment as the source image.

- Computes the intersection between the two images, creates an image window for each one, and stores the image windows in **roi1_** and **roi2_**. We use the term *roi*, meaning region of interest, which aptly describes what these images represent. **roi1_** will be identical to **src1** if no destination is specified, or if the destination was the same size or larger than the source image. **roi1_** and **roi2_** are stored as member functions to keep the object as generic as possible. We thought about passing the computed images as parameters to **process()**, but derived classes might require other arguments as well so we decided against it.

- Calls **process()** to perform the image processing operation, which occurs inside a **try** block to catch any exceptions that might be thrown. The **catch** block does no special processing, other than to rethrow the error.

❖ INTERSECT()

The **intersection()** method does nothing but call a global **intersect()** function. We added numerous **intersect()** functions to the global name space to encourage developers to use them for other purposes. The **intersect()** function is shown here.

```
apIntersectRects intersect (const apRect& src, const apRect& dst)
{
  apIntersectRects overlap;
  apRect srcOverlap = src;
  if (!dst.isNull())
    srcOverlap = srcOverlap.intersect (dst);

  overlap.src = srcOverlap;
  overlap.dst = srcOverlap;
  return overlap;
}
```

❖ PROCESS()

We provide the **process()** function to allow derived classes to define their own processing behavior, if necessary. We create a **placeholder** variable so that the compiler will call **function_** with the appropriate arguments, as shown:

```
virtual void process ()
{
  R placeholder;
  if (function_)
    function_ (placeholder, roi1_, roi2_);
}
```

We have kept this object, and the other objects like it, in a separate file to promote their use. The actual image processing operations are kept in separate files, based on what the functions do.

❖ COPY()

Let's get back to our **copy()** example and look at how we handle its implementation. We start by designing the actual image processing operation, making sure that its function prototype matches the **Function** definition in **apFunction_s1d1**. We show two implementations of our copy function. Note that neither function requires the template parameter, **R**, so this parameter is ignored.

■ **ap_copy()** defines the generic copy function and uses assignment to copy pixels from the source image to the destination image, as shown here.

```
template<class R, class T1, class T2, class S1, class S2>
void ap_copy (const R&, const apImage<T1,S1>& src1,
              apImage<T2,S2>& dst1)
{
  typename apImage<T1,S1>::row_iterator i1;
  typename apImage<T2,S2>::row_iterator i2;
  unsigned int w = src1.width ();
  const T1* p1;
  T2* p2;
  for (i1=src1.row_begin(), i2=dst1.row_begin(); i1 !=src1.row_end();
       i1++, i2++) {
    p1 = i1->p;
    p2 = i2->p;
    for (unsigned int x=0; x<w; x++)
      *p2++ = static_cast<T2>(*p1++);
  }
}
```

■ **ap_copyfast()** makes the assumption that **memcpy()** can be used to duplicate pixels, as long as source and destination images share the same data type. **ap_copyfast()** is slightly more complicated, because it uses **typeid()** to determine if the source and destination image share the same pixel type. To properly use **typeid()**, make sure that any compiler flags that enable Run-Time Type Information (RTTI) are set. The **ap_copyfast()** function is shown here.

```
template<class R, class T1, class T2, class S1, class S2>
void ap_copyfast (const R&, const apImage<T1,S1>& src1,
                  apImage<T2,S2>& dst1)
{
```

```
    typename apImage<T1,S1>::row_iterator i1 = src1.row_begin();
    typename apImage<T2,S2>::row_iterator i2 = dst1.row_begin();
    unsigned int w = src1.width();
    unsigned int bytes = w * src1.bytesPerPixel ();
    const T1* p1;
    T2* p2;

    if (typeid(T1) == typeid(T2)) {
      // We're copying like datatypes so use memcpy for speed
      // This assumes T1 and T2 are POD (plain old data) types
      for (; i1 != src1.row_end(); i1++, i2++) {
        p1 = i1->p;
        p2 = i2->p;
        memcpy (p2, p1, bytes);
      }
    }
    else {
      // We have to do a pixel by pixel copy
      for (; i1 != src1.row_end(); i1++, i2++) {
        p1 = i1->p;
        p2 = i2->p;
        for (unsigned int x=0; x<w; x++)
          *p2++ = static_cast<T2>(*p1++);
      }
    }
  }
```

The assumption that **memcpy()** can be used to duplicate pixels is usually, but not always, valid. For example, what if you had an image of **std::string** objects? It may sound absurd, but it demonstrates that blindly copying memory is not always appropriate.

Our final version of **copy()**, written using the generic **ap_copy()**, is shown here.

```
    template<class T1, class S1, class T2, class S2>
    void copy (const apImage<T1,S1>& src, apImage<T2,S2>& dst)
    {
      apFunction_s1d1<T2,T1,T2,S1,S2> processor (ap_copy);
      processor.run (src, dst);
    }
```

As implemented, **copy()** addresses the issues raised when the source and destination images are specified and the pixel types may or may not be different. Note that **T2** is passed as a parameter, **R**, which defines all of the template parameters; however, the copy function can ignore it. In addition, **copy()** offers improved performance when the pixel types match. (See the earlier discussion in Section 6.3.1 on page 204.)

In the case where the source image is specified and the copy should create the destination image, we can create an overloaded version of **copy()** to take advantage of **ap_copyfast()**, as shown.

```
    template<class T1, class S1>
    apImage<T1,S1> copy (const apImage<T1,S1>& src)
    {
      apImage<T1,S1> dst;

      apFunction_s1d1<T1,T1,T1,S1,S1> processor (ap_copyfast);
      processor.run (src, dst);
```

```
      return dst;
   }
```

To demonstrate that we can use the STL generic algorithms with **apImage<>**, we rewrite **copy()** using **std::copy()**, as shown. The destination image must be allocated before calling **std::copy()**, since **apImage<>** does not support input iterators.

```
   template<class T1, class S1>
   apImage<T1,S1> copy_stl (const apImage<T1,S1>& src)
   {
     apImageLocker<T1,S1> srcLocking (src);

     apImage<T1,S1> dst (src.boundary(), src.alignment());
     std::copy (src.begin(), src.end(), dst.begin());

     return dst;
   }
```

While this function may be easier to write, it also slows greatly during execution. Using our 2.0 GHz Intel Pentium 4 processor-based machine, the performance for allocating and copying a 1024x1024 8-bit monochrome image is as follows: **copy()** takes 4 milliseconds, while **copy_stl()** takes 16 milliseconds. Both functions produce the identical image as output.

6.3.3 Processing Two Source Images

Many image processing functions operate on two source images and produce a single output image. We provide the following two source image processing operations:

- **intersect()**
- **add()**
- **operator+**
- **sub()**
- **operator-**

Let's look at a few of these operations. We can use **apFunction_s1d1** as a template to add a new object that computes the intersection of three images (the two source images and the destination image, if any). There are two images that supply source pixels to the image processing function. If a valid destination image is specified, its boundary information helps determine which source pixels to use in the image processing routine.

Our new object, **apFunction_s1s2d1**, takes on a slightly more complicated form, because there are now two additional template parameters to refer to the additional image used by these operations. This brings the total number of parameters to seven, but for most uses only four are needed. The **apFunction_s1s2d1** object is shown here.

```
   template<class R, class T1, class T2, class T3,
           class S1=apImageStorage<T1>, class S2=apImageStorage<T2>,
           class S3=apImageStorage<T3> >
   class apFunction_s1s2d1;
```

❖ INTERSECT()

Let's look at the **intersect()** method, which is shown here. Note that we have removed a few virtual functions, compared to **apFunction_s1d1**, because we do not expect derived classes to be necessary.

```
apIntersectRects intersect (const apRect& src1, const apRect& src2,
                            const apRect& dst)
{
  apIntersectRects overlap;
  // Setup our src and dst regions we have to work with
  apRect srcOverlap = src1;
  srcOverlap = srcOverlap.intersect (src2);
  if (!dst.isNull())
    srcOverlap = srcOverlap.intersect (dst);

  overlap.src = srcOverlap;
  overlap.dst = srcOverlap;
  return overlap;
}
```

❖ ADD() AND OPERATOR+

Now let's look at the **add()** operation. As we demonstrated with **copy()**, **add()** uses the **apFunction_s1s2d1** class to add the contents of two images and store the result in a third. **ap_add2()** is the function that performs this operation. And like **copy()**, we can ignore the intermediate storage specifier (**R** in this case).

```
template<class R, class T1, class T2, class T3,
         class S1, class S2, class S3>
void ap_add2 (const apImage<T1,S1>& src1,
              const apImage<T2,S2>& src2,
              apImage<T3,S3>& dst1)
{
  // Operate on each pixel
  typename apImage<T1,S1>::row_iterator i1 = src1.row_begin();
  typename apImage<T2,S2>::row_iterator i2 = src2.row_begin();
  typename apImage<T3,S3>::row_iterator i3 = dst1.row_begin();
  unsigned int w = src1.width ();
  const T1* p1;
  const T2* p2;
  T3* p3;
  for (; i1 != src1.row_end(); i1++, i2++, i3++) {
    p1 = i1->p;
    p2 = i2->p;
    p3 = i3->p;
    for (unsigned int x=0; x<w; x++)
      *p3++ = add2<T3> (*p1++, *p2++);   // *p3++ = *p1++ + *p2++;
  }
}
```

ap_add2() iterates row by row, and uses our generic **add2()** function to construct each destination pixel. We use **add2()** so that we can easily handle overflow detection (if we use **apClampedTmpl<T>** as parameters), or other optimizations based on pixel type.

The user-callable functions are now easy to write. The only assumption that we make is with **operator+**, where the destination image is given the same pixel type and alignment as the first image specified. The implementation of **add()** and **operator+** is shown here.

```
template<class T1, class T2, class T3,
         class S1, class S2, class S3>
void add (const apImage<T1,S1>& src1,
          const apImage<T2,S2>& src2,
          apImage<T3,S3>& dst1)
{
  apFunction_s1s2d1<T3,T1,T2,T3,S1,S2,S3> processor (ap_add2);
  processor.run (src1, src2, dst1);
}

template<class T1, class T2, class S1, class S2>
apImage<T1,S1> operator+ (const apImage<T1,S1>& src1,
                          const apImage<T2,S2>& src2)
{
  // Get our types from the first parameter
  apImage<T1,S1> dst;
  add (src1, src2, dst);
  return dst;
}
```

6.3.4 Processing Images with Neighborhood Operators

A *neighborhood operator* is one where the content of many source pixels affects the contents of a single destination pixel. One of the most common types of neighborhood operations is called *convolution*. In convolution, the value of a pixel in the resulting filtered image is computed as a weighted sum of its neighboring pixels. The matrix of weights used in the summing operation is called a *kernel*.

We provide the following convolution kernels:

- Low-pass kernel for eliminating noise
- Laplacian kernel for sharpening edges
- High-pass kernel for sharpening edges
- Gaussian kernel for smoothing edges

Low-Pass Kernel for Noise Elimination

Noise in an image may come from such phenomena as photographic grain. Noise often appears as random pixels interspersed throughout the image that have a very different pixel value than those pixels immediately surrounding them (or the neighboring pixels).

Figure 6.6 illustrates the application of a noise-smoothing filter.

Original Image   Filtered Image

Figure 6.6: Low-Pass Averaging Filter

There are many different algorithms for smoothing noise in an image. Noise in an image generally has a higher spatial frequency because of its seeming randomness. We use a simple low-pass spatial filter to reduce the effects of noise through an averaging operation. Each pixel is sequentially examined and, in the 3x3 kernel we use, the pixel value is determined by averaging the pixel value with its eight surrounding neighbors.

Given a point (**x,y**) we average nine pixels in a 3x3 neighborhood surrounding this point. This 3x3 kernel is shown here.

$$D(x,y) = \frac{1}{9} \begin{bmatrix} 1 & 1 & 1 \\ 1 & 1 & 1 \\ 1 & 1 & 1 \end{bmatrix}$$

This kernel is sequentially centered over each pixel. The value of each pixel and its surrounding neighbors are multiplied and then summed. Finally, the average value is computed using the following formula:

```
D(x,y) = (S(x-1,y-1)+S(x,y-1)+S(x+1,y-1)+
          S(x-1,y)  +S(x,y)  +S(x+1,y)+
          S(x-1,y+1)+S(x,y+1)+S(x+1,y+1)) / 9;
```

Figure 6.7 shows how this kernel is used to reduce the noise on a single pixel in an image.

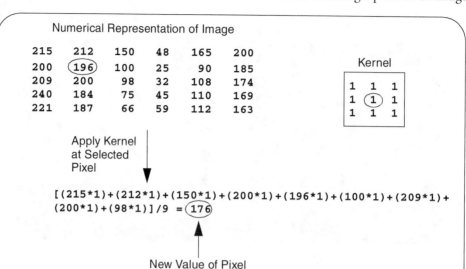

Figure 6.7: Low-Pass Filter

This function is easy to write, until you consider the boundary conditions. Consider a source image with an origin of (**0,0**). In Figure 6.7, the origin has a pixel value of **215**. To compute the destination point in the filtered image at (**0,0**), our equation shows that we need information from pixels that do not exist (for example, **s(-1,-1)**). We cannot compute a pixel when the data does not exist.

This boundary condition can be handled in a number of different ways. One very common solution is to set all boundary pixels to **0** (black). We recommend a different, more generalized solution that has several advantages. By effectively optimizing the problem to determine which pixels are needed to compute the destination (or filtered) image, our solution allows developers to ignore complicated boundary solutions.

Here's how it works. We compute the intersection of the source and destination image, taking the size of the kernel into account. Our **intersection()** function computes which pixels to process. In our example, the kernel size is **3** (using the 3x3 kernel above). The **intersection()** function assumes the kernel size is odd, making it possible to center the kernel over the pixels to process. The function is as follows:

```
apIntersectRects intersect (const apRect& src,
                            unsigned int xKernelSize,
                            unsigned int yKernelSize,
                            const apRect& dst)
{
  apIntersectRects overlap;
  if (xKernelSize < 1 || yKernelSize < 1)
    return overlap;
```

```
    // Expand the dst region to indicate pixels we would "like"
    // to have in our image.
    int xExpansion = (xKernelSize-1) / 2;
    int yExpansion = (yKernelSize-1) / 2;
    apRect dstRegion = dst;
    dstRegion.expand (xExpansion, yExpansion);

    // The source pixels we'll use is just the intersection
    apRect srcRegion = src;
    srcRegion = srcRegion.intersect (dstRegion);

    // We're done if there is no overlap or the overlap
    // area is not big enough.
    if (srcRegion.isNull() ||
        srcRegion.width()  < xKernelSize ||
        srcRegion.height() < yKernelSize)
      return overlap;

    // The destination pixels we'll have is handled by
    // shrinking (i.e. eroding) the source region
    dstRegion = srcRegion;
    dstRegion.expand (-xExpansion, -yExpansion);

    overlap.src = srcRegion;
    overlap.dst = dstRegion;
    return overlap;
  }
```

As you can see, this function is very different from the simple intersection operations we have written so far. Let's apply this function using an example with our 3x3 kernel. Assume that both the source and destination images have an origin at (**0,0**) and are 640x480 pixels in size as shown in Figure 6.8.

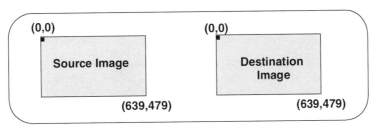

Figure 6.8: Source and Destination Images

1. Determine if the kernel size is too small, and therefore no intersection exists. This is a degenerate case. In our example, the kernel size of **3** is fine.

2. Determine which pixels the destination image needs in order to compute an output value for every pixel in the image. To do this, we increase the size of the destination region to show the pixels that are needed from the source image to fill the destination.

For our 3x3 kernel, this amounts to expanding the size of the destination region by one pixel in all directions, as shown in Figure 6.9.

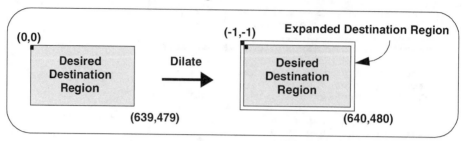

Figure 6.9: Find the Destination Region

This is also called a *dilation* operation. The destination region has an origin at (**0,0**) and is 640x480 pixels in size. The expanded region has an origin at (**-1,-1**) and is 642x482 pixels in size.

3. Intersect this expanded destination region with the source region to find out exactly which pixels are available in the source image. This produces an intersection region at (**0,0**) of size 640x480 pixels, as shown in Figure 6.10.

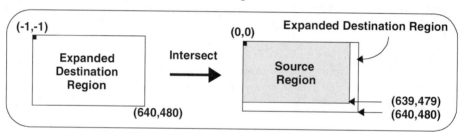

Figure 6.10: Find the Available Source Image Pixels

4. Return a null **apRect** is there is no intersection or if the intersection is too small.

5. Compute the actual destination pixels that will be manipulated. We determine this by reducing the size of the source region by the one pixel in all dimensions as shown in Figure 6.11.

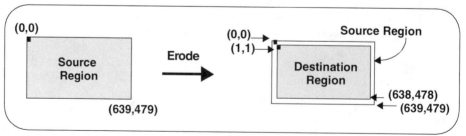

Figure 6.11: Find the Available Destination Image Pixels

This is also called an *erosion* operation. Eroding this region shows what pixels in the destination region can be computed, with an origin at (**1,1**) and 638x478 pixels in size.

This says what we already know: if the source and destination images are the same size, there is a one pixel border surrounding the destination image that cannot be computed. Under common operating conditions, these calculations result in a long, but simple, result. It has much more utility when you need to process a region of interest of a larger image. With larger images, the destination image can often be filled with valid results, since the source image contains all of the necessary pixels.

Our neighborhood processing is similar to the one source image, one destination image case we discussed earlier. Our image processing class, `apFunction_s1d1Convolve`, is derived from `apFunction_s1d1` to take advantage of our modular design. Besides taking additional parameters, this object overrides the member functions that compute the intersection and creates a destination if none was specified.

We can write a general purpose convolution routine by writing our processing function to take an array of kernel values and a divisor. For example, the following kernel is what our image framework uses to compute a low-pass averaging filter:

$$D(x,y) = \frac{1}{9} \begin{bmatrix} 1 & 1 & 1 \\ 1 & 1 & 1 \\ 1 & 1 & 1 \end{bmatrix}$$

```
template<class R, class T1, class T2,
         class S1, class S2>
void ap_convolve_generic (const R&, const apImage<T1,S1>& src1,
                          const char* kernel, unsigned int size,
                          int divisor, apImage<T2,S2>& dst1)
{
  typename apImage<T1,S1>::row_iterator i1 = src1.row_begin();
  typename apImage<T2,S2>::row_iterator i2 = dst1.row_begin();

  typename apImage<T1,S1>::row_iterator i1k;

  unsigned int h = src1.height() - (size-1);
  unsigned int w = src1.width()  - (size-1);

  const T1* pk;
  const char* k;
  T2* p2;
  R sum;
  unsigned int x, y, xk, yk;

  for (y=0; y<h; y++, i1++, i2++) {
    p2 = i2->p;
    for (x=0; x<w; x++) {
      sum = 0;
      i1k = i1;
      k = kernel;
      for (yk=0; yk<size; yk++) {
        pk = i1k->p + x;
        for (xk=0; xk<size; xk++)
          sum += static_cast<R>(*pk++) * (*k++);
        i1k++;
      }
      if (divisor == 1)
```

```
        *p2++ = apLimit<T2> (sum);   // Prevent wrapping
      else {
        sum /= divisor;
        *p2++ = apLimit<T2> (sum);   // Prevent wrapping
      }
    }
  }
}
```

As you can guess, convolution is a fairly slow process, at least when compared with simple point processing routines. This function is somewhat dense and needs some further explanation.

- There are four loops in this function. The outer loops step pixel by pixel in the destination image. The inner two loops perform the neighborhood operation on the source image, by multiplying a kernel value by the source pixel value and accumulating this term in **sum**.

- **R** is the datatype used to represent intermediate computations. **sum** is a variable of type **R** that is used during the computation of each destination pixel. If we did not have the forethought to add this template parameter, **R**, then **sum** would have been of type **T2** (the destination pixel type) and would have likely caused pixel overflows.

- When you call a convolution function, you must explicitly specify the datatype of **R**.

- Once **sum** is computed, it is scaled by the divisor, which is **9** in our example, to create the output pixel value. Some convolution kernels have a divisor of 1, and we can achieve much higher performance by making this a special case. For example, we saw a 10% performance improvement for a 1024x1024 image when we added this optimization.

- **apLimit<>** is used to prevent pixel overflows. Unlike many of our image processing functions, where the user can select special data types to prevent overflow (by use **apClampedTmpl<>**), convolution always enforces this constraint.

- Kernel values are expressed as a **char**. This is sufficient for most convolution kernels. However, some large kernels, especially Gaussian filters, may have values that do not fit. If this is the case, you will need your own **convolve()** function that defines the kernel as a larger quantity.

Fortunately, all of these details are hidden. To perform convolution, you can simply call the **convolve()** function and explicitly specify **R**. Its definition is shown here.

```
template<class R, class T1, class T2, class S1, class S2>
void convolve (const apImage<T1,S1>& src1,
               const char* kernel, int size, int divisor,
               apImage<T2,S2>& dst1)
{
  apFunction_s1d1Convolve<R,T1,T2,S1,S2> processor
(ap_convolve_generic);
  processor.run (src1, kernel, size, divisor, dst1);
}
```

Our example using an averaging low-pass filter now looks like the following:

```
apImage<Pel8> src
...
apImage<Pel8> dst;
char kernel[] = { 1, 1, 1, 1, 1, 1, 1, 1, 1 };
convolve<Pel32> (src, kernel, 3, 9, dst);
```

If you call **convolve()** without specifying a value for **R** (i.e., as in **convolve<Pel32>**), the compiler will generate an error to remind you to add one.

Laplacian Kernel for Sharpening Edges

The edge of an object is indicated by a change in pixel value. Typically, there are two parameters associated with edges: *strength* and *angle*. The strength of an edge is the amount of change in pixel value when crossing the edge. Figure 6.12 illustrates strength by the length of the arrows. The angle is the angle of the line as drawn perpendicular to the edge. Figure 6.12 illustrates angle by the direction of the arrows.

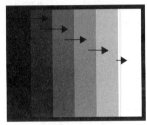

Varying Strength

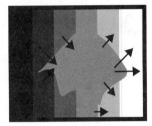

Varying Angle and Strength

Figure 6.12: Edge Definition

There are many methods for sharpening edges. A very effective and simple image processing technique is to ignore the angle and use the strength to sharpen the edges. You can accomplish edge sharpening by using a Laplacian mask (or kernel) in a convolution operation on the image. The *Laplacian kernel* generates peaks where edges are found. Our framework provides the following Laplacian kernel:

$$D(x,y) = \begin{bmatrix} -1 & -1 & -1 \\ -1 & 8 & -1 \\ -1 & -1 & -1 \end{bmatrix}$$

If we sum of all the values in the kernel, we see that they sum to zero. This means that when this kernel is run over a constant, or slowly varying image, the output will be zero or close to zero. However, when the kernel is run over a region where strong edges exist (the center pixel tends to be brighter or darker than surrounding pixels), the output can be very large. Figure 6.13 illustrates the application of an edge sharpening filter.

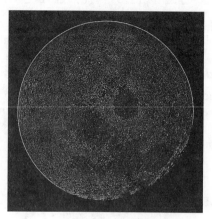

Original Image   Filtered Image

Figure 6.13: Laplacian Filter

We can write a function that is similar to **ap_convolve_generic**, but uses this specific Laplacian kernel, as shown.

```
template<class R, class T1, class T2, class S1, class S2>
void ap_convolve_3x3laplacian (const R&,
                               const apImage<T1,S1>& src1,
                               const char* /*kernel*/,
                               unsigned int /*size*/,
                               int /*divisor*/,
                               apImage<T2,S2>& dst1)
{
  typename apImage<T1,S1>::row_iterator i1 = src1.row_begin();
  typename apImage<T2,S2>::row_iterator i2 = dst1.row_begin();

  unsigned int h = src1.height() - 2;
  unsigned int w = src1.width()  - 2;

  const T1* p1;
  const T1* pk;
  T2* p2;
  R sum;
  unsigned int x, y;

  // Elements to skip from end of one row to start of next
  unsigned int pitch = (i1->bytes / sizeof (T1)) - 3;

  for (y=0; y<h; y++, i1++, i2++) {
    p1 = i1->p;
    p2 = i2->p;
    for (x=0; x<w; x++) {
      sum = 0;
      pk = p1 + x;
```

```
              sum -= *pk++;
              sum -= *pk++;
              sum -= *pk++;
              pk += pitch;

              sum -= *pk++;
              sum += (*pk++) * 8;
              sum -= *pk++;
              pk += pitch;

              sum -= *pk++;
              sum -= *pk++;
              sum -= *pk++;

              *p2++ = apLimit<T2> (sum);   // Prevent wrapping
          }
      }
  }
```

Many of the function arguments are ignored. By keeping the arguments identical for any
filtering routine, we can reuse our framework with only the expense of a few wasted
parameters. Note that this function still works for arbitrary pixel types. Although we have
hard-coded the kernel operator into the function, we have made no additional assumptions
about the pixel type.

The function works as follows:

- It unrolls the two inner loops that are inside **ap_convolve_generic** and explicitly
  computes the summation of the kernel using the source pixels.

- It uses the variable **pitch** to specify the number of pixels to skip after we process one
  line of input pixels to get to the start of the next line. Precomputing this value allows us
  to quickly skip from one line to the next.

While this function efficiently processes monochrome data types, it is slower for color
images. To address this issue, we can take advantage of template specialization and we can
define a special version of **ap_convolve_3x3laplacian** that works with **apRGB** (an 8-bit
RGB image). To do this, we not only unroll the two inner loops, but we also explicitly
compute the RGB values. This function is not difficult to write and it produces a dramatic
increase in speed, as shown here.

```
template<>
void ap_convolve_3x3laplacian (const apRGBPel32s&,
                               const apImage<apRGB>& src1,
                               const char* /*kernel*/,
                               unsigned int /*size*/,
                               int /*divisor*/,
                               apImage<apRGB>& dst1)
{
  apImage<apRGB>::row_iterator i1 = src1.row_begin();
  apImage<apRGB>::row_iterator i2 = dst1.row_begin();

  unsigned int h = src1.height() - 2;
  unsigned int w = src1.width()  - 2;
```

```cpp
const apRGB* p1;
const apRGB* pk;
apRGB* p2;
apRGBPel32s sum;
unsigned int x, y;

// Elements to skip from end of one row to start of next
unsigned int pitch = (i1->bytes / sizeof (apRGB)) - 3;

for (y=0; y<h; y++, i1++, i2++) {
  p1 = i1->p;
  p2 = i2->p;
  for (x=0; x<w; x++) {
    sum = 0;
    pk = p1 + x;

    sum.red   -= pk->red;
    sum.green -= pk->green;
    sum.blue  -= pk->blue;
    pk++;
    sum.red   -= pk->red;
    sum.green -= pk->green;
    sum.blue  -= pk->blue;
    pk++;
    sum.red   -= pk->red;
    sum.green -= pk->green;
    sum.blue  -= pk->blue;
    pk++;

    pk += pitch;

    sum.red   -= pk->red;
    sum.green -= pk->green;
    sum.blue  -= pk->blue;
    pk++;
    sum.red   += 8*pk->red;
    sum.green += 8*pk->green;
    sum.blue  += 8*pk->blue;
    pk++;
    sum.red   -= pk->red;
    sum.green -= pk->green;
    sum.blue  -= pk->blue;
    pk++;

    pk += pitch;

    sum.red   -= pk->red;
    sum.green -= pk->green;
    sum.blue  -= pk->blue;
    pk++;
    sum.red   -= pk->red;
    sum.green -= pk->green;
    sum.blue  -= pk->blue;
    pk++;
    sum.red   -= pk->red;
    sum.green -= pk->green;
    sum.blue  -= pk->blue;
    pk++;

    *p2++ = apLimit<apRGB> (sum);   // Prevent wrapping
```

```
        }
      }
    }
```

The **template<>** prefix to the function tells the compiler that this is a specialization. You have to pay careful attention to the arguments, since you are replacing generic parameter types with explicit ones. You will still have to specify the template, **R**, although this value is hard-coded as **apRGBPel32s** in the function. It is important that this value is signed, because the Laplacian kernel contains both positive and negative values.

There is one more small change to our template specialization for **ap_convolve_3x3laplacian**. As we discussed in *class Versus typename* on page 25, we cannot use the keyword **typename** in our specialization without generating an error. The line from our generic template definition:

```
typename apImage<T1,S1>::row_iterator i1 = src1.row_begin();
```

must be changed to:

```
apImage<apRGB>::row_iterator i1 = src1.row_begin();
```

To use the Laplacian filter, you can simply call the **laplacian3x3()** function and, as with **convolve()**, explicitly specify the **R** template parameter. The definition of **laplacian3x3()** is shown here.

```
template<class R, class T1, class T2, class S1, class S2>
void laplacian3x3 (const apImage<T1,S1>& src1,
                   apImage<T2,S2>& dst1)
{
  apFunction_s1d1Convolve<R,T1,T2,S1,S2> processor
    (ap_convolve_3x3laplacian);
  char* kernel = 0;
  unsigned int size = 3;
  int divisor = 1;
  processor.run (src1, kernel, size, divisor, dst1);
}
```

Table 6.1 shows the performance results when computing the Laplacian of a 1024x1024 **apRGB** image, with and without specialization, on our Intel Pentium 4 processor-based test platform, running at 2.0 GHz.

Table 6.1: 1024x1024 Laplacian Performance Results

Test	Execution Time
convolve<apRGBPel32s>() general purpose convolution	683 milliseconds
laplacian3x3<apRGBPel32s>() without the **apRGB** specialization	270 milliseconds
laplacian3x3<apRGBPel32s>() with the **apRGB** specialization	90 milliseconds

As you can see from the results, this specialization was clearly advantageous. We have removed numerous loops in our RGB specialization, which explains the performance gain. As you would expect, calling any of the three functions produces the identical image as output.

High-Pass Kernel for Sharpening Edges

Another way to sharpen edges, especially those in scanned photographs, is to use a convolution operation with a high-pass kernel. High-pass kernels enhance pixel differences and effectively sharpen edges. Our framework provides the following high-pass kernel:

$$D(x,y) = \begin{bmatrix} -1 & -1 & -1 \\ -1 & 9 & -1 \\ -1 & -1 & -1 \end{bmatrix}$$

If we sum of all the values in the kernel, we see that they sum to one. This means that when this kernel is run over a constant, or slowly varying image, the output will be very close to the original pixel values. In areas where edges are found (i.e., the pixel values vary), the output values are magnified. Figure 6.14 illustrates the application of a high-pass edge sharpening filter.

Original Image

Filtered Image

Figure 6.14: High-Pass Filter

Gaussian Kernel for Smoothing Edges

You can use a convolution operation with a Gaussian kernel to smooth the edges in your image. This technique usually produces a superior result to the low-pass kernel we presented on page 219. Our framework provides the following Gaussian kernel:

$$D(x,y) = \frac{1}{16} \begin{bmatrix} 1 & 2 & 1 \\ 2 & 4 & 2 \\ 1 & 2 & 1 \end{bmatrix}$$

Like our general convolution kernel, the Gaussian kernel uses summing and averaging to assign new values to pixels in the filtered image. The effect is that the strong edge differences are reduced, giving the filtered image a softer or blurred appearance. This is useful for reducing contrast or smoothing the image to eliminate such undesired effects as noise and textures. Figure 6.15 illustrates the application of a Gaussian edge smoothing filter.

Original Image   Filtered Image

Figure 6.15: Gaussian Filter

6.3.5 Generating Thumbnails

We could not end a section on image processing routines without reviewing our global **thumbnail()** function in its final form. This is a stand-alone function. **thumbnail()**

always computes the destination image. Figure 6.16 illustrates the application of the **thumbnail()** function.

Original Image

Thumbnail Image

Figure 6.16: Thumbnail Function

The **thumbnail()** function is as shown.

```
template<class R, class T1, class S1>
apImage<T1,S1> thumbnail (const apImage<T1,S1>& src1,
                          unsigned int factor)
{
  apImageLocker<T1,S1> srcLocking (src1);
  apImage<T1,S1> dst;

  if (src1.isNull())
    return dst;

  apRect boundary (src1.x0(), src1.y0(),
                   src1.width()/factor, src1.height()/factor);
  dst = apImage<T1,S1> (boundary, src1.alignment());

  typename apImage<T1,S1>::row_iterator s;
  typename apImage<T1,S1>::row_iterator d;
  typename apImage<T1,S1>::row_iterator s1;
  unsigned int w = dst.width ();
  const T1* sp;
  T1* dp;
  R sum;

  // Iterate over pixels in the destination
  for (d=dst.row_begin(), s=src1.row_begin(); d != dst.row_end();
       d++, s+=factor) {
    dp = d->p;
    for (unsigned int x=0; x<w; x++) {
      sum = 0;
      s1 = s;
      for (unsigned int dy=0; dy<factor; dy++, s1++) {
        sp = s1->p + x*factor;
        for (unsigned int dx=0; dx<factor; dx++)
          sum += *sp++;
      }
```

```
        *dp++ = apLimit<T1> (sum / (factor*factor));
    }
  }

  return dst;
}
```

6.4 Finalizing Interfaces to Third-Party Software

A decade ago, most software solutions were completely proprietary, in that all aspects of the application were developed in-house. There were plenty of software libraries available for purchase, but they were usually expensive or were considered inferior — not because they didn't perform the intended function, but because they were not developed in-house. This "not invented here" syndrome created large in-house development groups that often duplicated functionality available elsewhere. The actual expense of developing these packages was enormous, especially considering that all maintenance was performed by the organization. Most of these issues vanished due to shrinking budgets and the advent of open-source software.

Modern software takes advantage of existing libraries to speed development and minimize the maintenance issues. It is now considered good design practice to design applications with interfaces that leverage existing code. We use the word *delegates* to refer to third-party software packages to which we delegate responsibility.

6.4.1 File Delegates

We have created a very flexible and extensible image processing framework. However, it still lacks the capability of interacting with the outside world. Unless our package can import and export images using many of the popular image formats, our framework is of little use.

There are many image storage formats, including JPEG, GIF, PNG, and TIFF. They all have their advantages and disadvantages, so supporting a single format is of limited use. We will design a simple interface so new file formats can be added with little difficulty. This design can be used by most image formats, although it may not take advantage of all the features of an individual format. Figure 6.17 provides an overview of the file delegate strategy.

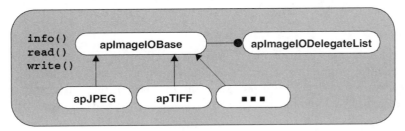

Figure 6.17: File Delegate Interface Design

We create a base class, **apImageIOBase**, that defines the services we want and then we derive one class from **apImageIOBase** for every file format we want to support. **apImageIOBase** defines three essential methods, **info()**, **read()**, and **write()**, that check the file format and handle the actual reading and writing of each file format, respectively, as shown.

```
class apImageIOBase
{
public:
  virtual apDelegateInfo info (const std::string& filename) = 0;

  template<class T, class S>
  void read (const std::string& filename, apImage<T,S>& image);

  template<class T, class S>
  void write (const std::string& filename, apImage<T,S>& image,
              const apDelegateParams& params = sNoParams)

  // Default copy constructor and assignment operators ok.
protected:
  apImageIOBase ();
  virtual ~apImageIOBase ();

  static apDelegateParams sNoParams;
};
```

❖ INFO()

info() determines whether a file is of the specified format and, if known, can provide the size. **info()** returns a structure, **apDelegateInfo**, which is shown here.

```
struct apDelegateInfo
{
  bool         isDelegate;    // true if delegate knows this format
  apRect       boundary;      // Image boundary (if known)
  unsigned int bytesPerPixel; // Bytes per pixel (if known)
  unsigned int planes;        // Number of planes (if known)
  std::string  format;        // Additional image format information
};
```

The optional field, **format**, is used to hold other information about a storage format. This is particularly important when an object, like **apDelegateInfo**, is shared among many objects. This prevents **apDelegateInfo** from containing a large number of fields, most of which are particular to a single image format. None of the image formats we support use the **format** member, but it is still good practice to include it for future use.

❖ READ()

The **read()** function reads an image into the specified **apImage<>** object. This is an excellent example of using templates inside a non-template object. The user can specify an image of any arbitrary type, and **read()** returns an image of that type. Most applications would use **info()** to determine the image type before using **read()** to read the image data from a file.

A very nice feature of **read()** is that it lets you pass it the name of a file containing a color image, and you receive a monochrome image in return. The color image is read, but converted to the monochrome image and returned.

❖ WRITE()

write() takes an **apImage<>** object and saves it in a particular image format. Optional parameters can be passed in an **apDelegateParams** structure:

```
struct apDelegateParams
{
  float        quality;        // Quality parameter
  std::string params;          // Other parameters

  apDelegateParams (float qual=70.) : quality (qual) {}

};
```

As with **apDelegateInfo**, we only place common functions directly in the structure. We added the **quality** parameter, because it is needed when JPEG images are stored, but other storage formats might use this parameter. We made **quality** a **float** to make it as useful as possible (although this is an integer value for JPEG compression). **params** is intended to hold format-specific parameters and prevents the structure from getting too large.

You may have wondered why the **read()** and **write()** methods are not **virtual**. The answer is that it is illegal. A member template function cannot be defined this way. Our definitions for **read()** and **write()**, however, will call virtual functions. The complete definition for **apImageIOBase** looks like this.

```
class apImageIOBase
{
public:
  virtual apDelegateInfo info (const std::string& filename) = 0;

  template<class T, class S>
  void read (const std::string& filename, apImage<T,S>& image)
  {
    if (typeid(apImage<apRGB>) == typeid(image))
      image = readRGB (filename);
    else if (typeid(apImage<Pel8>) == typeid(image))
      image = readPel8 (filename);
    else
      copy (readRGB (filename), image);
  }

  template<class T, class S>
  void write (const std::string& filename, apImage<T,S>& image,
              const apDelegateParams& params = sNoParams)
  {
    if (typeid(apImage<apRGB>) == typeid(image))
      write (filename, image.storage(), params);
    else if (typeid(apImage<Pel8>) == typeid(image))
      write (filename, image.storage(), params);
    else {
      apImage<apRGB> rgb = image;
      write (filename, rgb.storage(), params);
    }
  }
```

```
    virtual apImage<apRGB> readRGB (const std::string& filename) =0;
    virtual apImage<Pel8>  readPel8(const std::string& filename) =0;
    // File formats have limited ways that files are stored. These
    // functions read RGB and 8-bit monochrome images.

    virtual bool write (const std::string& filename,
                        const apRectImageStorage& pixels,
                        const apDelegateParams& params) = 0;

    // Default copy constructor and assignment operators ok.
protected:
    apImageIOBase ();
    virtual ~apImageIOBase ();

    static apDelegateParams sNoParams;
};
```

Our class makes the assumption that most images are stored in files. Our implementation has virtual functions, **readRGB()** and **readPel8()**, to read a color or monochrome (8-bit) image from the specified file. These are the two most important formats for our use. It would be a pretty simple matter to add additional functions as needed. For example, **readPel32()** might be useful for applications with 16- or 32-bit monochrome images. Before adding such a function, make sure that the image file format you are using supports such a resolution.

When you look at the **read()** method, you can see how it figures out whether to call **readRGB()** or **readPel8()**. By using **typeid()**, we are able to convert from a non-virtual member template to a regular virtual function. When you have the ability to enable or disable Run-Time Type Identification (RTTI), as with Microsoft compilers, you will need to enable RTTI so that this function works properly. **readRGB()** is called if the pixel type is not a **Pel8** or **apRGB**, since a color image is more generic than a monochrome image.

To implement a new file delegate, you have to implement **info()**, **write()**, **readRGB()**, and **readPel8()**, although often **readPel8()** can simply call **readRGB()**.

Note that it is possible to extend this interface to include files that are stored in memory, but that is beyond the scope of this book.

File Delegate List

It is very nice to have a separate object to save or restore our **apImage<>** objects in each file format. However, it is better if we can maintain a current list of available file formats. Using our standard **gOnly()** technique, we write a repository object, **apImageIODelegateList**, to keep track of which file delegates are loaded, as shown here.

```
class apImageIODelegateList
{
public:
    static apImageIODelegateList& gOnly ();

    apImageIOBase* getDelegate (const std::string& type);
    void setDelegate (const std::string& type, apImageIOBase* object);

    apImageIOBase* findDelegate (const std::string& filename);
```

```
private:
  typedef std::map<std::string, apImageIOBase*> map;
  typedef map::iterator iterator;

  map map_;    // Mapping of file type to a delegate to handle it

  static apImageIODelegateList* sOnly_;

  apImageIODelegateList ();
};
```

With this object, we can see whether a particular file format can be read or written. **getDelegate()** returns a pointer to a file delegate object if the specified file type name exists. The type name is simply the standard file suffix used by a file format (i.e., **jpg** for a JPEG file).

You can extend **apImageIODelegateList** by adding **read()** and **write()** methods to handle all known file formats. These methods would find an appropriate delegate for the specified file, and then would call the delegate's corresponding **read()** or **write()** method to handle the file.

JPEG File Delegate

One of the most common file formats is Joint Photographic Expert's Group (JPEG). JPEG can store both monochrome and color images at various levels of compression. This format is considered *lossy*, meaning that if you save an image as a JPEG file, and then read it back, the image will be close but not identical to the original. For images intended for human viewing, this is usually acceptable, especially if you limit the amount of compression. However, for many applications, including medical imaging and machine vision, a lossy compression method should be avoided.

C and C++ API's are freely available and can be built on many platforms. Like most frameworks, we are using the Independent JPEG Group implementation (**http://www.ijg.org**). This is a pretty complicated API with many options. If this library does not already exist on your system and pre-compiled binaries are not available, you will need to do the following:

1. Download the JPEG library from the Web site or the CD-ROM included with this book.

2. Unpack the files onto your system.

3. Read the building and installation instructions that come with the distribution.

4. Build and install. For UNIX systems, this is as easy as typing **make** as the first command, followed by **make install** as the second.

The JPEG library is C-based and uses callback functions when errors or warnings occur. For our purposes, we define callback functions that generate C++ exceptions that we later catch in our file delegate object, as shown:

```
class apJPEGException : public apException
{
public:
  apJPEGException (std::string name="")
    : apException ("apJPEGException: " + name) {}
};
```

We define a JPEG callback function to receive error information and to generate an exception:

```
void local_error_exit (jpeg_common_struct* cinfo)
{
  char msg[1024];
  sprintf (msg, "error_exit: %d", cinfo->err->msg_code);
  throw apJPEGException (msg);
}
```

jpeg_common_struct is an internal JPEG structure that contains information about the JPEG file, including any error information.

apJPEG is our file delegate object that creates an interface between our **apImageIOBase** interface and the JPEG library. Its definition is shown here.

```
class apJPEG : public apImageIOBase
{
public:
  static apJPEG& gOnly ();

  virtual apDelegateInfo info (const std::string& filename);

  virtual apImage<apRGB> readRGB  (const std::string& filename);
  virtual apImage<Pel8>  readPel8 (const std::string& filename);

  virtual bool write (const std::string& filename,
                      const apRectImageStorage& pixels,
                      const apDelegateParams& params = sNoParams);

  // Default copy constructor and assignment operators ok.
private:
  static apJPEG* sOnly_;

  apJPEG ();
  ~apJPEG ();
};
```

The implementation of these functions requires knowledge of the JPEG API. A rough outline of the implementation is as follows:

```
apImage<apRGB>  apJPEG::readRGB  (const std::string& filename)
{
  apImage<apRGB> rgbImage;

  struct jpeg_decompress_struct cinfo;
```

```
    FILE *infile;
    if ((infile = fopen(filename.c_str(), "rb")) == NULL) {
      return rgbImage;
    }

    // Install our callback functions to stub out warning messages
    // and generate our exception when an error occurs.
    ...

    // Read header information
    try {
      jpeg_read_header(&cinfo, TRUE);
      ...
    }
    catch (apJPEGException&) {
    }
    ...
    fclose(infile);
    return rgbImage;
  }
```

We place a **try** block around all of the JPEG API functionality. By doing this we can treat the JPEG library as a black box. We either get the image data we want, or else the **catch** block catches any errors generated by the JPEG library. Most file delegate functions are similar to this one.

We only need a single instance of any file delegate class, and **gOnly()** takes care of this for us. Instead of using **apJPEG** directly, we access this object by means of the **apImageIODelegateList** class. This gives us a way to automatically update our list of available file delegates, because having to manually update this list whenever a file delegate is added or subtracted is prone to error. Our solution is to take advantage of static initialization by defining a static function that adds the delegate to **apImageIODelegateList**:

```
  class apJPEG_installer
  {
  public:
    static apJPEG_installer installer;
  private:
    apJPEG_installer ();
  };
```

In our source file, we add:

```
  apJPEG_installer apJPEG_installer::installer;
  apJPEG_installer::apJPEG_installer ()
  {
    apImageIODelegateList::gOnly().setDelegate ("jpg",
                                                &apJPEG::gOnly());
  }
```

During static initialization, **apJPEG_installer::installer** is initialized by calling the **apJPEG_installer** constructor, which adds the JPEG file delegate to the list of supported file types. **apImageIODelegateList::gOnly()** and **apJPEG::gOnly()** ensure that the Singleton objects are constructed.

Get in the habit of not referencing **apJPEG** directly. The preferred method is:

```
apImageIOBase* delegate;
delegate = apImageIODelegateList::gOnly().getDelegate ("jpg");
if (delegate) {
  ...
}
```

This lookup converts the file type, **.jpg** in this case, to the object that handles this file format. This approach is clearly advantageous when you need to manage many file formats.

The method **readRGB()** does more than it appears. This function returns an **apImage<apRGB>** image, but it must be capable of reading the information contained in the file. The JPEG format can store an image in multiple ways, two of which are supported by our class. Using the nomenclature of the JPEG standard, the two color spaces that we support are a 24-bit color image (same as **apImage<apRGB>**), and an 8-bit monochrome image (same as **apImage<Pel8>**). **readRGB()** handles both cases and converts grayscale data to colors if necessary.

readPel8() could look very similar to **readRGB()**, in that it converts color data as it is received to monochrome. However, we do not have to worry about performance as much with save and restore operations, so we can take a huge shortcut:

```
apImage<Pel8> apJPEG::readPel8 (const std::string& filename)
{ return readRGB (filename);}
```

Since **readRGB()** can read both JPEG storage formats, we can simply convert the color image returned from **readRGB()** into an image of type **apImage<Pel8>**. The compiler handles the conversion from an **apImage<apRGB>** object to **apImage<Pel8>** by using the **apImage<>** copy constructor (defined inline in the **apImage<>** class definition):

```
template<class T1, class S1>
apImage (const apImage<T1,S1>& src)
{
  // Our copy() function does exactly what we want
  copy (src, *this);
}
```

By carefully creating the copy constructor and assignment operator in terms of different template parameters, we can reuse our **copy()** function.

TIFF File Delegate

The Tag Image File Format (TIFF) is another popular image format. It includes many internal formats for storing both color and monochrome images. It can store images in both lossy and loss-less fashion. The **apTIFF** object works like **apJPEG**, in that it handles the most common cases of reading and writing a TIFF image. We handle the warning or error callback issue in the same way by constructing an exception object, **apTIFFException**. Like the JPEG library, the C source code is freely available for this format from **http://www.libtiff.org** or on the CD-ROM included with this book.

6.4.2 Image Delegates

There are many third-party image processing packages available. The primary reasons to use third-party libraries is to broaden functionality and improve performance.

❖ INTEL IPP

In our examples, we use the Intel Integrated Performance Primitives (IPP) library, which contains a large number of highly optimized, low-level functions that run on most Intel microprocessors. Once you take a look at the results of running a Laplacian filter with a 3x3 kernel on a 1024x1024 image, you'll understand why we have chosen this library.

Table 6.2 shows the performance results you can expect using our framework's wrapper functions to call the corresponding Intel IPP functions. Note that we performed these tests on our Intel Pentium 4 processor-based test platform running at 2.0 GHz.

Table 6.2: IPP Library Performance Results, 1024x1024 Image

Test	Pel8 image	apRGB image
Calling Intel IPP functions through our wrapper function	4 milliseconds `IPPLaplacian3x3<Pel8>`	11 milliseconds `IPPLaplacian3x3<apRGB>`
Convolution routine for Laplacian filtering with 3x3 kernel	45 milliseconds `laplacian3x3<>`	90 milliseconds `laplacian3x3<>`
General purpose convolution routine	89 milliseconds `convolve<>`	683 milliseconds `convolve<>`

❖ GENERIC CONVOLUTION FUNCTION

Before we deal with the specifics of IPP, let's discuss the broader design issue of how to interface any external library with our framework. To explore this issue, let's use our generic **convolve()** function and see how it changes, given different design strategies. Our original definition for **convolve()** is:

```
template<class R, class T1, class T2, class S1, class S2>
void convolve (const apImage<T1,S1>& src1,
               const char* kernel, int size, int divisor,
               apImage<T2,S2>& dst1)
{
  apFunction_s1d1Convolve<R,T1,T2,S1,S2> processor
                                  (ap_convolve_generic);
  processor.run (src1, kernel, size, divisor, dst1);
}
```

Strategy 1: A Fully Integrated Solution

If you want to fully integrate our framework with a third-party library, such that they operate as a single piece of code, we would need to modify our generic `convolve()` function as follows:

```
template<class R, class T1, class T2, class S1, class S2>
void convolve (const apImage<T1,S1>& src1,
               const char* kernel, int size, int divisor,
               apImage<T2,S2>& dst1)
{
  if (!thirdPartyFramework()) {
    apFunction_s1d1Convolve<R,T1,T2,S1,S2> processor
                                       (ap_convolve_generic);
    processor.run (src1, kernel, size, divisor, dst1);
  }
  else {
    thirdPartyFramework()->convolve (...);
  }
}
```

We modify `convolve()` to query `thirdpartyFramework()`, which returns a pointer to an external library, or `0` if none is available.

Let's consider the issues with this strategy. Our example shows that the external `convolve()` function is always called if an external `convolve()` function is available. What happens if the external function is less efficient than our built-in version? Our function definition should really include some kind of logic to determine which particular image processing function should be called.

In addition, our function assumes that as long as the third-party library exists, it must also support convolution. We should make sure to not only query the existence of the library, but also to verify that it supports convolution.

These changes are not unique to `convolve()`; rather, we would need to make similar changes to all image processing functions that we would like to use with our third-party library.

And given the extensiveness of the changes, it is unlikely that the third-party library will exactly support our definition of an image. In our example, `thirdpartyFramework()` must return an object, which takes `apImage<>` objects as parameters and converts them, as needed, to an image format that is compatible with the image format used by the third-party library.

It is a very expensive proposition to make two distinct pieces of code act together as one, requiring numerous changes throughout the framework. This makes the solution prone to errors and difficult to maintain or extend.

We attempted to create a tightly integrated design that was very similar to how we handled file delegates. Although we don't highlight all the details in the book, we created a mapping object that would track which processing functions were available. We also looked at modifying our interface functions, like `laplacian3x3<>`, to detect whether an alternative version was available. This scheme quickly became unworkable because of the number of changes this approach forced us to make to the entire framework. Since many applications should be able to use our framework directly, without the need for any image delegates, we decided to abandon this strategy.

Because of these issues, we decided that the integration of a third-pary library should happen at a higher level. Let's explore a loosely coupled solution that does just that.

Strategy 2: A Loosely Coupled Solution

Let's look at a solution that provides a very loose coupling of our framework and a third-party library. We will leave both our framework and the third-party library unchanged. Instead, we will create interface functions and objects that convert our **apImage<>** references to a form compatible with the third-party library. In this solution, our original **convolve()** function also remains completely unchanged, as do all of the other image processing functions. To fully explore this solution, we use concrete examples with Intel IPP as the third-party library.

❖ IMAGES AND MEMORY ALIGNMENT

It turns out that the image definitions and memory alignment capabilities of the two frameworks are very compatible. In the IPP, an image is an array of image pixels, rather than a separate, well-defined structure. In **apImage<>**, our image storage also requires an array of image pixels. The memory alignment capabilities of **apImage<>** are also supported in the IPP.

IPP routines pass the *pitch* (or *step*, as the IPP documentation calls it) between rows. This is the number of bytes needed to move from one pixel in the image to the pixel just below it on the following row. While the IPP does not have specific memory alignment requirements, some alignments will result in higher performance because of the architecture of the Intel processors. Unless you must squeeze out every bit of performance, you can safely ignore the alignment details and simply let the libraries handle the alignment issues.

If you really must be concerned about every bit of performance, here are some issues to consider. Neighborhood processing routines, such as convolution, require preprocessing to determine which pixels in the operation are used. (See our discussion regarding intersections on page 213 for more information.) It is not possible to guarantee that the regions of interest (ROIs) being processed will be aligned for optimal performance. But this does not mean that the obvious solution of creating a temporary image will result in the performance gains of an aligned image. Using an aligned image adds four processing steps: creating temporary image(s), copying the pixels from the input images to the temporary images, copying the result to the destination image, and, finally, deleting the temporary image(s).

Interfacing **apImage<>** to other image processing libraries will not always be this easy. If you are fortunate, as we are in this example, the complexity will be limited to converting between the **apImage<>** data structure and the third-party library. However, if the third-party library uses an incompatible storage format, the underlying image data must be converted. Regardless of the complexity, you should always implement an interface object to encapsulate the details.

❖ TRAITS

Our interface object, **apIPP<>,** converts an **apImage<>** object into a form usable by the Intel library. Converting images is a simple operation in our case. IPP, however, is a C-interface library that contains hundreds of functions. Therefore, it is very useful to encapsulate some of these related datatypes into *traits* classes. Using traits, you can define one or more properties (or traits) for a datatype.

Let's start by reviewing our **IPPTraits<>** object, which maps an **apImage<>** pixel type to one used by the IPP, as shown.

```
template<class T> struct IPPTraits
{
  typedef T ipptype;  // Intel IPP  type for this apImage type
};

template<> struct IPPTraits<apRGB>
{
  typedef Ipp8u ipptype;
};

template<> struct IPPTraits<apRGBPel32s>
{
  typedef Ipp32s ipptype;
};
```

Even though we have called this a traits class, this object only contains a single **typedef.** We did this because the object will grow over time as other image-specific quantities are added. The generic version of **IPPTraits<>** defines a value, **ipptype,** to be the same type as the **apImage<>** pixel type. This works as expected for monochrome data types, but we must define specializations for our color data types to correctly map the **apImage<>** pixel types to the corresponding ones in the IPP.

For example, **apImage<apRGB>** defines an image of RGB pixels. However, the IPP considers this to be an image of bytes, taking three consecutive bytes as a color pixel. While the memory layouts are identical, the compiler will generate an error if we try to pass an **apRGB** pointer to an IPP function. So, we define a specialization that uses the native pixel types (**Ipp8u** for an 8-bit unsigned integer and **Ipp32s** for a 32-bit signed integer) for the IPP.

❖ APIPP<>

apIpp<> encapsulates our **apImage<>** objects and converts them into a form compatible with the IPP as shown here.

```
class apIPPException : public apException
{
public:
  apIPPException (std::string name="")
    : apException ("apIPPException: " + name) {}
};

template<class T, class S=apImageStorage<T> >
```

```
class apIPP
{
public:
  typedef typename IPPTraits<T>::ipptype ipptype;

  enum eType {
    eIPP_Unknown = 0,       // Unknown or uninitialized type
    eIPP_8u_C1   = 1,       // 8-bit monochrome
    eIPP_32s_C1  = 2,       // 32-bit (signed) monochrome
    eIPP_8u_C3   = 3,       // 8-bit RGB
    eIPP_32s_C3  = 4,       // 32-bit (signed) RGB
  };

  apIPP (apImage<T,S>& image);
  ~apIPP () { cleanup ();}

  apIPP (const apIPP& src);
  apIPP& operator= (const apIPP& src);
  // We need our own copy constructor and assignment operator.

  ipptype* base      ()
    { return reinterpret_cast<ipptype*>(align_.base());}
  const ipptype* base () const
    { return reinterpret_cast<ipptype*>(align_.base());}
  // Base address of image data, in the proper pointer type

  IppiSize imageSize () const
  { IppiSize sz; sz.width = align_.width();
    sz.height = align_.height(); return sz;}
  // IPP image size (suitable for use in IPP routines)

  unsigned int pitch () { return align_.begin()->bytes;}
  // Pitch (spacing, in bytes, between rows)

  void syncImage ();
  // Called after image processing to sync up the image with the
  // aligned image, if necessary
protected:
  void createIPPImage ();
  // Convert the apImage<> image, if necessary, to a form for IPP

  void cleanup ();
  // Cleanup any memory allocated to the intel image object

  apImage<T,S>& image_;    // Our storage object (A reference)
  apImage<T,S>  align_;    // Our aligned image
  eType         type_;     // Image type
};
```

apIPP<> keeps a reference to the passed image, rather than a copy of the image. This is to ensure that any changes made to **image_** will be reflected in the original image. Holding onto a copy of the image, even though the image storage uses reference counting, will not work. Reference counting does avoid making copies of the underlying pixel data, but it cannot guarantee that two images will always point to the same storage.

align_ is an image which is aligned in memory to take advantage of performance improvements in the IPP. Both **align_** and **image_** will refer to the same image pixels, unless **createIPPImage()** generates a temporary image to enhance performance.

❖ CREATEIPPIMAGE()

createIPPImage() is called by the constructor and allows IPP functions to use the **apImage<>** pixel data. The implementation does little more than use Run-Time Type Identification (RTTI) to map the pixel type to the IPP datatype name, as shown.

```
template <class T, class S>
void apIPP<T,S>::createIPPImage ()
{
  // Cleanup any existing Intel object
  cleanup ();

  align_ = image_; // No special memory alignment by default

  // Figure out our datatype
  if (typeid(T) == typeid(Pel8)) {
    type_ = eIPP_8u_C1;
  }
  else if (typeid(T) == typeid(Pel32s)) {
    type_ = eIPP_32s_C1;
  }
  else if (typeid(T) == typeid(apRGB)) {
    type_ = eIPP_8u_C3;
  }
  else if (typeid(T) == typeid(apRGBPel32s)) {
    type_ = eIPP_32s_C3;
  }
  else {
    throw apIPPException ("Unsupported image type");
  }
}
```

❖ SYNCIMAGE()

After any image processing step that changes **align_**, the **syncImage()** method should be called to make sure that **image_** accurately reflects the results of the operation. If **align_** and **image_** point to the same storage, nothing needs to be done. The definition of **syncImage()** is shown here.

```
template <class T, class S>
void apIPP<T,S>::syncImage ()
{
  if (align_.base() != image_.base())
    copy (align_, image_);
}
```

❖ GENERIC INTERFACE TO FILTERING FUNCTIONS

Now that we have **apIPP<>** to interface our **apImage<>** object with the IPP data structures, we can turn our attention to writing an interface to some of its image processing functions.

We create a generic object, **apIPPFilter<>**, that defines an interface that can be used with most IPP filtering functions. Most of the IPP functions are similar to the following prototype:

```
IppStatus prototype (const ipptype* src, int srcStep,
                     ipptype* dst, int dstStep,
                     IppiSize roi, IppiMaskSize mask);
```

In this example, **prototype()** takes a source pixel pointer and step size (bytes between neighboring rows in the image), destination pixel pointer and step size, image size (**IppiSize**), and filter size (**IppiMaskSize**).

IPPFilter<> defines the call operator, **operator()**, to perform a specific image filtering operation. The definition of **IPPFilter<>** is shown here.

```cpp
template<typename T, IppiMaskSize S> class IPPFilter
{
public:
  typedef typename IPPTraits<T>::ipptype ipptype;
  typedef IppStatus  (__stdcall *fixedFilterFunction)(
                                   const ipptype* /*pSrc*/,
                                   int /*srcStep*/,
                                   ipptype* /*pDst*/,
                                   int /*dstStep*/,
                                   IppiSize /*dstRoiSize*/,
                                   IppiMaskSize /*mask*/);

  IppStatus operator() (const apImage<T>& src, apImage<T>& dst)
   {
     if (src.isNull())
       return ippStsNoErr;

     apImageLocker<T> srcLocking (src);

     apImage<T> source = src;
     apImage<T> dest    = dst;

     eMethod method = eRegular;

     // If destination is specified, use it in computing the overlap.
     if (dest.isNull()) {
       // Our destination size is smaller than the source, but aligned
       int size = IPPMaskSizeTraits<S>::xSize;
       int expansion = (size-1) / 2;
       apRect region = src.boundary ();
       region.expand (-expansion, -expansion);

       dst = apImage<T> (region, src.alignment());
       dest = dst;
       method = eCreatedDest;
     }
     else if (src.isIdentical (dst)) {
       // In-place operation
       dest = duplicate (source, apRectImageStorage::e16ByteAlign);
       method = eInPlace;
     }
     else if (source.boundary() != dest.boundary()) {
       // Restrict output to the intersection of the images
       dest.window   (src.boundary());
       source.window (dest.boundary());
       method = eWindow;
     }

     // Lock destination after it is created (if necessary)
     apImageLocker<T> dstLocking (dst);

     // Compute the overlap between the images
     apIntersectRects overlap = intersect (src.boundary(),
            IPPMaskSizeTraits<S>::xSize, IPPMaskSizeTraits<S>::ySize,
            dst.boundary());

     // Return a null image if there is no overlap
```

```
      if (overlap.dst.isNull()) {
        dstLocking.unlock ();
        dst = dst.sNull;
        return ippStsNoErr;
      }

      // Work only within the overlap area
      apImage<T> roi1 = src;
      apImage<T> roi2 = dst;
      roi1.window (overlap.dst);
      roi2.window (overlap.dst);

      apIPP<T> s (roi1);
      apIPP<T> d (roi2);

      // Call the IPP function
      IppStatus status = func_ (s.base(), s.pitch(), d.base(),
                                d.pitch(), s.imageSize(), S);

      d.syncImage ();

      // Post-processing
      switch (method) {
      case eInPlace:
        copy (dest, source);
        dst = dest;
        break;
      default:
        break;
      }

      return status;
    }

  protected:
    enum eMethod { eRegular, eInPlace, eCreatedDest, eWindow};

    IPPFilter (fixedFilterFunction f) : func_ (f) {}

    fixedFilterFunction func_;
};
```

IPPFilter<> is fairly straightforward. The **typedef ipptype** is identical to the one we find in the traits class, **IPPTraits<>**, and is defined to make it easier to refer to the IPP datatype. Note that you must use **typename** to equate **ipptype** with the corresponding type in **IPPTraits<>**.

The **typedef fixedFilterFunction** defines what the IPP filter functions will look like, and matches the **prototype()** function shown earlier on page 242.

You pass the desired IPP filter function to **IPPFilter<>** in its constructor, so that it can be used by **operator()**.

You may notice that we are only using a single template parameter, **T**, when referring to **apImage<>**, and we are relying on using the default values for the other parameter. If your images require non-default versions of the other parameter, you can modify this object very easily.

operator() allows some flexibility in how the destination argument is specified, as follows:

- If an output image is specified, the returned image will be the intersection of the source and destination regions.

- If no destination image is specified, a destination image is created to be the same size as the source image. This destination image will have the same alignment as the source image.

- If the destination image is identical to the source image, the operation is performed in place. Internally, this creates a temporary image before the image processing is performed.

To keep track of what kind of processing is needed, the **eMethod** enumeration defines all of the possible states we may encounter.

operator() performs the following four steps:

1. Convert the source image to the IPP format.

2. Convert the destination image to the IPP format.

3. Call the IPP function **func_()** to compute the filtered image.

4. Synchronize our result with the destination image, in case a copy of the image was made for alignment reasons.

These steps are handled by the following four lines of code:

```
apIPP<T> s (roi1);
apIPP<T> d (roi2);
IppStatus status = func_ (s.base(), s.pitch(), d.base(),
                          d.pitch(), s.imageSize(), S);

d.syncImage ();
```

❖ DERIVED OBJECTS FOR SPECIFIC FILTERING OPERATIONS

You can now derive objects from **IPPFilter<>** to define objects for specific Intel IPP image processing functions. For example, we derived an object that defines 3x3 and 5x5 Laplacian filtering operations, as follows:

```
template<typename T> class IPPLaplacian3x3
  : public IPPFilter<T, ippMskSize3x3>
{
public:
  typedef typename IPPFilter<T, ippMskSize3x3>::fixedFilterFunction
                                           fixedFilterFunction;
  static IPPLaplacian3x3 filter;
protected:

  IPPLaplacian3x3 (fixedFilterFunction f)
    : IPPFilter<T,ippMskSize3x3> (f) {}
};

IPPLaplacian3x3<Pel8>  IPPLaplacian3x3<Pel8>::filter
                              (ippiFilterLaplace_8u_C1R);
```

```
IPPLaplacian3x3<apRGB> IPPLaplacian3x3<apRGB>::filter
                                 (ippiFilterLaplace_8u_C3R);


template<typename T> class IPPLaplacian5x5
  : public IPPFilter<T, ippMskSize5x5>
{
public:
  typedef typename IPPFilter<T, ippMskSize5x5>::fixedFilterFunction
                                                fixedFilterFunction;
  static IPPLaplacian5x5 filter;
protected:

  IPPLaplacian5x5 (fixedFilterFunction f)
    : IPPFilter<T, ippMskSize5x5> (f) {}
};

IPPLaplacian5x5<Pel8>  IPPLaplacian5x5<Pel8>::filter
                              (ippiFilterLaplace_8u_C1R);
IPPLaplacian5x5<apRGB> IPPLaplacian5x5<apRGB>::filter
                              (ippiFilterLaplace_8u_C3R);
```

In the example above, you can see how our framework interfaces with the Intel IPP function, `ippiFilterLaplace_8u_C3R()`, to compute the Laplacian image of an 8-bit RGB image.

We can see how easy it is to use our image delegate by looking at a comparison of techniques for computing the Laplacian image of an 8-bit RGB image. To compute the Laplacian image using our framework, we write:

```
apImage<apRGB> src;
apImage<apRGB> dst;
laplacian3x3<apRGBPel32s> (src, dst);
```

When we rewrite this example using our image delegate, the code looks similar; however, the template parameter now specifies the pixel type instead of the internal pixel type required by our framework. The rewritten example that computes the Laplacian image of an 8-bit RGB image is as follows:

```
apImage<apRGB> src;
apImage<apRGB> dst;
IPPLaplacian3x3<apRGB>::filter (src, dst);
```

If we call the function, `laplacian3x3<>`, we call our built-in routine to compute the Laplacian image of an input image. If we call `IPPLaplacian3x3<apRGB>::filter()`, we call the IPP version of the same filtering operation.

An additional advantage in this particular example, is that both versions return the identical image results, because the Intel IPP library has the same boundary behavior as our framework. You cannot always count on this behavior from a third-party library, however, and it is best to leave it up to the application to choose the appropriate function.

Extending the Loosely Coupled Solution

Our loosely coupled strategy gives us the freedom to call functionality either in our image framework or from image delegates, depending on the application requirements. Many applications need to call both kinds of functions, depending upon such issues as the availability of image delegate run-time libraries, performance requirements, or accuracy requirements.

You can extend our loosely coupled design to create a framework, using inheritance, that enables the libraries to work efficiently together. Your application's framework may look similar to the following:

```
class Image
{
public:
  virtual void create (unsigned int width, unsigned int height);

  virtual Image laplacian3x3 ();

protected:
  apImage<Pel8> image_;
};
```

We have left out most details, but the idea is to create a wrapper object that manages a specific type of **apImage<>** (in this case, it is an 8-bit monochrome image). You can place whatever processing support you need in this object, or you can create a number of separate functions to add this functionality. These functions are all **virtual** functions, allowing derived classes to override their behavior as needed.

To handle the specifics of a third-party framework, such as the IPP, you create a derived object like **IPP_Image**, as shown:

```
class IPP_Image : public Image
{
public:
  virtual void create (unsigned int width, unsigned int height);

  virtual Image laplacian3x3 ();

protected:
  apIPP<Pel8> ipp_;
};
```

The derived object, **IPP_Image** in this example, can be very selective in what functions it overrides, and in what contraints it chooses to enforce. Your application will use **Image** when functionality from **apImage<>** is desired, and it will use **IPP_Image** when functionality from both **apImage<>** and the image delegate (IPP in this case) is needed.

Our Recommended Strategy

During our design phase, we spent a long time analyzing our image framework to determine whether or not to build hooks for third-party image processing packages. We explored a fully integrated design that was very similar to how we handled file delegates. There were many issues that arose from our design efforts, and we highlighted a few of them in the section *Strategy 1: A Fully Integrated Solution* on page 238. This design proved difficult to manage, and required extensive changes that rendered the use of image delegates more like a built-in feature instead of its intended purpose as an extension.

Based on the issues that arose, we decided that the fully integrated design was unsuitable. We explored a second strategy in the section *Strategy 2: A Loosely Coupled Solution* on page 239, which provided a loosely coupled connection between our framework and a third-party library (in this case, the Intel IPP). We found this to be a successful strategy that not only allowed us to build a general purpose framework, but also gave us the ability to provide additional tools, through a third-party libary, that are necessary for building robust applications.

6.5 Summary

In this chapter, we finalized the design and implementation of the image class, the global image functions, and the third-party interfaces (also called delegates). We showed many examples where methods could also be implemented to leverage generic STL algorithms, in addition to using those supplied with the image framework. We also made extensive use of templates to define the constructs needed by our final image class, including clamping data types to prevent overflows. This required an exception-safe locking mechanism, which we fully discussed.

When we described global image processing functions, we provided a brief overview of the algorithms, and then showed concrete implementations to support the algorithms. We also provided visual feedback of the original image and the subsequently filtered image, letting you decide the usefulness of any particular operation.

Finally, we discussed the appropriate design for integrating third-party software libraries with the image framework. We showed a file delegate for supporting other file types, such as JPEG or TIFF, and we showed an image delegate for supporting third-party image processing libraries (Intel IPP, in our example). In addition to providing coding examples, this section compared alternative techniques of using third-party software packages, and contrasted their effects on implementation and future expandability.

In Chapter 7, we proceed to create a unit test framework to ensure the accuracy of the global imaging functions you are now able to add. We also discuss specific techniques, showing coding examples of each, for improving the performance of your code.

IN THIS CHAPTER

C++ Concepts
Performance Tuning
Macros
Timing Your Code
Real-Time Performance Issues
GUI Considerations

Image Framework Concepts
Unit Test Framework

7

Testing and Performance

No software development effort is complete until you do some testing and performance tuning. This chapter provides guidelines for unit tests and creates a framework for automatically running them. In addition, we provide thirteen specific techniques that you can apply to your code to optimize performance.

7.1 Unit Tests

Unit tests are small pieces of software that test specific conditions in your source code. Typically, it is the developer's responsibility to write and maintain unit tests. Unit tests are often used to test such conditions as boundaries, unusual data types, interfaces between components, and any complex operation that needs to be continually verified as the software changes. Unit tests should be run regularly as the software is being built. Each development team uses their own methodology for building software. We recommend that the following simple rules be applied for working with unit tests:

■ Any piece of code checked into the main code base must have a corresponding unit test.

■ Code cannot be checked into the main code base until it passes its unit tests.

■ Unit tests should be kept current, being updated as the code is updated.

■ Unit tests should be part of a framework that runs regularly (every night, every week, and so on) and reports meaningful results.

A unit test can be something as simple as:

```
int main()
{
    ... test some stuff
  return 0;
}
```

A simple framework can lend organization to your unit test strategy. We include a unit test framework with the following features:

- Each piece of functionality can be placed in a separate test function so it can be tested in isolation. New tests can be added by simply creating a new function.

- A few simple macros are included that make it easy to verify certain conditions and report any that are not correct.

- All exceptions are caught and reported as errors.

7.1.1 Using the Unit Test Framework

This section provides an overview of how you use the unit test framework that we provide.

1. Write one or more unit test functions using the functionality provided:

`UTFUNC()`	Creates a unit test function of the specified name and adds the function name to the list of functions to run. `UTFUNC()` actually creates a small object, but this detail is hidden.
`setDescription()`	Specifies what the unit test does. This string is displayed when the test is run.
`VERIFY()`	Verifies that a specified condition is true. If the condition is true, nothing is output. If the condition is false, an error is generated and the specified condition is displayed as the message when this function is run.

2. Run the unit test functions. The execution time is computed and any exceptions are caught. If a unit test has no `VERIFY()` statements, the result is set to `eUnknown`. If an exception is thrown, the unit test result is set to `eFailure`. Possible results for unit tests are as follows:

`eNotRun`	The default state if the unit test has not been run.
`eRunning`	The unit test is currently running.
`eUnknown`	A unit test that has no `VERIFY()` statements is labeled as unknown.
`eSuccess`	The unit test had no failures.
`eFailure`	The unit test had one or more failures.

3. Use `main()` to call `apUnitTest::gOnly().run()`, which runs all of the unit tests in the framework object. The results are then written to the console (or other stream). `main()` also returns the cumulative state of the unit test framework object as `0` if there are any failures or unknowns, or as `1` if there are only successes.

► **EXAMPLE** ───

We have written unit tests for almost every component we present in this book. All unit tests are included on the CD-ROM. Here, we use one of the **apBString** unit tests as an example:

```
UTFUNC(Pel8)
{
    setDescription ("Pel8 tests");

    Pel8 b;
    Pel16 w;
    Pel32 l;
    Pel32s ls;
    float f;
    double d;
    std::string s;

    apBString bstr;
    bstr << (Pel8) 123;

    bstr >> b;  bstr.rewind ();
    bstr >> w;  bstr.rewind ();
    bstr >> l;  bstr.rewind ();
    bstr >> ls; bstr.rewind ();
    bstr >> f;  bstr.rewind ();
    bstr >> d;  bstr.rewind ();
    bstr >> s;  bstr.rewind ();

    VERIFY (b == 123);
    VERIFY (w == 123);
    VERIFY (l == 123);
    VERIFY (ls== 123);
    VERIFY (f == 123);
    VERIFY (d == 123);
    VERIFY (s.compare ("123") == 0);

    bstr >> b;
    VERIFY (bstr.eof());
}
```

This function tests that a byte can be written to the binary string and then read back in multiple formats, to verify that the conversions were made correctly.

───◄

You can use the provided framework to write your own unit tests. Our framework encourages you to write a number of small, isolated tests instead of a large complex test. We strongly recommend that you test as much as possible in your unit tests, as we demonstrate in the following portion of the **apRect** unit test:

```
UTFUNC(rect)
{
    setDescription ("Rect");

    apRect rect (0, 1, 2, 3);
    VERIFY (rect.x0() == 0);
    VERIFY (rect.y0() == 1);
    VERIFY (rect.width() == 2);
```

```
      VERIFY (rect.height() == 3);
      ...
  }
```

This function is testing trivial inline functions and the **apRect** constructor. Do not assume that this simply works, or that other test functions will indirectly test these member functions. You should test these functions directly. Here is the unit test for the **apRect** default constructor:

```
UTFUNC(defaultctor)
{
  setDescription ("default ctor");

  apRect rect;
  VERIFY (rect.x0() == 0);
  VERIFY (rect.y0() == 0);
  VERIFY (rect.width() == 0);
  VERIFY (rect.height() == 0);
  ...
}
```

Your unit test file contains one or more **UTFUNC()** functions as well as a **main()** function. If you want to include any custom pre- or post-processing, you can do so, as follows:

```
int main()
{
  // Add any pre-processing here
  bool state = apUnitTest::gOnly().run ();
  // Add any post-processing here
  apUnitTest::gOnly().dumpResults (std::cout);
  return state;
}
```

apUnitTest is a Singleton object that contains a list of all unit tests to run. The results for each unit test are stored internally and can be displayed when **dumpResults()** is called. Unit test functions should not generate any output on their own, unless that is the point of the test. Any extra input/output can skew the execution time measurements.

7.1.2 Design of the Unit Test Framework

Figure 7.1 illustrates the overall design of the unit test framework.

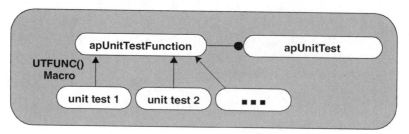

Figure 7.1: Unit Test Framework Design

There is a base class, **apUnitTestFunction**, from which unit tests are derived using the **UTFUNC()** macro. There is a unit test framework object, **apUnitTest**, that maintains a list of all the unit tests, runs them, and displays the results. Each of these components is described in this section.

apUnitTestFunction Base Class

Each unit test is derived from the **apUnitTestFunction** base class using the **UTFUNC()** macro. The complete **apUnitTestFunction** base class is shown below.

```
class apUnitTestFunction
{
public:
  apUnitTestFunction (const std::string& name);

  enum eResult {eNotRun, eRunning, eUnknown, eSuccess, eFailure};

  const std::string& name        () const { return name_;}
  eResult            result      () const { return result_;}
  double             elapsed     () const { return elapsed_;}
  const std::string& message     () const { return message_;}
  const std::string& description () const
  { return description_;}
  std::string        resultString () const;

  void setDescription (const std::string& s) { description_ = s;}

  void run (bool verbose = false);
  // Run this unit test. Called by the unit test framework
protected:
  virtual void test() = 0;
  // All unit tests define this function to perform a single test

  bool verify (bool state, const std::string& message="");
  // Fails test if state is false. Used by VERIFY() macro

  void addMessage (const std::string& message);
  // Adds the message string to our messages

  bool        verbose_;     // true for verbose output

  eResult     result_;      // Result of this unit test
  std::string name_;        // Unit test name (must be unique)
  std::string description_; // Description of function
  std::string message_;     // Message, usual a failure message
  double      elapsed_;     // Execution time, in seconds
};
```

The **run()** method runs a single unit test, measures its execution time, creates a catch handler to deal with any unexpected exceptions, and determines the result. Note that the actual unit test is defined within the **test()** method.

The implementation of the **run()** method is shown here.

```
void apUnitTestFunction::run ()
{
  std::string error;

  apElapsedTime time;
```

```
    try {
      test ();
    }
    catch (const std::exception& ex) {
      // We caught an STL exception
      error = std::string("Exception '") + ex.what() + "' caught";
      addMessage (error);
      result_ = eFailure;
    }
    catch (...) {
      // We caught an unknown exception
      error = "Unknown exception caught";
      addMessage (error);
      result_ = eFailure;
    }
    elapsed_ = time.sec ();

    // Make sure the test() function set a result or set eUnknown
    if (result_ != eSuccess && result_ != eFailure)
      result_ = eUnknown;
  }
```

Note that the source code also includes a verbose mode to display immediate results, which we have removed for the sake of brevity.

apUnitTest Object

Our unit test framework object, **apUnitTestObject**, maintains a list of unit tests, runs all of the unit tests in order, and displays the results of those tests. Its definition is shown here.

```
class apUnitTest
{
public:
  static apUnitTest& gOnly ();

  bool run (bool verbose = false);
  // Run all the unit tests. Returns true if all tests are ok

  void dumpResults (std::ostream& out);
  // Dump results to specified stream

  int size () const { return static_cast<int>(tests_.size());}
  const apUnitTestFunction* retrieve (int index) const;
  // Retrieves the specific test, or NULL if invalid index

  void addTest (const std::string& name,
                apUnitTestFunction* test);
  // Used by our macro to add another unit test

private:
  apUnitTest ();
  static apUnitTest* sOnly_;  // Points to our only instance

  std::vector<apUnitTestFunction*> tests_; // Array of tests
};
```

A **std::vector** maintains our list of unit tests. The **run()** method steps through the list, in order, and executes all the unit tests, as shown.

```
bool apUnitTest::run ()
{
  bool state = true;

  for (unsigned int i=0; i<tests_.size(); i++) {
    apUnitTestFunction* test = tests_[i];
    test->run ();
    if (test->result() != apUnitTestFunction::eSuccess)
      state = false;
  }
  return state;
}
```

▶ EXAMPLE

In this example, we look at the output for the **apBString** unit test. (Note that we include the complete source code for the **apBString** unit test on the CD-ROM.) Running the unit test produces the following output:

```
Unit Test started at  Thu Jul 04 23:39:46 2002

Unit Test finished at Thu Jul 04 23:39:46 2002

Test 1: Success : ctor : Constructor and simple accessor tests: 0 sec
Test 2: Success : Pel8 : Pel8 tests : 0 sec
Test 3: Success : Pel16 : Pel16 tests : 0 sec
Test 4: Success : Pel32 : Pel32 tests : 0 sec
Test 5: Success : Pel32s : Pel32s tests : 0 sec
Test 6: Success : float : float tests : 0 sec
Test 7: Success : double : double tests : 0 sec
Test 8: Success : string : string tests : 0 sec
Test 9: Success : eof : eof tests : 0 sec
Test 10: Success : data : data tests : 0 sec
Test 11: Success : bstr : bstr tests : 0 sec
Test 12: Success : dump : dump tests : 0 sec
Test 13: Success : point : point tests : 0 sec
Test 14: Success : rect : rect tests : 0 sec

Passed: 14, Failed: 0, Other: 0
```

The execution times are all reported as **0** because each test is very simple. This unit test framework is portable across many platforms and the results are similar on each platform.

We can simulate a failure by adding a simple unit test function to our framework, as shown:

```
UTFUNC (failing)
{
  setDescription ("Always will fail");
  VERIFY (1 == 2);
}
```

The output would include these additional lines:

```
Test 15: ***** Failure ***** : failing : Always will fail : 0 sec
  Messages:
1 == 2

Passed: 14, Failed: 1, Other: 0
```

Notice that the conditional is included as part of the failure message.

Macros in the Unit Test Framework

The unit test framework uses two macros: **UTFUNC()** and **VERIFY()**. In general, we tend to avoid macros; however, they are very useful in our unit test framework. Figure 7.2 provides a quick overview of the syntax used in macros.

Macro Syntax

- Begins with #**define** and looks somewhat like a function definition. Any arguments are listed between parentheses.

- Requires a continuation character, \, on every line except the last of a multi-line macro. A macro ends when it sees the first newline character, **\n**.

- Uses **##** as a merging operator to combine the information on either side of the operator. For example: **a##b = ab**.

- Uses **#** as the stringization operator to convert an argument into a string. For example: **#a = "teststring"**.

Figure 7.2: Overview of Macro Syntax

Note that parameters used in macros are not checked for syntax; rather, they are treated as plain text. Parameters can contain anything, even unbalanced braces. This can result in very obscure error messages that are difficult to resolve.

The **UTFUNC()** macro creates a unit test function of the specified name by deriving an object from the **apUnitTestFunction** base class. **UTFUNC()** is defined as follows:

```
#define UTFUNC(utx)                                    \
class UT##utx : public apUnitTestFunction             \
{                                                      \
UT##utx ();                                            \
static UT##utx sInstance;                              \
void test ();                                          \
};                                                     \
UT##utx UT##utx::sInstance;                            \
UT##utx::UT##utx () : apUnitTestFunction(#utx)        \
{                                                      \
   apUnitTest::gOnly().addTest(#utx,this);            \
}                                                      \
void UT##utx::test ()
```

For example, the preprocessor expands the **UTFUNC(rect)** macro into the following code:

```
class UTrect : public apUnitTestFunction
{
UTrect ();
static UTrect sInstance;
void test ();
```

```
};
UTrect UTrect::sInstance;
UTrect::UTrect () : apUnitTestFunction("rect")
{
   apUnitTest::gOnly().addTest("rect",this);
}
void UTrect::test ()
```

Every unit test function creates a new object with one static instance. These objects are constructed during static initialization, and automatically call **addTest()** to add themselves to the list of unit test functions to be run. Note that the last line of the expanded macro is the **test()** method, and your unit function becomes its definition.

The **VERIFY()** macro is much simpler than **UTFUNC()**. It verifies that a specified condition is true. Its definition is as follows:

```
#define VERIFY(condition) verify (condition, #condition)
```

Let's look at the following example:

```
VERIFY (rect.x0() == 0);
```

The preprocessor expands this macro into the following code:

```
verify(rect.x0() == 0, "rect.x0() == 0");
```

The **VERIFY()** macro calls a **verify()** method that is defined in the **apUnitTestFunction** base class, as shown.

```
bool apUnitTestFunction::verify (bool state,
                                const std::string& message)
{
  if (!state) {
    result_ = eFailure;
    addMessage (message);
    if (verbose_)
      std::cout << " FAILURE " << name_.c_str() << " : "
                << message.c_str() << std::endl;
  }
  else if (result_ != eFailure)
    // Make sure we mark the unit test success, if possible.
    result_ = eSuccess;
  return state;
}
```

state is the result of the conditional expression. If the result is **false**, a failure message, including the string of the conditional, is written to an internal log. This failure message is displayed after all of the unit tests have been run.

setDescription() is a method that lets you include more descriptive information about the test. It is very useful if you have a number of tests and wish to clarify what they do.

7.1.3 Extending the Unit Test Framework

The unit test framework that we have included is only a beginning of a complete solution. We recommend using this framework as a basis to construct a fully automated unit test framework that runs unit tests at regular intervals, such as each night. An automated framework would do the following:

■ Obtain the most recent sources for your application. This involves obtaining a copy of the sources from whatever configuration management package you use.

■ Compile and build any intermediate libraries.

■ Compile each unit test.

■ Execute all unit tests, capture the results, and record which unit tests fail.

■ Generate a report, including a summary or detailed information about the tests.

■ Email the report to the appropriate software developers and engineers.

Our experience is that at least half of all unit test failures are not actually failures in the objects being tested. Failures tend to occur when an object has been modified, but the unit test lags behind.

  When updating your code, update the unit test at the same time.

7.2 Performance Tuning

Writing efficient code is something of an art. Efficiency is not about rewriting your application in assembly code or anything that drastic. Efficiency is about writing software that meets whatever design criteria you set for it. If a design specification states that an application should "run as fast as possible," you need to rewrite the specification. It is far better to say that particular operations need to execute in a specific amount of time (on a specific platform). For many applications, especially image processing ones, performance is a very important issue. However, it is surprising how many design documents do not address performance in a concrete way.

Let's look at it another way. If you want to train to become a sprinter, you know that you need to run very fast for a relatively short period of time. If you were to write a list of goals for yourself, would you include a statement that says you should "run as fast as possible"? Of course you wouldn't. You would probably say that you need to be able to run a certain distance in a certain amount of time. And based on this goal, you can set up a training program to meet it.

Writing software is no different. You need to have plausible goals and then you can design a plan to reach them. Your goals can be difficult, but not impossible, to achieve. Sometimes a goal may seem impossible, but further investigation reveals it is actually possible, though extremely challenging. Having a goal that is well defined is absolutely essential for getting the performance you need from your application. See [Bulka99] for useful information on writing efficient C++ code.

7.2.1 General Guidelines

It is not always easy to decide when you need to worry about performance. Our recommendation is to assume that a piece of software does not have any special performance criteria unless you know this statement to be false. Avoid writing a highly optimized piece of software to solve a timing problem that may not even be a problem. It is better to design a reasonable solution first, and then discover that it must run faster. This iterative approach to design helps you reduce development time and wasted effort. It is true that you can have cases where your product does not meet the expectations of its testers on the first iteration, but this is what an iterative design approach is all about. The product design specification needs to be as clear as possible regarding the desired functionality and performance of the application.

For example, let us look at how a customer interacts with a graphical user interface (GUI). We see that the overhead of the framework and the way you write your code often has little effect on performance. The customer communicates with the software by making various requests in the form of mouse or other pointer manipulation or keyboard input. For complicated interfaces, these requests occur at no more than one request per second. The steps that the software takes to process such a request can be listed as a series of events:

1. Receive the event.

2. Invoke the event handler responsible for the event.

3. Process the event.

4. Update the user interface.

If the customer generates events at the rate of one request per second, then this sequence of events, including updating the user interface, must happen in no more than half that time. Where did this number, .5 seconds, come from? It is simply a guess based upon our perception of how customers operate such systems.

Now, without worrying about specific operating systems or GUI implementations, we can make some assumptions about how long it takes to handle each of the above steps. Receiving and invoking an event handler is a fast operation, even when written in a general purpose C++ framework. This step comprises a number of table lookups, as well as one or more virtual function calls to locate the owner of an event. It certainly does not consume a lot of time. Processing the event is strictly an application-specific task, as is updating the user interface. The amount of overhead that can be tolerated in this example is fairly large. The customer will have a very hard time distinguishing between one millisecond and 50 milliseconds.

As a contrasting example, let's look at a real-time system that has hard performance requirements. As opposed to the previous example, where there is a person waiting to see results updated on the screen, these results are needed in a certain period of time, or else the information is useless. The framework's overhead, as well as how the processing is written, is important. However, it is not so obvious how much overhead is acceptable.

We have found that dealing with percentages makes it easier to gauge how overhead can be tolerated. If your processing function does not spend 98 to 99 percent of its time doing actual work, you should examine your design more closely. For example, for very fast processing cycles, say five milliseconds, the framework overhead should be kept to less than 100 microseconds. For slower real-time systems that require about 50 milliseconds to execute, overhead should be less than one millisecond. The design of each of these systems will be very different.

To measure overhead for an image processing system, or other system that performs a repeated calculation on a number of samples, it is customary to compute the overhead on a per row or per pixel basis. Let us assume that we must perform one or more image processing steps on a 512x512 pixel image. If we want to keep the total overhead to one millisecond, the per-row overhead can be no more than two microseconds. Two microseconds is quite a bit of time for modern processors, and this permits numerous pointer manipulations or iterator updates. We are not so lucky if we have a goal of only two-tenths of a microsecond per row. In this case, you should consider optimizing your code from the onset of the design.

If you find this calculation too simplistic for your taste, you can write some simple prototypes to measure the actual performance on your platform and decide if any code optimization is needed. Since many image processing functions are easy to write, you can get a sense for how much time the operation takes. Our unit test framework is a convenient starting point, since the framework computes and reports the execution time of each unit test function. To get started, you would need to write at least two functions. The first function would contain the complete operation you want to test. The second function would contain just the overhead components. The execution time of the first test function tells us how long the image processing takes, while the second tells us if the overhead itself is significant. If our unit test framework was more complicated than it is, we would also need a third function to measure the overhead of the unit test framework itself. But, since the framework is so simple, its overhead is negligible.

7.2.2 Thirteen Ways to Improve Performance

Without getting specific about the dynamics of your application, we offer thirteen techniques that you can use to improve the overall performance of your software.

Performance Checklist

✔ **Measure performance with release builds and not debugging builds.**

✔ **Compute only those items that you need.**

✔ **Compute or fetch items only once.**

✔ **Use integer instead of floating point when possible.**

✔ **Know the objects being used in time-critical code, especially copy constructors and assignment operators.**

✔ **Remove all debugging and log-generating code from your time-critical code once it is fully debugged.**

✔ **Deliver release versions of your software internally as early as possible.**

✔ **Avoid excessive operations with heavyweight objects, like the standard library string class.**

✔ **Precompute quantities to speed up run-time calculations.**

✔ **Avoid system calls and heap allocations in time-critical sections of code.**

✔ **Minimize locks in time-critical sections of code.**

✔ **Develop an efficient algorithm that works correctly before you start fine tuning your code. Use unit tests to ensure that tuning hasn't broken anything.**

✔ **Use a profiler to find out where the biggest performance problems are before doing a lot of small optimizations.**

Figure 7.3: Performance Checklist

Each of these techniques is described in more detail in this section.

■ Measure performance with release builds, not debugging builds. Debug builds usually have more overhead from the optimizations that are employed, the maintaining of debugging symbols, and the code intended only for debugging. The difference in execution time between release and debug builds can be enormous. For compilers, such as Microsoft Developer Studio, switching between either type of build is easy. For UNIX makefiles, make sure that debugging symbols are excluded and that optimizations are enabled.

- Compute only those items that you need, especially in functions that take a long time to execute or are called frequently by your application. It is very common to write a function with the desire to be complete. If you find that certain functions are returning quantities that are never used, you should investigate whether these quantities are needed at all.

  For example, suppose you have a function that computes the mean and standard deviation of a number of samples. If you always find yourself throwing out the standard deviation value, then you have to ask yourself why you are computing it. There is no reason why you cannot have two similar functions: one that computes just the mean of a sample set, and another that computes the mean and standard deviation.

- Compute or fetch items only once. It is better to explicitly use a local variable in your function than to assume your compiler can divine which quantities are invariant. For example:

```
for (unsigned int y=0; y<image.height(); y++)
  for (unsigned int x=0; x<image.width(); x++)
    // ...
```

  In this example, the **height()** member is called once for every row in the image. **width()** is called for every pixel in the image. In this particular example, **height()** is a simple inline method, but this is not always the case. If you are concerned about performance, you can rewrite this loop as:

```
unsigned int h = image.height ();
unsigned int w = image.width ();
for (unsigned int y=0; y<h; y++)
  for (unsigned int x=0; x<w; x++)
    // ...
```

  In this loop, we call **width()** and **height()** only once and save their value in a variable. Most of our performance improvement comes from saving the width variable, but it is good programming practice to write symmetrical code and save both. You may be surprised at how a series of these savings can affect the overall performance.

- Use integers instead of floating point when possible. This used to be much more important than it is now, but many microprocessors have more integer registers than floating point ones, and they can be used in many more ways. On embedded platforms, you might also consider using the smallest integer format possible.

  For example, if you need to sum all the pixels in an image row, you might be able to use an **unsigned short** instead of an **unsigned int**. In our own development projects, we usually consider the size of most variables and use one of a sufficient size, but no larger. As an aside, we ignore this rule for counter variables and just use an **int** or **unsigned int**.

- Know and understand the objects you are using in time-critical code. For example, you don't want a copy constructor or assignment operator to take the bulk of the processing time. If objects are anything other than very simple, try using references (**const** if possible) or pointers to avoid copies. This is not a big concern with our `apImage<>` object because it takes advantage of reference counting.

- Remove all debugging and log generation code from time critical code, once you have it debugged. Otherwise, make sure you use `#if` to compile this code only for debug builds.

- Deliver release versions of your application internally as early as possible. Internal users can provide valuable feedback to you regarding performance of which you may not be aware. There's nothing like a real user banging on the system to bring performance issues to light.

- Avoid excessive operations with heavyweight objects, like the standard library string class. Many operations, like searching a large string for a substring, should be called as few times as possible. For example, if you are parsing through a large string, keep track of the last index where you found a match, so that you only need to search from that point in the string.

- Precompute quantities to speed up run-time calculations. This can be as simple as precomputing quantities to improve loop performance, to caching values that remain invariant for longer periods of time. We'll use a very obvious example to demonstrate this technique. Image rotation is a common image processing function that can be implemented in a variety of ways. If you use a brute force method, the processing loop to rotate the image on a pixel-by-pixel basis looks something like this:

```
for (unsigned int y=0; y<image.height(); y++)
  for (unsigned int x=0; x<image.width(); x++) {
    double xprime = cos(angle) * x - sin(angle) * y;
    double yprime = sin(angle) * x + cos(angle) * y;
    // ...
  }
```

We can easily compute the constant values outside of the loop and considerably improve run-time performance with code similar to this:

```
double sine   = sin(angle);
double cosine = cos(angle);
double xprime, yprime;
for (unsigned int y=0; y<image.height(); y++)
  for (unsigned int x=0; x<image.width(); x++) {
    xprime = cosine * x - sine   * y;
    yprime = sine   * x + cosine * y;
    // ...
  }
```

- Avoid system calls and heap allocations in time-critical sections of code. Wherever possible, pre-allocate the memory needed by your routine, since heap allocation is a highly variable process. Defer calls to third-party and operating system functions if they are such that they may take a long time to execute.

- Minimize locks in time-critical sections of code. The process of locking is fast only if no one currently owns the lock. A section of code can potentially wait forever before it acquires the lock.

■ Develop an efficient algorithm that works correctly before you start fine tuning your code. Use unit tests to ensure that the tuning hasn't broken anything. There are many ways to solve the same problem. You may find that optimizing a poorly designed, well-implemented algorithm will never be as efficient as a well-designed, poorly implemented algorithm.

■ Use a profiler to find out where the biggest performance problems are before doing a lot of small optimizations. Often 90 percent of the execution time for an operation takes place in only 10 percent of the code. Make sure you are spending your time optimizing the right section of code.

7.2.3 Image-Specific Improvements

Image processing algorithms can be optimized in many ways because of their symmetry. To demonstrate this, we'll start with a simple function that computes the sum of all pixels in an image and optimize it in a number of iterations.

❖ SLOW

The easiest way to write this, and probably the slowest, is:

```
UTFUNC(slow)
{
   setDescription ("Slow version");

   apRect boundary (0, 0, 512, 512);
   apImage<Pel8> byteImage (boundary);
   byteImage.set (1);

   unsigned int sum = 0;

   for (unsigned int y=0; y<byteImage.height(); y++) {
       for (unsigned int x=0; x<byteImage.width(); x++) {
       sum += byteImage.getPixel (x, y);
     }
   }

   VERIFY (true);   // So this test will pass
}
```

We can rewrite this to take advantage of our iterators. Because this version runs so quickly, we have to run it multiple times to get reported execution times greater than zero.

❖ ORIGINAL

The rewritten function is as follows:

```
UTFUNC(original)
{
   setDescription ("Original version, sum all pixels");

   apRect boundary (0, 0, 512, 512);
   apImage<Pel8> byteImage (boundary);
   byteImage.set (1);

   // Run many times to get an accurate measurement
   for (int iterations=0; iterations<1000; iterations++) {
```

```
        unsigned int sum = 0;

        apImage<Pel8>::row_iterator i;
        for (i=byteImage.row_begin(); i != byteImage.row_end(); i++) {
          const Pel8* p = i->p;
          for (unsigned int x=0; x<byteImage.width(); x++) {
            sum += *p++;
          }
        }
      }

    VERIFY (true);   // So this test will pass
  }
```

❖ OVERHEAD

Now, we rewrite the **original** function, so that it has the same setup, but performs no image processing, in order to measure overhead. Note that we perform one trivial operation per row, to make sure that the compiler doesn't optimize the loop for us.

```
    UTFUNC(overhead)
    {
      setDescription ("Overhead version, sum all pixels");

      apRect boundary (0, 0, 512, 512);
      apImage<Pel8> byteImage (boundary);
      byteImage.set (1);

      for (int iterations=0; iterations<1000; iterations++) {
        unsigned int dummy = 0;

        apImage<Pel8>::row_iterator i;
        for (i=byteImage.row_begin(); i != byteImage.row_end(); i++) {
          const Pel8* p = i->p;
          dummy += *p++; // Prevents compiler optimization of loop
        }
      }
      VERIFY (true);   // So this test will pass
    }
```

The execution time of **original** includes the execution time of the unit test framework, as well as the actual image processing operation. The execution time of **overhead** also includes the unit test framework overhead, but only includes the overhead portion of the image processing operation, and not the actual time required for the operation. If the overhead of the unit test framework is significant, then we need a third function that measures the overhead of the unit test framework. Because our framework has very low overhead, we can skip this third test.

❖ ORIGINAL_WIDTH

Let's further optimize the function by removing **width()** from the loop and placing it into a local variable, as shown.

```
    UTFUNC(original_width)
    {
      setDescription ("Original version with width()");

      apRect boundary (0, 0, 512, 512);
```

```
    apImage<Pel8> byteImage (boundary);
    byteImage.set (1);

    for (int iterations=0; iterations<1000; iterations++) {
      unsigned int sum = 0;
      unsigned int w = byteImage.width();

      apImage<Pel8>::row_iterator i;
      for (i=byteImage.row_begin(); i!=byteImage.row_end(); i++) {
        Pel8* p = i->p;
        for (unsigned int x=0; x<w; x++) {
          sum += *p++;
        }
      }
    }
    VERIFY (true);   // So this test will pass
  }
```

Let's do one more optimization.

❖ ORIGINAL_UNROLLED

We can do some basic loop unrolling by expanding the inner loop, so that multiple pixels are handled in each iteration, as shown.

```
    UTFUNC(original_unrolled)
    {
      setDescription ("Original version with unrolling optimization");

      apRect boundary (0, 0, 512, 512);
      apImage<Pel8> byteImage (boundary);
      byteImage.set (1);

      for (int iterations=0; iterations<1000; iterations++) {
        unsigned int sum = 0;
        unsigned int w = byteImage.width() / 8;

        apImage<Pel8>::row_iterator i;
        for (i=byteImage.row_begin(); i!=byteImage.row_end(); i++) {
          Pel8* p = i->p;
          for (unsigned int x=0; x<w; x++) {
            sum += *p++;
            sum += *p++;
            sum += *p++;
            sum += *p++;
            sum += *p++;
            sum += *p++;
            sum += *p++;
            sum += *p++;
          }
        }
      }
      VERIFY (true);   // So this test will pass
    }
```

As written, this version works for images whose width are multiples of eight pixels. Extending this to work with an arbitrary pixel value would not be difficult.

Execution Results

We ran these tests using Microsoft Visual Studio 7.0 on an Intel Pentium 4 processor-based machine, running at 2.0 GHz. Table 7.1 shows the times for a single iteration. The actual times are lower than this, because we shut off optimization to prevent the compiler from optimizing the loops.

Table 7.1: Performance Test Results

Test	Execution Time
slow	156 milliseconds
original	1.33 milliseconds
original_width	1.23 milliseconds
original_unrolled	1.03 milliseconds

Comparing the **original** version to **original_unrolled** shows over a 20 percent decrease in execution time. This is a significant gain for such a simple function. However, the inner loop for most image processing functions is more complicated. We measured the overhead of executing the loops and found it to be 0.03 milliseconds, or about 3 percent of our most optimized example.

Let's look at some of the execution times for our existing image processing functions. Table 7.2 shows the execution times for a Laplacian filter running on a 1024x1024 8-bit monochrome image.

Table 7.2: Image Processing Test Results

Test	Execution Time
convolve()	89 milliseconds
laplacian3x3()	51 milliseconds
Intel IPP	4 milliseconds

convolve() is our general-purpose convolution routine that contains a number of nested loops and fetches the kernel values from an array, resulting in the longest execution time. **laplacian3x3()** only has two loops, because it uses hard-coded statements to compute the output value for each pixel in the image, and this reduces the execution time significantly. The **Intel IPP** routine directly uses the power of the Intel Pentium 4 processor to achieve the fastest execution time.

7.2.4 A Note About Timing Your Code

Measuring the execution time of critical sections of your code is not always a simple task, especially if you want to establish the worse-case execution time. In our previous examples, we measured the average time, because we ran a number of iterations, and then divided the total execution time by the number of iterations. Here are some of the reasons why this value will not be the worst case:

■   You really need to measure the slowest code path in your code to get the worst case time. Our filter example is very simple, yet it has several possible code paths. For example, you should let the filter function determine the size and allocate the destination image. Likewise, if you are using a clamped pixel type, you should test your filter so that every pixel in the image causes an overflow.

■   Multithreaded and multiprocess designs "steal" processor time from the code you are trying to measure. If these threads or processes are not part of the actual application, you should test your function in isolation. If you are utilizing other threads or processes in your design, you won't be able to get actual worst-case values until you simulate these conditions in your unit test. You will also need to compute the execution time of each iteration and store the worst case value.

■   Interrupt service routines should also be considered if you are working with an embedded system that has more than simple interrupt routines. Like we mentioned above, you will need to measure the worst case execution time by simulating the actual conditions.

The timing routines defined in **time.h** provide standard, but very coarse, measurements of elapsed time. Most platforms include higher resolution facilities to measure time, and if you are designing for a single platform, we encourage you to take advantage of them. For example, under Microsoft Windows, you can take advantage of timers that provide sub-microsecond resolution. Instead of using this functionality directly (**QueryPerformanceCounter**), you should create a generic wrapper object and reuse the interface on other platforms, as shown.

```
class apHiResElapsedTime
{
public:
  apHiResElapsedTime ();
  // Record the current time

  double usec () const; // Return elapsed time, in microseconds.
  double msec () const; // Return elapsed time, in milliseconds.
  double sec  () const; // Return elapsed time, in seconds

  void reset ();
  // Reset the current time

private:
  LONGLONG starting_;      // Starting time
};

apHiResElapsedTime::apHiResElapsedTime () : starting_ (0)
{ reset ();}
```

```
double apHiResElapsedTime::sec () const
{
  LARGE_INTEGER t, freq;
  QueryPerformanceCounter (&t);
  QueryPerformanceFrequency (&freq);

  return (double(t.QuadPart - starting_)) / freq.QuadPart;
}

void apHiResElapsedTime::reset ()
{
  LARGE_INTEGER t;
  QueryPerformanceCounter (&t);

  starting_ = t.QuadPart;
}
```

7.3 Summary

In this chapter, we provide a practical strategy for integrating unit tests into your software development cycle. We design a complete unit test framework, providing the details on why certain C++ constructs were used in the implementation. We provide guidelines for extending the framework to work in your software development environment. We also include a short primer on macros, as the implementation of the unit test framework relies on two macros.

We also focus on performance issues, both in the context of soft performance constraints (of typical applications) and hard performance constraints (of real-time systems). We detail specific techniques, providing a checklist on page 261, that you should consider in any domain to improve the run-time performance.

In Chapter 8, we explore those topics that we felt warranted more detailed discussion than we could provide at the time they were introduced in the book. These topics include: copy on write, caching, **explicit** keyword usage, **const**, and pass by reference. We also include a section on extending the image framework with your own processing functions. Because we thought it might be of interest, we've highlighted some routines that work particularly well for enhancing your digital photographs.

8

Advanced Topics

In this chapter, we explore topics that we touched on earlier, but strongly warrant further discussion. In addition to going into detail about specific C++ constructs, we discuss ways that our image processing framework can be extended.

8.1 Memory Issues

As we have seen, memory management is extremely important when dealing with images. Even in cases where image buffers are already allocated, inefficient use of memory can cause heap fragmentation that can only lead to problems. This is especially true for embedded systems, because restarting an application or rebooting the system is not an option. In this section, we discuss numerous memory issues and look at ways to improve performance and reliability.

8.1.1 Copy on Write

The `apAlloc<>` class we introduced in Chapter 3 uses reference counting to allow multiple objects to share the same underlying memory. This class has a `duplicate()` method that forces the object to have its own copy of the data. `duplicate()` does nothing if the buffer is not shared (i.e., the reference count is `1`). Consider the following example:

```
apAlloc<unsigned char> buffer1 (100000);
...
apAlloc<unsigned char> buffer2 = buffer1;
buffer2[0] = 0;
```

Objects `buffer1` and `buffer2` share the same underlying memory. What if we want to change `buffer2` without affecting `buffer1`? We can manually do this by changing the last lines of the previous example to be as follows:

```
buffer2.duplicate ();
buffer2[0] = 0;
```

This can become very time intensive if we have to manually duplicate memory every time we plan on changing the contents of a buffer. This is where copy-on-write semantics can help. We can extend our **apAlloc<>** class to add this capability, but we will also be faced with some limitations. This topic is discussed fully in *More Effective C++*. See [Meyers96].

Our **apAlloc<>** class defines **operator[]** as:

```
template<class T, class A>
T& apAlloc<T, A>::operator[] (long index)
{
  if (index < 0 || index >= size())
    throw std::range_error ("Index out of range");

  return *(data() + index);
}
```

There is also a corresponding **const** version that is identical. At first glance, it may appear that we can just call **duplicate()** inside the non-**const** version to duplicate the buffer if it is shared. However, there is a problem with this, as shown in the following example:

```
apAlloc<unsigned char> buffer (100);
cout << buffer[0] << endl;
buffer[0] = 5;
```

In both cases, the non-**const** version of **operator[]** is called. The decision about whether the **const** or non-**const** version is called does not depend on whether **operator[]** appears on the left-hand side (lvalue) or right-hand side (rvalue). This means that we need to find another solution so that **duplicate()** will be called only when necessary.

You can rewrite the example to make sure that the **const** and non-**const** versions are called at the appropriate times. We use a **const apAlloc<>** object whenever we only read the contents of the object, as follows:

```
apAlloc<unsigned char> buffer (100);
const apAlloc<unsigned char> buffer2 = buffer;
cout << buffer2[0] << endl;
buffer[0] = 5;
```

This is not the way to practically design commercial software. It puts too much burden on the developer to ensure whether the **const** or non-**const** version of a function is called. And worse, a single mistake in the implementation can mean that unnecessary memory duplications are made that slow down the application.

In *More Effective C++* [Meyers96], Meyers discusses a technique of using proxy classes to decide how **operator[]** is being used (either as an lvalue or rvalue). This technique requires that we return a class object that, based on operator overloading, determines which form is being called. While this solves the problem, it does add some additional complexity.

Leaving out copy-on-write semantics from our **apAlloc<>** class was done on purpose. Providing the compiler with enough information to always do the right thing makes the

apAlloc<> class much more complicated. The last thing we want to do is write code that may become difficult to maintain because of its complexity. We believe it is much better to specify what **apAlloc<>** does and what it does not do.

A Practical Solution

If you really must have copy-on-write in **apAlloc<>**, here is an alternative way to do it. It does require an additional step, but fortunately, the compiler will always complain if you should forget. The **const** methods to access data are no problem:

```
const T* data () const;
const T& operator[] (long index) const;
```

These functions will never be used as an lvalue. If you look at **apAlloc<>**, the non-**const** versions look almost identical to the **const** versions. In our design, we handle things differently. Instead of defining a non-**const** version of **data()**, we define **dataRW()** as:

```
T* dataRW ();
```

The **RW** suffix indicates that the pointer is for reading and writing. By moving the decision of what kind of pointer is needed from the compiler to the developer, we remove the confusion about what is happening, since we no longer offer two versions of a **data()** function.

operator[] also looks different because it takes an **apIndex** object as an argument, rather than a simple numerical index as shown:

```
T& operator[] (const apIndex& index);
```

The definition of **apIndex** is as follows:

```
class apIndex
{
public:
  explicit apIndex (unsigned int index) : index_ (index) {}
  operator unsigned int () const { return index_;}
private:
  unsigned int index_;
};
```

apIndex is really just a proxy for an **unsigned int**. It is critical that we use the **explicit** keyword in the constructor, to prevent the compiler from implicitly using this constructor to convert an integer into an **apIndex** object. If this were to ever happen, the non-**const** version of **operator[]** might incorrectly be called.

Our code now changes very little, as shown:

```
template<class T, class A>
T& apAlloc<T, A>::operator[] (const apIndex& apindex)
{
  unsigned int index = apindex;
  if (index >= size())
    throw std::range_error ("Index out of range");
  return *(data() + index);
}
```

Although we do not show it here, it is now possible to modify **operator[]** to duplicate the memory if the reference count is greater than one. You would add a flag in the object that enables and disables the copy-on-write behavior, instead of doing it unconditionally.

Our sample code is now slightly different, with references to **buffer[0]** being replaced by **buffer[apIndex(0)]**, as shown:

```
apAlloc<unsigned char> buffer (100);
cout << buffer[0] << endl;
buffer[apIndex(0)] = 5;
```

If we rewrote the last line of this example as:

```
buffer[0] = 5;
```

the compiler would issue an error, because a non-**const** reference can only be returned when an **apIndex** object is used. Using the **apIndex** type as an array index lets the compiler know that you intend to modify the array. This solution, although not perfect, lets us minimize the complexity of our **apAlloc<>** object.

8.1.2 Caching Issues

When dealing with image processing operations, it is very useful to minimize the number of intermediate images that must be computed. Although we believe caching to be a useful capability, we decided not to include it in our image framework, as it increased the difficulty of managing objects and placed more responsibility on the developer. That said, we still believe it to be a useful technique, and we present a strategy here if you should wish to extend the framework to include caching.

▶ **EXAMPLE** ───

Let's take an example of an image processing function and look at how caching makes it more efficient. The following function computes a histogram of all pixels in the image. The histogram always has 256 entries and represents the number of times each pixel value occurs. Our function converts the image to an 8-bit monochrome image before the histogram is computed. The **histogram()** function is as follows:

```
template<class T>
unsigned int* histogram (const apImage<T> image)
{
  static unsigned int counts[256];
  for (unsigned int index=0; index<256; index++)
    counts[index] = 0;

  apImage<Pel8> mono;
  copy (image, mono);

  apImage<Pel8>::row_iterator i;
  for (i=mono.row_begin(); i!=mono.row_end(); i++) {
    Pel8* p = i->p;
    for (unsigned int x=0; x<mono.width(); x++)
      counts[*p++]++;
  }
  return counts;
}
```

This simple function is deficient in a few ways (for example, it duplicates the image even if it already is of type **Pel8**), but this is not relevant for our discussion. Let's look at how we might use such a function:

```
int main ()
{
  apRect boundary (0, 0, 1024, 1024);
  apImage<apRGB> src (boundary);
  src.set (apRGB(1,2,3));

  unsigned int* h = histogram (src);

  for (unsigned int i=0; i<256; i++)
    std::cout << i << ": " << h[i] << std::endl;

  return 0;
}
```

On the surface, **histogram()** computes an array of values given an image. The fact that it computes a temporary image is hidden. However, computing this temporary image can consume quite a bit of time. The way we have defined **histogram()**, it always computes an **apImage<Pel8>** image. One obvious performance enhancement is to test if the image is already an image of type **Pel8**. If so, there is no need to copy this image. For other image types, however, a copy is always necessary.

histogram() discards the temporary image when it is no longer needed. However, what happens if another call to **histogram()** is made, or another image processing step needs an image of the same type? The answer is that this image is computed every time it is needed. What we really want is a framework that can store temporary images so that they can be reused as needed.

A General Purpose Caching Framework

Our need to cache intermediate copies of images can be generalized into a generic framework. It should have the following features:

- Before computing a derived object, consult a list of cached objects to see if it is available.

- If the object is available, return the cached copy.

- If the object is not available, compute this quantity, then save it in the cache.

After we discuss the general framework, we apply it to an image processing example, where we attach a cache object to each instance of an image to hold the list of available images.

❖ CACHING OBJECT

apCache keeps track of one or more cached quantities, called **apCacheEntryBase*** objects. Each of these cached quantities is maintained as an object derived from **apCacheEntryBase**, as shown.

```
class apCacheEntryBase;   // Forward declaration

class apCache
{
public:
  enum eDeletion { eAll, eStateChange, eDataChange};
  // Each entry can decide when it will get deleted from the cache

  typedef std::map<std::string, apCacheEntryBase*> Cache;
  // Our map of related images, by name

  apCache ();
  ~apCache ();

  void add (const std::string& key, apCacheEntryBase* cacheEntry);
  // Add an item in the cache, or replace an existing item

  apCacheEntryBase* find (const std::string& key);
  // Retrieve a cache item, or 0 if not found

  void clear (eDeletion deletion = eAll);
  // Clear items in our cache. By default, they all are cleared
protected:
  Cache cache_;      // List of cached items
};
```

❖ ADDING CACHED OBJECTS

apCache uses a **std::map** object to map a string to an **apCacheEntryBase** object. Every object that is added to the cache has a unique string. This string is used by other objects to query and fetch a cached object, as shown:

```
void apCache::add (const std::string& key,
                   apCacheEntryBase* cacheEntry)
{ cache_[key] = cacheEntry;}

apCacheEntryBase* apCache::find (const std::string& key)
{
  Cache::iterator i = cache_.find (key);
  if (i == cache_.end())
    return 0;

  return (i->second);
}
```

❖ DELETING CACHED OBJECTS

It is equally important to decide when information should be deleted from the cache. For example, if a function changes the original image that was used to compute a derived quantity, the cached image is no longer valid and must be recomputed. **apCache** has a limited understanding of what is contained in its cache. The **clear()** method is included to delete items from the cache, as shown.

```
void apCache::clear (eDeletion deletion)
{
  // Delete some or all of our objects. This loop is different
  // because we can't delete the iterator we're on.
  // See Meyers, Effective STL, Item 9
  Cache::iterator i;
```

```
    for (i=cache_.begin(); i!=cache_.end();) {
      apCacheEntryBase* entry = i->second;
      if (deletion == eAll || entry->deletion() == eAll ||
          entry->deletion() == deletion) {
        delete (i->second);
        cache_.erase (i++);
      }
      else
        ++i;
    }
  }
```

You decide what items are deleted by using the state of the cached object and the value of **deletion**, which can be any of the following:

- **eAll** - All items should be deleted from the cache.

- **eStateChange** - The state of the object has changed. If this cache contained images, it means that the pixel data has not changed, but other features, such as its origin point, have changed.

- **eDataChange** - The object's data has changed. If this cache contained images, it means that the actual pixels of the parent image have been altered.

Note that, as the comment indicates, the loop must be written this particular way, since it is possible to delete the current item we are examining in **cache_**.

 Placing references in your code or indicating ways to get more information is very useful to anyone using your code.

❖ BASE CLASS FOR CACHED OBJECTS

Now we can look at the objects that actually get cached. We have seen that **apCache** keeps track of zero or more **apCacheEntryBase*** objects. The main purpose of **apCacheEntryBase** is to act as the base class for any cache object, as shown here.

```
    class apCacheEntryBase
    {
    public:
      apCacheEntryBase (apCache::eDeletion deletion);
      virtual ~apCacheEntryBase ();

      apCache::eDeletion deletion () const { return deletion_;}

    protected:
      apCache::eDeletion deletion_;
    };
```

apCache maintains pointers to objects derived from **apCacheEntryBase** in **cache_**. We use pointers to avoid copies, since these cached objects might contain very large and difficult to copy features. **apCache::clear()** calls **delete** on these pointers in order to free them.

Templates once again allow us to be very flexible about what is contained in a cache entry, as shown here.

```
template<class T>
class apCacheEntry : public apCacheEntryBase
{
public:
  apCacheEntry (T& object,
                  apCache::eDeletion deletion = apCache::eAll)
    : apCacheEntryBase (deletion), object_ (object) {}
  virtual ~apCacheEntry () {}

  T object () { return object_;}

protected:
  T object_;
};
```

As you can see, one copy of the cached item, **object**, is made during construction when it gets stored in **object_**. The deletion criteria can also be specified, with the default behavior that any changes to the parent object cause the entry to be deleted. Cached elements are returned as base class objects. They must be cast in order to retrieve the specific information contained inside. This is not a problem, since the function that is trying to access this value is also capable of storing it, so the function must understand the details.

As you might expect, there are a number of important issues that you must understand when writing code that caches derived objects. Let's look at example to clarify things.

▶ EXAMPLE

Let's rewrite the **histogram()** function we used in our previous example. Instead of caching an **apImage<>** object, we will store an **apImageStorage<>** object because it contains all the necessary information, as shown.

```
apCache cache; // Stand-alone cache for testing

template<class T>
unsigned int* histogram (const apImage<T> image)
{
  static unsigned int counts[256];
  for (unsigned int index=0; index<256; index++)
    counts[index] = 0;

  apImage<Pel8> mono;

  std::string cacheKey ("Pel8");
  apCacheEntry<apImageStorage<Pel8> >* entry ;

  // Retrieve or store our Pel8 image in the cache
  apCacheEntryBase* cached = cache.find (cacheKey);
  if (!cached) {
    // This item is not in the cache. Compute it and cache it
    copy (image, mono);
    apImageStorage<Pel8> storage = mono.storage ();
    entry = new apCacheEntry<apImageStorage<Pel8> > (storage);
    cache.add (cacheKey, entry);
```

```
  }
  else {
    entry = static_cast<apCacheEntry<apImageStorage<Pel8> >*>
            (cached);
    mono = apImage<Pel8>(entry->object());
  }

  apImage<Pel8>::row_iterator i;
  for (i=mono.row_begin(); i!=mono.row_end(); i++) {
    Pel8* p = i->p;
    for (unsigned int x=0; x<mono.width(); x++)
      counts[*p++]++;
  }

  return counts;
}
```

This technique makes the **histogram()** function more complicated, but also more efficient. **cacheKey** is the string name we use to see if an image is already in the cache. We use **apCache::find()** to see if the item is already in the cache.

If the item is not in the cache (i.e., **cached** is zero), we compute the monochrome image and save it in the cache. The template parameter for our **apCacheEntry** is **apImageStorage<Pel8>**, as shown.

```
copy (image, mono);
apImageStorage<Pel8> storage = mono.storage ();
entry = new apCacheEntry<apImageStorage<Pel8> > (storage);
cache.add (cacheKey, entry);
```

(Note: If we were really adding this to the image framework, we would have used something more complicated than just **Pel8** as the name of the key. We would have combined the **typeid()** and any special storage alignment of the image.)

If the item was in the cache, we make **mono** point to the storage object we obtain from the cache, as shown.

```
entry = static_cast<apCacheEntry<apImageStorage<Pel8> >*> (cached);
mono = apImage<Pel8>(entry->object());
```

The rest of the **histogram()** function remains the same. While caching is clearly a useful performance and efficiency enhancement, it is also obvious that it makes the design more complex. These trade-offs have to be considered when approaching the design of your application.

Adding a Cache to the Image Object

To add caching to our image object, **apImage<>**, we need to make every instance of **apImage<>** contain an **apCache** instance. We must also modify every image processing function that uses an intermediate image, to first check if the image is already available in the cache before computing it.

And, we still have to worry about making sure the cache is cleaned up when the image is changed. Let's take a look at how we might add caching to our image object.

We start by adding a number of new methods to **apImage<>** to manage the **apCache** object, **cache_**, as shown:

```
void clearCache (apCache::eDeletion deletion = apCache::eAll)
{ cache_.clear (deletion);}

apCacheEntryBase* readCache (const std::string& key);
void writeCache (const std::string& key, apCacheEntryBase* object);
```

Now we need to modify every function that can change the image data or state. For example, our assignment operator must add **cache_.clear()** to make sure the cache removes all items, as shown:

```
template<class T, class S>
apImage<T,S>& apImage<T,S>::operator= (const apImage& src)
{
  apImageLocker<T,S> srcLocking (src, false); // Lock state

  // Make sure we don't copy ourself!
  if (storage_ != src.storage_) {
    apImageLocker<T,S> locking (*this, false); // Lock our state
    storage_ = src.storage_;
    cache_.clear ();                           // Clear our cache
  }
  return *this;
}
```

Statements like this must be carefully placed in all functions that can modify the image. A single mistake can keep an old version of the image in the cache.

If your application computes the same types of images many times, then you should consider adding caching at the application level of your design. In this case, it would be a mistake to add this functionality within the image object. Making **apImage<>** cache every image it computes would mean that many of the cached images would never be used. The point of caching is to reduce the number of times we compute temporary images. Caching unused images would defeat the whole purpose.

If you are still not convinced, consider objects with very long lifetimes. These objects are used for many operations and persist in the system for a long time. If these objects cache quantities that are only used once, the application can find itself exhausting memory, without the addition of yet another component to make sure that cached entries do not stay around too long.

In this section, we have highlighted only some of the changes required to add caching to the image framework by means of the **apImage<>** object. Instead of adding caching to **apImage<>**, you should consider caching certain images in your application, such as:

- Monochrome images derived from color images or vice-versa. Since many image processing operations are written to only work on one type of image, caching a copy of it is a good idea if you expect to perform numerous computations on it.

- Images with a specified image alignment. We have said many times that some algorithms run faster when their storage is aligned in memory. If you take the time to compute an image with a specific alignment, you should consider caching a copy in your code to use it again. Our Intel IPP interface is a perfect example. If you pass an improperly aligned image to an **IPPFilter<T>** object, a copy of this object is made. If possible, you should consider caching if you expect to call many **apIPP** methods using the same image.

8.2 Language Construct Issues

In this section, we provide some guidelines and examples for applying such C++ language constructs as:

- **explicit** keyword
- **const**
- passing by reference (both **const** and non-**const**)

8.2.1 Explicit Keyword Usage

In the image framework, we use the **explicit** keyword to prevent undesired conversions. Usually, you want the compiler to automatically convert an object from one type to another. Whenever you see an object of one type being compared or manipulated with an object of another type, you know there are two things that can be occurring:

- The compiler is using a defined conversion operator to convert the object from one type to another.

- The compiler is using a constructor to make the conversion.

At times, it is undesirable for the compiler to implicitly convert an object from one type to another. If the compiler finds a way to perform an implicit conversion, it will do so, regardless of whether or not the conversion is correct. After all, the compiler does not understand the specific meaning of a constructor, only that it can be used to perform a conversion. Let's look at an example where using **explicit** can address these issues.

► **EXAMPLE**

Let's create a **testString** object. This object is nothing but a wrapper around **std::string** with a single operation, as shown.

```
class testString
{
public:
  testString ();
  testString (const std::string& s) : string_ (s) {}
  testString (const char* s) : string_ (s) {}
  testString (int size, const char c=' ') : string_ (size, c) {}

  testString operator+ (const testString& src)
  {
    std::string result = string_ + src.string_;
    return result;
  }

  std::string fetch () const { return string_;}
private:
  std::string string_;
};
```

You can use **testString** objects in a number of ways:

```
testString();                          // An empty string
testString("Hello World");             // Contains "Hello World"
std::string s("Hello World");
testString(s);                         // Contains "Hello World"
testString(10);                        // Contains 10 spaces
```

You can also use them to do some useful string manipulations:

```
testString a ("Hello ");
testString b ("World");
testString c = a + b;
testString d = a + "World";
```

c and **d** both contain "Hello World". The last line is particularly useful to succinctly combine two strings, even though the second string is not a **testString** object.

With this usefulness, comes some pitfalls. For example, you can also write:

```
testString d = a + 5;
```

While the intention of this line is completely unclear, the compiler will successfully compile it. This line of code produces the same results as:

```
testString spaces (5);
testString d = a + spaces;
```

d will contain **"Hello   "**. The compiler is able to convert the integer value **5** to a **testString** because a constructor exists that takes an integer value and a second value as a default. This is where the **explicit** keyword can help. **explicit** can be used even when the constructor takes more than one argument, if the arguments have default values. If we modify our class such that the constructor is as follows:

```
explicit testString (int size, const char c=' ')
: string_ (size, c) {}
```

then the compiler will not compile the unclear line of code, instead appropriately generating an error, such as:

```
binary '+' : no operator found which takes a right-hand operand of
type 'int' (or there is no acceptable conversion)
```

During Template Instantiation

Another place where **explicit** can remove confusion is during template instantiation. When you define a template object, you create a generic template that can be used for any data type. It is not uncommon to create a template object with the intention of using only a few specific data types. A problem can occur when a new data type is used for the first time.

You can use a technique, like we do, of letting the compiler tell you what functionality is missing that prevents a template instantiation from working. The compiler will try to do simple conversions automatically, and it is possible that it will successfully create an instantiation by applying the incorrect conversions.

If you do have a single argument constructor, or a constructor that the compiler will treat as if it had a single argument, you should review whether or not the compiler is making the appropriate conversion. To ensure that it does, use the **explicit** keyword. If the compiler finds that you are attempting this conversion, and this is your intention, explicitly call the constructor rather than removing the **explicit** keyword.

8.2.2 Const Usage

We sometimes get sloppy with **const** during prototyping and in unit tests. Before releasing our software, we go back to the unit tests and change the code, such that any object that is not altered by a method is defined as **const**. We define a method as being **const** if it looks like a **const** object to the client (i.e., the code using this object). The compiler enforces that there can be no changes to the **const** object.

▶ **EXAMPLE**

Let's look at an example where we need to be able to change the value of a variable within a **const** function.

```
class apTest
{
public:
  apTest () : value_ (0), counter_ (0) {}
  void set (int v)  { value_ = v;}
  int  get () const { counter_++; return value_;}
  ...
```

```
private:
  int value_;
  int counter_;
};
```

apTest is a simple repository for an integer, **int**, accessed by means of **get()** and **set()** methods. However, the object also keeps track of the number of times that **get()** is called. From the standpoint of the code that uses **apTest**, the **get()** method is constant.

However, in this example there is an internal variable, used for debugging or perhaps caching, that is changing. Because of this, the compiler will not allow you to define this function as **const**. This is where the **mutable** keyword is used. The **mutable** keyword defines a variable that can be changed inside a **const** function. This is exactly what we are trying to do. All we have to do is define **counter_** as:

```
mutable int counter_;
```

and the compiler accepts the function. This is much better than the alternative, before **mutable** was available, as shown:

```
int get () const
{
  apTest* obj = const_cast<apTest*>(this); // Get non-const pointer
  obj->counter_++;
  return value_;
}
```

In addition, if you didn't have the **const_cast<>** operator, you would be forced to write this line of code as shown:

```
apTest* obj = (apTest*)this;
```

Clearly, using **mutable** is the preferred solution for allowing changes to a variable inside a **const** function.

Guidelines

Here are simple guidelines for using **const**:

- Use **const** references for any function arguments that do not change. The **const** portion will tell the compiler to make sure the value is not altered, and the reference will prevent the copy constructor from getting called when the function is called. An example is:

```
void set (const std::string& string);
void set (const apImage<T>& image);
```

- Examine all functions to see if they can be made **const**. It is easy to miss them. By labeling a function as **const**, the compiler becomes responsible for making sure this condition is true. There are some occasions where you will have to make a few changes in order to use **const**, but it is worth it. For example, suppose you have the following members in a class:

```
std::vector<int> v;
int sum () const
{
   int s = 0;
   std::vector<int>::const_iterator i;
   for (i=v.begin(); i!=v.end(); i++)
     s += *i;
   return s;
}
```

Since the method is **const**, you must use a **const_iterator** instead of just an **iterator**. If you forget, the compiler will remind you. However, in some cases, such as when templates are used, the error messages can be difficult to decipher. See [Meyers01].

■ Return internal values from a **const** method as **const**. For example (from **apImage<>**):

```
const S& storage () const;
const T* base    () const;
```

■ Add a second method that returns a non-**const** version when a **const** method must be accessed by a non-**const** member. For example (from **apImage<>**):

```
const T* rowAddress (unsigned int y) const;
T*       rowAddress (unsigned int y);
```

8.2.3 Pass by Reference Usage

We saw in the last section that the use of **const** and passing by reference are often used together. References can be used in numerous ways, both as return values and arguments. There are some combinations, however, that should be used sparingly. In this section, we review all of the combinations and provide guidelines for their use.

Returning a const Reference

This is one of the most common uses for references. By making the return value **const**, you can safely return object variables without copying them. Copies should be avoided whenever possible, even if that object uses reference counting, like our image storage class does.

Returning a Non-const reference

Returning a non-**const** reference to an internal variable gives full access, without restriction, to that variable. By design, returning a non-**const** reference is done in the assignment operator (**operator=**), prefix increment (**operator++**), and prefix decrement (**operator--**), in addition to other places in the language. You should be very careful when using this feature, as it is easy to misuse the reference that is returned. If you see this construct in your code, you should redesign it, as follows.

If you are returning a reference because an external function needs to access it, consider using friendship instead. Obviously, you cannot return a non-**const** reference in a **const** function. In general, if you are returning a non-**const** reference, it is most likely a bug in your code unless you have deliberately and carefully applied this construct. If you do use non-**const** references, be sure to comment it in your code so that others are clear about your intentions.

Passing by const Reference

This is also a very common use for references. Arguments passed by **const** reference avoid the copy issue. It also helps the function prototype become self-documenting. For example, the **duplicate()** functionality in our image framework looks like this:

```
template<class T1, class S1>
apImage<T1,S1> duplicate (const apImage<T1,S1>& src,
                          apRectImageStorage::eAlignment align);
```

The **const** reference clearly indicates that this is a source image as opposed to an output image.

Passing by Reference

Passing by reference is a perfectly acceptable practice. Usually when you see an argument passed by reference (not **const** reference), you can assume it is used as a return value. When you have more than one output parameter, you can either return one parameter normally with the rest returned by setting reference arguments, or you can return a structure. We use both types, depending upon the application. If you only have two pieces of information to return, returning a **std::pair<>** is a great way of handling this.

During Template Instantiation

We frequently use references to assist the compiler during template instantiation. By using references to pass the destination information, the proper template instantiation can occur, as shown in the following example. We chose to use a slightly different definition, but we could have written our **add2()** functions as:

```
template<class T1, class T2, class T3>
void add2 (const T1& s1, const T2& s2, T3& d1)
{ d1 = s1 + s2;}
```

Returning Multiple Values

The other use of references is for returning multiple values. For example, you might have a function like:

```
bool getValue (int index, std::string& value);
```

getValue() returns the status of the operation, and if successful, **value** is set to the appropriate string. For functions that only return two values, we find this type of construct acceptable. However, if you have additional results, you should create a structure to hold all the results, as shown.

```
struct results
{
  bool          status;
  std::string value;
  // other results
};

results getValue (int index);
```

The Boost Graph library has an interesting construct, called **tie()**, that allows you to treat the values of a **std::pair<>** as two separate pieces of data. See [Siek02]. Using this construct, you can write:

```
std::pair<int, float> someFunction();
int i;
float f;
tie(i, f) = someFunction();
```

8.3 Extending the Framework

In this section, we provide some simple techniques for extending the image framework that is presented throughout this book and contained fully on the CD-ROM. By showing a few examples, we hope to make it easier for you to add your own image processing functions and to enhance your digital photographs.

8.3.1 Adding Image Processing Functions

We have gone into a great deal of detail in this book describing how to design an image processing framework. We have added a small set of image processing functions to demonstrate how the framework holds together. In the image processing world, most software packages offer a rich set of functionality. In this section we will provide some insight into how you can incorporate more features into our framework.

Neighborhood Operations

A *neighborhood operation* is one that uses a relatively small set of pixels in the source image to generate a pixel in the destination image. The Laplacian and Gaussian filters we presented in Chapter 6 are examples of neighborhood operators. We presented a flexible filter framework that other neighborhood routines can use with little or no modification. The framework dealt with all the special boundary conditions and took care of the intersection operations to determine exactly which pixels needed to be processed.

Our image processing filters, such as Laplacian and Gaussian, use kernels that are always square with an odd width and height. The kernel is always centered over the corresponding pixels in the image, removing any ambiguity over which pixels are used. There are other neighborhood routines, however, where this restriction does not work.

To handle these cases, we have to generalize our definition in two ways. First, we need to add an origin point to the kernel to specify how the neighborhood operation is computed. Figure 8.1 shows a 2x2 kernel and its origin.

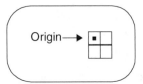

Figure 8.1: 2x2 Kernel

Second, we have to relax the restriction of the kernel being square, so that any rectangular kernel can be used. Figure 8.2 shows a 1x3 rectangular kernel and its origin.

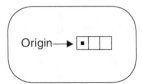

Figure 8.2: 1x3 Kernel

Because of these generalizations, we have to change how we determine which pixels to process. Figure 8.3 shows how we determine which source and destination pixels to use for a 640x480 image using a 1x3 kernel.

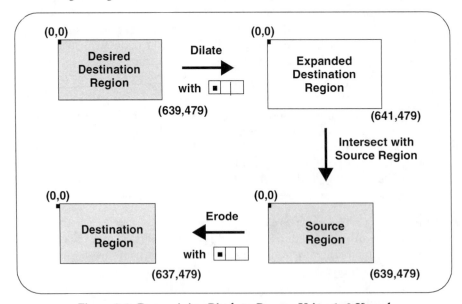

Figure 8.3: Determining Pixels to Process Using 1x3 Kernel

In addition to image convolution, there are a number of other image processing operations that use neighborhood operators, such as morphology. Note that dilation and erosion, which are indicated in Figure 8.3, are subsequently discussed within the context of morphology.

Morphology

Morphology operations manipulate image data by performing operations on a region around each pixel. These regions are called *structuring elements* because they do not contain information other than a description of the pixel neighborhood. If you apply the morphological filter we provide to your images, you will find that the image becomes darker and that small defects in the image are removed, as shown in Figure 8.4.

Original Image   Filtered Image

Figure 8.4: Morphology Filter

Morphology operations were initially defined for binary images (i.e., each pixel is either on or off), and performed simple OR and AND operations between pixels in the source image to decide the state of each destination pixel.

Grayscale morphology extends the original definition to work with non-binary pixel data. These operators typically use a min or max operator to compare pixels in the source image.

The structuring elements used in morphology do not have to be rectangular. A common structuring element is a cross with its origin in the center that uses the immediate neighbors around every pixel, as shown in Figure 8.5.

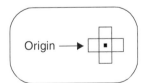

Origin ⟶

Figure 8.5: Cross Structuring Element

The *erosion* operator (or *min* operator) tends to shrink the objects in an image by removing pixels along the boundary between the object and its background. The complimentary operator is the *dilation* operator (or *max* operator), which tends to expand the size of an object.

Let's write a simple morphology operator with the following assumption: we will use a cross structuring element so that we can extend our existing convolution operation to perform morphology. Even though the structuring element is a cross, the intersection operations are identical to those used in our 3x3 kernel. Since we are using an existing operation, there are many parameters that we can ignore. The structuring element is hard-coded into our filter function, as shown here.

```
template<class R, class T1, class T2, class S1, class S2>
void ap_erode_cross (const R&, const apImage<T1,S1>& src1,
                     const char* /*kernel*/, unsigned int /*size*/,
                     int /*divisor*/, apImage<T2,S2>& dst1)
{
  typename apImage<T1,S1>::row_iterator i1 = src1.row_begin();
  typename apImage<T2,S2>::row_iterator i2 = dst1.row_begin();

  unsigned int h = src1.height() - 2;
  unsigned int w = src1.width()  - 2;

  const T1* p1;
  T2* p2;
  unsigned int x, y;

  // Elements to skip between rows
  unsigned int pitch = (i1->bytes / sizeof (T1));

  for (y=0; y<h; y++, i1++, i2++) {
    p1 = i1->p + (pitch + 1); // Center the pixel
    p2 = i2->p;
    for (x=0; x<w; x++) {
      *p2++ = apMin( apMin( apMin( apMin(*p1, *(p1-1)), *(p1+1)),
                                          *(p1-pitch)), *(p1+pitch));
      *p1++;
    }
  }
}
```

The biggest difference between this morphology operation and the convolution operation is how the output pixels are computed:

```
*p2++ = apMin( apMin( apMin( apin(*p1, *(p1-1)), *(p1+1)),
                                    *(p1-pitch)), *(p1+pitch));
```

We call our own **apMin()** function rather than **min()**, because **min()** is not defined uniformly by compilers. If you want this function to work correctly with **apRGB** images, you will need to define a specialization, as we did with convolution, or you will need to write a **min()** function that works with **apRGB**.

To perform an erosion using a cross structuring element, you can simply call the **erodeCross()** function. Its definition is shown here.

```
template<class T1, class S1>
void erodeCross (const apImage<T1,S1>& src1,
                 apImage<T1,S1>& dst1)
{
  apFunction_s1d1Convolve<T1,T1,T1,S1,S1> processor
                                       (ap_erode_cross);

  char* kernel = 0;
  unsigned int size = 3;
  int divisor = 1;
  processor.run (src1, kernel, size, divisor, dst1);
}
```

Like with many image processing operations, you should experiment to determine what settings work best in your application.

Sobel

Another popular convolution filter is the Sobel operator. This is similar to Laplacian, but it finds the edges in the image by applying two kernels to each pixel. If you only take the magnitude of these two results, you have an image similar to that produced by the Laplacian filter. However, you can also use this information to determine the angle of any edge in the image. This angle information is then mapped to a binary value and written like any image pixel. Even though this angle is very rough, it works surprisingly well when the image has little noise in it. Figure 8.6 demonstrates the effects of using the Sobel operator that we provide.

Original Image

Filtered Image

Figure 8.6: Sobel Filter (Magnitude)

The Sobel filter differs from the Laplacian filter, in that it tends to produce two peaks at every edge in the image. This is the result of using the following two convolution kernels during processing:

$$X = \begin{bmatrix} -1 & 0 & 1 \\ -2 & 0 & 2 \\ -1 & 0 & 1 \end{bmatrix} \qquad Y = \begin{bmatrix} 1 & 2 & 1 \\ 0 & 0 & 0 \\ -1 & -2 & -1 \end{bmatrix}$$

Although you can compute a separate image with each kernel and then compute the output image, it is much more efficient to do this in a single step. Given the values **x** and **y**, you can compute the output pixel values using the following equations:

$$Magnitude = \sqrt{(x^2 + y^2)}$$

$$Angle = \tan^{-1}(y/x)$$

We can use our convolution framework to design this filter, as long as we return only a single image from each call. Since the Sobel angle image is of limited use, we implement it as a separate function. Here is the generic Sobel magnitude function:

```
template<class R, class T1, class T2, class S1, class S2>
void ap_convolve_3x3sobelmag (const R&,
                        const apImage<T1,S1>& src1,
                        const char* /*kernel*/,
                        unsigned int /*size*/, int /*divisor*/,
                        apImage<T2,S2>& dst1)
{
  typename apImage<T1,S1>::row_iterator i1 = src1.row_begin();
  typename apImage<T2,S2>::row_iterator i2 = dst1.row_begin();

  unsigned int h = src1.height() - 2;
  unsigned int w = src1.width()  - 2;

  const T1* p1;
  const T1* pk;
  T2* p2;
  R sumx, sumy;
  R pel;
  unsigned int x, y;

  // Elements to skip from end of one row to start of next
  unsigned int pitch = (i1->bytes / sizeof (T1)) - 3;

  for (y=0; y<h; y++, i1++, i2++) {
    p1 = i1->p;
    p2 = i2->p;
    for (x=0; x<w; x++) {
      sumx = sumy = 0;
      pk = p1 + x;

      pel = *pk++;
      sumx -= pel;
      sumy += pel;
      sumy += 2 * (*pk++);
      pel = *pk++;
      sumx += pel;
      sumy += pel;
      pk += pitch;

      sumx -= 2 * (*pk++);
      pk++; // Skip this pixel
      sumx += 2 * (*pk++);
      pk += pitch;

      pel = *pk++;
```

```
        sumx -= pel;
        sumy -= pel;
        sumy -= 2 * (*pk++);
        pel = *pk++;
        sumx += pel;
        sumy -= pel;

        sumx = static_cast<R>(sqrt(static_cast<double>(sumx*sumx +
                                                       sumy*sumy)));
        *p2++ = apLimit<T2> (sumx);   // Prevent wrapping
      }
    }
  }
```

When you write a function like this, you will often find that there are optimizations you can make. We took advantage of zero kernel elements to eliminate the unnecessary arithmetic: six of the 18 total kernel elements are zero, so ignoring them saves about one-third of the processing time.

Our magnitude calculation at the end of the loop is as follows:

```
    sumx = static_cast<R>(sqrt(static_cast<double>(sumx*sumx +
                                                   sumy*sumy)));
```

We use a **double** to compute the magnitude, which is then cast to the appropriate type. However, this does not work properly for RGB data types because the compiler will implicitly convert the RGB quantity to a grayscale value. As with the morphology filter, we have written an RGB specialization to correctly handle this case. It is included on the CD-ROM.

We can also write more specializations to further optimize our Sobel filter. For example, the magnitude calculation can hurt performance on embedded platforms in particular because of the floating point operations that are used. For a pixel type of **Pel8**, for example, you could add a lookup table to convert the **x** and **y** values to a magnitude with a single lookup. This table does consume memory (64 kilobytes if an exhaustive table is stored), but can be well worth it to make this calculation run faster. You can also use approximations, depending on the purpose of the filtered images. For example, the magnitude calculation can be approximated using absolute value, as shown:

```
    Magnitude = |x| + |y|
```

Fortunately, all these details are hidden. To use the Sobel magnitude filter, you can simply call the **sobel3x3mag()** function and explicitly specify **R**. Its definition is shown here.

```
    template<class R, class T1, class T2, class S1, class S2>
    void sobel3x3mag (const apImage<T1,S1>& src1,
                      apImage<T2,S2>& dst1)
    {
      apFunction_s1d1Convolve<R,T1,T2,S1,S2> processor
    (ap_convolve_3x3sobelmag);
      char* kernel = 0;
      unsigned int size = 3;
      int divisor = 1;
      processor.run (src1, kernel, size, divisor, dst1);
    }
```

Image Space Transforms

Another image processing category are those operations that transform images from one type to another. In Chapter 6, we showed how `copy()` can be used to change an image from one type into another. We used this function to convert between monochrome (`apImage<Pel8>`) and color images (`apImage<apRGB>`). When we talk about *image space transforms*, we are referring to the meaning of a pixel, rather than the data type of a pixel.

Let's look at two examples of useful transforms:

- A lookup table to map pixels from one value to another

- A color-space operator to convert an RGB (Red, Green, Blue) image to an HSI (Hue, Saturation, Intensity) image

Mapping Pixels

Lookup tables are a very common technique for mapping pixels from one value to another. For pixel types with a small number of values, such as `Pel8`, an array is used to contain the mapping between source and destination. For larger images, such as `apRGB`, this is not practical because there are 2^{24} possible values. A generic lookup table function is very easy to write, partly because only a single image is involved. The image is modified in-place and does not require any temporary image storage as shown.

```
template<class T, class S>
void convertLUT (apImage<T,S>& image, T* lut)
{
  typename apImage<T,S>::row_iterator i;

  for (i=image.row_begin(); i!=image.row_end(); i++) {
    T* p = i->p;
    for (unsigned int x=0; x<image.width(); x++)
      *p++ = lut[*p];
  }
}
```

There are problems when using this function for image types such as `apRGB`, because you must pass a lookup table of type `apRGB*`, which is difficult to compute.

Even if you could pass these arguments, the function would not work properly, because the line:

```
*p++ = lut[*p];
```

will try and use `*p` (an `apRGB` value) as an index to the lookup table. And yes, this does compile, because there is a conversion operator defined in `apRGBTmpl<T>` to convert a color pixel into a monochrome pixel (i.e., an integer value), as shown:

```
operator T () const
{ return (red + green + blue) / 3;}
```

Most unit tests will not catch this mistake unless it tests template functions for a variety of pixel types. We recommend that whenever you write template functions, do any of the following:

- Write specializations only for the pixel types you want to support.

- Write specializations that fail for the pixel types you want to exclude. For example:

```
template<> void convertLUT (apImage<apRGB>&, apRGB*)
{
    throw apUnsupportedException("convertLUT");
}
```

- Document the function to indicate which template arguments are known to work.

Converting Between Color Spaces

Many applications that handle color images require *image space conversion*, which is the conversion of an RGB image to another color space image and vice versa. In our framework, we have used **apRGBTmpl<>** to represent an RGB pixel. There are many color spaces that use a triplet (i.e., three values) to represent the value of a color pixel. The term *tristimulus value* is another way of describing this triplet.

When we defined **apRGBTmpl<>**, we considered making this name more generic. We decided against it because in most cases we are dealing with an RGB pixel. To define our new color space data type, we can reuse **apRGBTmpl<>** by defining a new **typedef**, as shown:

```
typedef apRGBTmpl<Pel8> apHSI;
```

We will use this **apHSI** definition to refer to a color pixel with hue, saturation, and intensity components. Keep in mind that this won't prevent the mixing of **apHSI** with **apRGB**, because they both are the same data types. You can either use the **red**, **green**, and **blue** components, or the generic sounding **ts1()**, **ts2()**, and **ts3()** to access the tristimulus values. The code that computes the conversion from RGB to HSI for one pixel is more complicated than the function that iterates over the output image. Figure 8.7 shows the equations used to convert RGB to HSI.

$$
H = \cos^{-1}\left\{ \frac{\frac{1}{2}[(R-G)+(R-B)]}{\left[(R-G)^2+(R-B)(G-B)\right]^{\frac{1}{2}}} \right\}
\qquad
S = 1-\left(\frac{3}{(R+G+B)}\right)[\min(R, G, B)]
$$

$$
I = \frac{1}{3}(R+G+B)
$$

Figure 8.7: Color Space Conversion Formulas

Figure 8.8 shows the conversion of an RGB image to its corresponding hue, saturation, and intensity images.

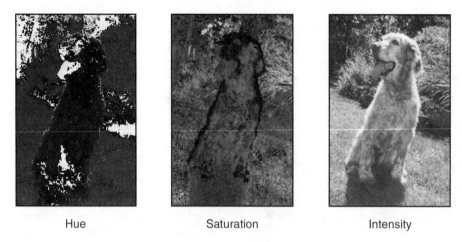

| Hue | Saturation | Intensity |

Figure 8.8: Image Conversion from RGB to HSI

We have split the problem into two pieces: first, we write a function, `RGB2HSI()`, to convert an RGB pixel into an HSI pixel; next, we write another function, also called `RGB2HSI()`, to convert an entire RGB image to an HSI image. Both are shown here.

```
template<class T>
apRGBTmpl<T> RGB2HSI (const apRGBTmpl<T>& pel)
{
  static double twoPi = asin(1.) * 4.;

  apRGBTmpl<T> hsi;
  double t;

  T r = pel.red;
  T g = pel.green;
  T b = pel.blue;

  if (r==g && r==b && g==b) // Degenerate case. Grayscale
    return apRGBTmpl<T> (0, 0, r);

  // Hue
  t = acos(.5 * ((r-g)+(r-b)) / sqrt((r-g)*(r-g) + (r-b)*(g-b)));
  double sum = r+g+b;
  if (b > g) t = twoPi - t;  // 2*pi - t; Gives us 4 quadrant answer
  hsi.red = static_cast<T>(t *
                          apLimitInfo<T>::sType.maxValue / twoPi);

  // Saturation
  t = 1. - 3. * min(r, min(g, b)) / sum;
  hsi.green = static_cast<T>(t * apLimitInfo<T>::sType.maxValue);

  // Intensity
  hsi.blue = (r + g + b) / 3;

  return hsi;
```

```
  }

template<class T>
void RGB2HSI (apImage<apRGBTmpl<T> >& image)
{
  typename apImage<apRGBTmpl<T> >::row_iterator i;

  unsigned int width = image.width();
  unsigned int x;
  apRGBTmpl<T>* pel;
  for (i=image.row_begin(); i!=row_image.end(); i++) {
    pel = i->p;
    for (x=0; x<width; x++) {
      *pel++ = RGB2HSI (*pel);
    }
  }
}
```

Our HSI pixel conversion function is far from optimized. We have chosen not to perform any optimizations because of the trade-off that occurs between accuracy and speed. As a generic implementation, this is fine. However, if you write a specialized version for **apRGB**, you should improve this function. The $\cos^{-1}()$ function is a candidate for a lookup table, in order to improve performance. The floating point arithmetic can also be converted to fixed point.

Image Geometry

Operations that deal with the geometry of an image, such as resizing or rotation, are used extensively in the image processing world. Like most algorithms, there are good ways and bad ways to solve these problems. Earlier, we used a **thumbnail()** function as a running example through the book because it is both easy to understand and implement. While **thumbnail()** is a resizing function and it has some usefulness, it does not go far enough to address the general problem.

In this section, we present a more robust image resizing operation. Most of our discussion is also applicable to image rotation, another important operation for image processing.

Image Resizing

We define image resizing as taking a source image of dimensions S_w x S_h and converting it to an output (or destination) image of dimensions D_w x D_h. There are two important things to note here. First, the destination image can either be larger or smaller than the source image. Second, the resizing operation does not have to respect the aspect ratio of the source image. *Aspect ratio* is the relationship between the height and width of an image, and is usually expressed as:

$$Aspect\ Ratio = \textbf{height / width}$$

For many applications, resizing the image is done such that the aspect ratio is preserved. By specifying either the width or height of the destination image, you compute the other dimension to keep the aspect ratio constant.

The right way to solve this problem is to think in terms of the destination image. For every pixel in the destination image, you want to find the appropriate pixels from the source image that contribute to it. When we write **resize()**, we will work with the geometry of the destination and compute a value for every pixel.

The wrong way to solve this problem is to think in terms of the source image. Depending on how the resizing is performed, a single source pixel can be used to compute multiple destination pixels. If you try and step through each source pixel, you must find all the destination pixels that are affected by it. The result will be a jagged looking image that may contain output pixels with no value.

Our implementation for **resize()** is slightly different than our other image processing operations, in that **resize()** allocates the destination image given the desired size. This decision is based upon how we expect **resize()** to be used in applications. We can ignore the origin point of the source image until we are finished, since this value is left unchanged.

For any pixel in the destination image, **D(x,y)**, we can find the corresponding pixel in the source image, **S(x',y')**, using the equations shown in Figure 8.9.

$$X_{scale} = S_w / D_w$$

$$Y_{scale} = S_h / D_h$$

$$D(x,y) = S (x * X_{scale} , y * Y_{scale})$$

Figure 8.9: Equations for Computing Corresponding Source Pixels

Notice that the desired source pixel usually has fractional pixel coordinates. The pixel at these coordinates does not exist in our discrete representation of the image, but we can perform an interpolation to find out its value.

If performance is a concern, you can do a *nearest neighbor interpolation*, whereby you choose the pixel in the source image that is closest to the desired point.

Figure 8.10 shows an image reduced by 75 percent using nearest neighbor interpolation.

Original Image   Resized Image

Figure 8.10: Nearest Neighbor Image Resizing

We recommend bilinear interpolation to determine the pixel value because the results are better. *Bilinear interpolation* refers to the fact that we use four pixels (two pixels in the x direction and two in the y direction) to determine the value of any arbitrary pixel. In contrast, nearest neighbor interpolation only chooses the nearest point, rather than computing the weighted average of the four pixels. Bilinear interpolation is fairly fast and produces good results, as shown in Figure 8.11.

Original Image   Resized Image

Figure 8.11: Bilinear Interpolation Image Resizing

Using bilinear interpolation, we compute a pixel at some fractional coordinate `S(x+dx,y+dy)`, where `dx` and `dy` are the fractional coordinates and `x` and `y` are the integer coordinates computed as shown in Figure 8.12.

```
S(x+dx,y+dy) = (1-dy)(1-dx)S(x,y) + (1-dy)(dx)S(x+1,y) +
               (dy)(1-dx)S(x,y+1) + (dx)(dy)S(x+1,y+1)
```

Figure 8.12: Bilinear Interpolation

Figure 8.13 shows a side-by-side comparison of the nearest neighbor technique and the bilinear interpolation technique. Notice how the edges are much smoother with the bilinear interpolation technique applied to the same image.

Nearest Neighbor Interpolation   Bilinear Interpolation

Figure 8.13: Nearest Neighbor Versus Bilinear Interpolation

With this information we can now write our `resize()` function to work with most datatypes. (Note that it does not support our `apRGB` datatype; you could support this datatype by writing a specialized version of this function.) We start by defining a function, `fetchPixel_BLI()`, to fetch a pixel from an image using floating point coordinates. The `BLI` suffix stands for bilinear interpolation. This is a useful stand-alone function that can also be reused in other applications. The `fetchPixel_BLI()` function is as follows:

```
template<class T, class S>
T fetchPixel_BLI (const apImage<T,S>& image, double x, double y)
{
    // getPixel() throws an error if the coordinates are out of range

    unsigned int x0 = static_cast<unsigned int>(x);
    unsigned int y0 = static_cast<unsigned int>(y);
    double dx = x-x0;
```

```
    double dy = y-y0;

    T p1 = image.getPixel (x0, y0);

    if (x >= image.width()-1 || y >= image.height()-1)
      return p1; // Overflow

    T p2 = image.getPixel (x0+1, y0);
    T p3 = image.getPixel (x0, y0+1);
    T p4 = image.getPixel (x0+1, y0+1);

    double pel = (1.-dy)*(1.-dx)*p1 + (1-dy)*dx*p2 + dy*(1-dx)*p3 +
                 dx*dy*p4;
    return static_cast<T>(pel);
}
```

In this function, we use four calls to **getPixel()** to compute the output pixel. We could write a faster version that computes the address of one point and then finds the remaining three values using simple pointer arithmetic. **fetchPixel_BLI()** does not have any explicit range checking because **getPixel()** throws an exception if the coordinates are out of range. To prevent any messy boundary condition issues, the function just returns the actual coordinate, even if it lies on the edge of the image.

We can also write the nearest-neighbor equivalent function, **fetchPixel_NN()**, which fetches the nearest integer pixel in the image, as follows:

```
template<class T, class S>
T fetchPixel_NN (const apImage<T,S>& image, double x, double y)
{
  unsigned int x0 = static_cast<unsigned int>(x+.5);
  unsigned int y0 = static_cast<unsigned int>(y+.5);
  return image.getPixel (x0, y0);
}
```

With this fetch capability, the **resize()** function only has to compute the destination image and fill it with values, as shown:

```
template<class T, class S>
apImage<T,S> resize (const apImage<T,S>& src, unsigned long width,
                     unsigned long height=0)
{
  if (width == 0 && height == 0)
    return src.sNull;

  // Maintain aspect ratio if only one value is given
  if (width == 0)
    width = src.width() * height / src.height();
  if (height == 0)
    height = src.height() * width / src.width();

  // Compute the destination window
  apRect boundary (src.x0(), src.y0(), width, height);
  apImage<T,S> dst (boundary);

  // Compute our starting point in the source image and the
  // steps we use to traverse it
  double sx;
  double sy = src.y0();
```

```
double xscale = static_cast<double>(src.width()) / width;
double yscale = static_cast<double>(src.height()) / height;

typename apImage<T,S>::row_iterator i;
T* p;
for (i=dst.row_begin(); i!=dst.row_end(); i++) {
  sx = src.x0();
  p = i->p;
  for (unsigned int x=0; x<width; x++) {
    *p++ = fetchPixel_BLI (src, sx, sy);
    sx += xscale;
  }
  sy += yscale;
}
return dst;
}
```

Image Rotation

Image rotation is similar to image resizing because it uses the same approach, in that pixels in the destination image are populated with pixels from the source image. The major difference is in how we compute which source pixels are needed. Image rotation is only one aspect of a more general purpose transformation called an affine transform. An *affine transform* handles image rotation, scaling, translation, and shear (non-uniform scaling). This may sound complicated, but the affine transform is really just a matter of applying one or more linear transformations to the pixel coordinates.

For example, to rotate pixels in an image by an angle, θ, around the origin of the image, you would apply the following computations:

```
x' = x*cos(θ) - y*sin(θ)
y' = x*sin(θ) + y*cos(θ)
D(x,y) = S(x',y')
```

Whether we apply just rotation, or perform an entire *six degrees of freedom* (x translation, y translation, x scale, y scale, rotation, and shear), we map a point in the destination image to one in the source image. Once we have these coordinates, we use bilinear interpolation to compute the actual value.

We have not included the implementation for an affine transform. To write this function, you must pay close attention to the boundary conditions. For example, if you take a source image and rotate it 45 degrees, there will be large areas in the destination image that do not have valid pixels. If you devise your algorithm correctly, you can ignore most of these regions and only compute those pixels that contribute to the output image.

8.3.2 Enhancing Digital Photographs

Most of the image processing functions we have implemented are very mathematical in nature. A destination image is computed with pixels from one or more source images. In this section we discuss an image processing method, called *unsharp masking*, that you can use with your digital photographs to make them appear crisper and in focus. We refer to this method as unsharp masking because it works by subtracting a smoothed (or unsharp) version of the image from the original.

If you have never used this method to sharpen images, you might be surprised by how well it works. You can take an image from a digital camera, for example, and once you see the processed photograph, the original may begin to look fuzzy to you. You can also use unsharp masking as a way to restore the sharpness of the edges in scanned photographs. Figure 8.14 shows the effects of unsharp masking.

Original Image   Filtered Image

Figure 8.14: Unsharp Masking

You can construct an unsharp mask using one or more basic filtering components that we already have developed. Other filters, such as the convolution filters, may make an image more useful for further analysis by removing noise, but they can't create a more visually appealing image, as an unsharp masking filter can.

There are a number of ways to filter an image using unsharp masking. One simple technique uses a Laplacian filter to find the high frequency edges, and then adds a portion of this value to the original image. Although this is a very simple implementation, it works erratically on many images.

We provide the class unsharp masking implementation, which involves running a low pass filter on the image and subtracting a percentage of it from the original. The steps we use to implement unsharp masking are as follows:

1. Run a low-pass filter on the image. As a rule of thumb, the larger the kernel, the better the results. We use a 5x5 Gaussian filter to blur the image, as shown in Figure 8.15.

    Note that you could also the 3x3 Gaussian filter we presented in Chapter 6, but it produces greater errors near high frequency edges.

$$D(x,y) = \frac{1}{179} \begin{bmatrix} 0 & 0 & 1 & 0 & 0 \\ 0 & 8 & 21 & 8 & 0 \\ 1 & 21 & 59 & 21 & 1 \\ 0 & 8 & 21 & 8 & 0 \\ 0 & 0 & 1 & 0 & 0 \end{bmatrix}$$

Figure 8.15: Kernel for 5x5 Gaussian Filter

2. Compute the output image, **D**, by combining the original image, **S**, and the Gaussian filter image, **G**, as follows: **D = k S + (1-k)G**

    If **k=0**, the output image is identical to the Gaussian image. If **k=1**, the output image is identical to the source image. If **k=2**, the output image is twice the original image, minus the Gaussian image. When **k>1** we achieve the intent of the unsharp mask, because we subtract a portion of the Gaussian filter from the original.

When **k=2**, we have a filter that usually produces reasonable results. We can rewrite our steps to produce this filter using a single convolution kernel, which is computed as shown in Figure 8.16.

$$D(x,y) = 2S - G$$

$$D(x,y) = 2 \begin{bmatrix} 0 & 0 & 0 & 0 & 0 \\ 0 & 0 & 0 & 0 & 0 \\ 0 & 0 & 1 & 0 & 0 \\ 0 & 0 & 0 & 0 & 0 \\ 0 & 0 & 0 & 0 & 0 \end{bmatrix} - \frac{1}{179} \begin{bmatrix} 0 & 0 & 1 & 0 & 0 \\ 0 & 8 & 21 & 8 & 0 \\ 1 & 21 & 59 & 21 & 1 \\ 0 & 8 & 21 & 8 & 0 \\ 0 & 0 & 1 & 0 & 0 \end{bmatrix}$$

$$D(x,y) = \frac{1}{179} \begin{bmatrix} 0 & 0 & -1 & 0 & 0 \\ 0 & -8 & -21 & -8 & 0 \\ -1 & -21 & 299 & -21 & -1 \\ 0 & -8 & -21 & -8 & 0 \\ 0 & 0 & -1 & 0 & 0 \end{bmatrix} S$$

Figure 8.16: Equations for a Single Unsharp Masking Kernel

There is a one small problem with using this single kernel. The convolution routines we developed in Chapter 6 use a **char** to store the kernel values. The value, **299**, does not fit. We could add a new version of **convolve()** to take larger kernels; however, an easier

approach is to solve the problem in steps, thus avoiding the limitation. Our solution is
shown below.

```
template<class R, class T1, class S1>
apImage<T1,S1> unsharpMask (const apImage<T1,S1>& src,
                           double strength=2.0)
{
  if (src.isNull())
    return src;

  // Compute our 5x5 gaussian (lopass) filter
  char kernel[] = { 0,  0,  1,  0, 0,
                    0,  8, 21,  8, 0,
                    1, 21, 59, 21, 1,
                    0,  8, 21,  8, 0,
                    0,  0,  1,  0, 0};
  apImage<T1,S1> gaussian;
  convolve<R> (src, kernel, 5, 179, gaussian);

  // Window our source image to be the same size
  apImage<T1,S1> srcWindow = src;
  srcWindow.window (gaussian.boundary());

  // Our destination is the same size as the gaussian
  apImage<T1,S1> dst (gaussian.boundary());

  // Compute our output using
  // strength * srcWindow + (1-strength) * gaussian
  typename apImage<T1,S1>::row_iterator s = srcWindow.row_begin ();
  typename apImage<T1,S1>::row_iterator d = dst.row_begin ();
  typename apImage<T1,S1>::row_iterator g = gaussian.row_begin ();

  unsigned int h = dst.height ();
  unsigned int w = dst.width ();

  unsigned int x, y;
  R sum;
  const T1* ps;
  const T1* pg;
  T1* pd;

  R pels, pelg;
  double gstrength = 1. - strength;

  for (y=0; y<h; y++, s++, d++, g++) {
    ps = s->p;
    pg = g->p;
    pd = d->p;

    for (x=0; x<w; x++) {
      pels = static_cast<R>(*ps++);
      pelg = static_cast<R>(*pg++);
      // The order is very important
      sum = (pels * strength) + (pelg * gstrength);
      *pd++ = apLimit<T1> (sum);   // Prevent wrapping
    }
  }

  return dst;
}
```

8.4 Summary

In this chapter, we provided in depth discussions of topics we felt warranted such treatment. These topics included copy on write, caching, **explicit** keyword usage, **const**, and pass by reference. We also spent some time showing you exactly how to take the image framework provided in the book and extend it with image processing functions to meet the needs of our application. And, for those of you who have an interest in imaging, we highlight some routines that work particularly well for enhancing your digital photographs.

Throughout the book, we've taken a simple test application and evolved it into a commercial-quality image framework by prototyping and later applying C++ constructs designed to meet the requirements. By following this path, we've been able to have detailed discussions on techniques, such as memory management, handle class idiom, reference counting, and template specialization, as they apply directly to solving real world problems. Some of the techniques we expected would end up as part of the final design, like the handle class idiom, proved to have no benefit; whereas other techniques, like template specialization, proved to have significant benefit. The evolution of the framework gave us a concrete code base in which to compare and contrast the usefulness of various C++ constructs. We would not have been able to accomplish this, with the same level of detail, through an abstract or theoretical discussion.

We hope that, in addition to the C++ discussions, you might also find the software provided with the book useful in your software development efforts. We've touched on a number of the utilities that are provided, including the image framework, a unit test framework, a resource manager for localization, and other third-party libraries and development tools. You will be able to find software updates at **http://www.appliedcpp.com**. Appendix B provides a detailed description of the contents of the CD-ROM.

Useful Online Resources

A.1 Software

This book's companion Web site:
`http://www.appliedcpp.com`

POSIX interface for Win32 platforms:
`http://sources.redhat.com/pthreads-win32`

Basis Technology's Rosette Core Library for Unicode:
`http://www.basistech.com`

International Components for Unicode's (ICU) open-source software package:
`http://oss.software.ibm.com/icu/index.html`

XML parser open-source toolkit:
`http://www.jclark.com/xml/expat.html`

Gnu `gettext` utility:
`http://www.gnu.org/manual/gettext`

DebugView freeware:
`http://www.sysinternals.com`

Standard C++ I/O Streams and Locales, by Angelika Langer & Klaus Kreft:
`http://home.camelot.de/langer/Articles/Internationalization/I18N.htm`

Independent JPEG Group's implementation of the JPEG file format:
`http://www.ijg.org`

Implementation of the TIFF file format:
`http://www.libtiff.org`

Intel Integrated Performance Primitives (IPP) library:
`http://www.intel.com/software/products/ipp/ipp30/`

A.2 Standards

POSIX, IEEE Std 1003.1-2001 specification:
`http://www.opengroup.org/onlinepubs/007904975/toc.htm`

Unicode Standard:
`http://www.unicode.org/standard/standard.html`

XML Standard:
`http://www.xml.org`

B

CD-ROM
Information

B.1 Contents

The attached CD-ROM contains the following high-level directories:

- **Delegates**

  This directory contains the libraries and/or the source code to build the libraries for the three delegates that were used in Chapter 6: the Intel Integrated Performance Primitives (IPP) image delegate, the JPEG file delegate, and the TIFF file delegate.

- **framework**

  This directory contains all of the source code, unit tests, and project and makefiles necessary to build and use the framework.

- **Prototypes**

  This directory contains the complete source code and unit tests for each of the three prototypes used in Chapter 3. In addition, this directory contains the complete test application that was designed and built in Chapter 2.

- **Utilities**

  This directory contains two useful utilities: the Sysinternals DebugView utility and the Intel C++ Compiler 7.0 for Windows.

B.2 Framework

The CD-ROM includes all of the source code for the image framework developed throughout this book. In addition, we provide the source code for the supporting unit tests, makefiles, and project files. The file hierarchy is shown here.

📁 **framework**

  📁 **common** — Source code for general purpose classes

  📁 **delegates** — Source code for file delegate classes

  📁 **image** — Source code for image classes

  📁 **include** — Header files

  📁 **thirdparty** — Header and library files for delegates on specific platforms

  📁 **unittests** — Unit test files for all components

  📁 **unix** — Source code files specific to UNIX platforms

  📁 **win32** — Source code files specific to Microsoft Windows platforms

Licensing Information

USE, DATA, OR PROFITS, WHETHER OR NOT ADVISED OF THE POSSIBILITY OF DAMAGE, AND ON ANY THEORY OF LIABILITY, ARISING OUT OF OR IN CONNECTION WITH THE USE OR PERFORMANCE OF THIS SOFTWARE.

B.3 Prototypes

The CD includes all of the source code and supporting unit tests for the prototypes developed in Chapter 3 and for the test application built and designed in Chapter 2. The file hierarchy is shown here.

📁 **Prototypes**

   📁 **Prototype1**   All files necessary for Prototype 1

   📁 **Prototype2**   All files necessary for Prototype 2

   📁 **Prototype3**   All files necessary for Prototype 3

   📁 **TestApplication**   All files necessary to build and run the test application

Licensing Information

B.4 Utilities

The CD-ROM includes two utilities: the Sysinternals DebugView utility and the Intel C++ Compiler 7.0 for Windows. The file hierarchy is shown here.

📁 **Utilities**

    📁 **DebugView**   See section B.4.1 for more information

    📁 **IntelC++Compiler**   See section B.4.2 for more information

B.4.1 DebugView Utility

The CD-ROM includes version 4.2 of the Sysinternals (**http://www.sysinternals.com**) DebugView utility for Windows. There is no charge to use this software at home or at work. Please review the licensing information included here.

Description

From the Sysinternals Web site: DebugView is an application that lets you monitor debug output on your local system, or any computer on the network that you can reach using TCP/IP. It is capable of displaying both kernel-mode and Win32 debug output, so you don't need a debugger to catch the debug output that your applications or device drivers generate, nor do you need to modify your applications or drivers to use non-standard debug output APIs.

DebugView works on Windows 95, 98, Me, NT 4, 2000, XP, and .NET Server.

Under Windows 95, 98, and Me, DebugView will capture output from the following sources:

- Win32 **OutputDebugString**
- Win16 **OutputDebugString**
- Kernel-mode **Out_Debug_String**
- Kernel-mode **_Debug_Printf_Service**

Under Windows NT, 2000, XP, and .NET Server, DebugView will capture:

- Win32 **OutputDebugString**
- Kernel-mode **DbgPrint**
- All kernel-mode variants of **DbgPrint** implemented in Windows XP and .NET Server

DebugView also extracts kernel-mode debug output generated before a crash from Window NT/2000/XP crash dump files if DebugView was capturing at the time of the crash.

Licensing Information

From the Sysinternals Web site: There is no charge to use this software at home or at work.

A commercial license is required to redistribute any of these utilities directly (whether by computer media, a file server, an email attachment, etc.) or to imbed them in or link them to another program. Sales of commercial licenses support Sysinternals product development and assure that this Web site continues to offer valuable, up-to-date tools. Established software companies redistribute these utilities and incorporate the code into their products because this offers the potential to save significant development time.

Sysinternals commercial licenses are priced according to the complexity of the licensed code and its role in the target application. If you are interested in licensing Sysinternals tools or source code for redistribution or for inclusion with or as part of a software product, please contact `licensing@sysinternals.com`.

B.4.2 Intel C++ Compiler

The CD-ROM includes the evaluation version of the Intel C++ Compiler 7.0 for Windows.

Description

The Intel C++ compiler makes it easy to get outstanding performance from all Intel 32 bit processors, including the Pentium 4 and Intel Xeon processors, and the 64-bit Intel Itanium processor. The compiler provides optimization technology, threaded application support, features to take advantage of Hyper-Threading technology, and compatibility with leading tools and standards to produce optimal performance for your applications.

Compatibility features include:

- Compatibility with IA-32 Microsoft Visual C++
- Plugs into IA-32 Microsoft Visual Studio environment

Advanced optimization features include:

- Floating-point instruction throughput
- Interprocedural Optimization (IPO)
- Profile-Guided Optimization
- Data prefetching
- Full support for Streaming SIMD Extensions 2 [IA32 only]
- Automatic vectorizer [IA32 only]
- Run-time support for Intel processor generations: processor dispatch [IA32 only]
- Predication [Intel Itanium architecture only]
- Branch prediction [Intel Itanium architecture only]
- Speculation [Intel Itanium architecture only]

- Software pipelining [Intel Itanium architecture only]

Multithreading application support including:

- OpenMP support
- Auto-Parallelization (Preview Feature)

Standards support includes:

- ISO C/C++ standard
- ANSI C/C++ standard

Debugger support includes:

- Enhanced Debugger from Intel (EDB)

Licensing Information

You can obtain the required license key by going to:
`http://www.appliedcpp.com/intel.html`

You can upgrade to a full license version of the Intel C++ Compiler 7.0 for Windows for a nominal fee at the same URL.

B.5 Delegates

The CD-ROM includes either the library or the source code to build the library for the image and file delegates that are fully discussed in Chapter 6. The file hierarchy is shown here.

   📁 **Delegates**

      📁 **IntelIPP**   See section B.5.1 for more information

      📁 **JPEG**   See section B.5.2 for more information

      📁 **TIFF**   See section B.5.3 for more information

B.5.1 Intel Integrated Performance Primitives (IPP)

The CD-ROM includes the evaluation version of the Intel Integrated Performance Primitives (Intel IPP) for Windows, version 3.0, for use on the Intel Pentium and Intel Itanium architectures. The Linux version is also provided on the CD-ROM. This is the image delegate that is fully described in Chapter 6.

Description

Intel Integrated Performance Primitives (IPP) is a cross-platform software library that provides a range of library functions for multimedia, audio codecs, video codecs (for example, H.263, MPEG-4), image processing (JPEG), signal processing, speech compression (i.e., G.723, GSM ARM*) plus computer vision as well as math support routines for such processing capabilities. Specific features include vector and image manipulation, image conversion, filtering, windowing, thresholding, and transforms, plus arithmetic, statistical, and morphological operations. A variety of data types and layouts are supported for each function. IPP minimizes data structures to give the developer the greatest flexibility for building optimized applications, higher level software components, and library functions.

The Intel IPP is a low-level layer that abstracts multimedia functionality from the processor. This allows transparent use of recent Intel architecture enhancements such as MMX technology, Streaming SIMD Extensions, Streaming SIMD Extensions 2, as well as Intel Itanium architecture and Intel XScale technology instructions.

Intel IPP is optimized for the broad range of Intel microprocessors: Intel Pentium 4 processor, the Intel Itanium architecture, Intel Xeon processors, Intel SA-1110 and Intel PCA application processors based on the Intel XScale microarchitecture.

Licensing Information

You can get the required license key by going to:
`http://www.apppliedcpp.com/intel.html`

You can upgrade to a full-license version of Intel IPP for a nominal fee at the same URL.

B.5.2 JPEG

The CD-ROM includes the files necessary to build the Independent JPEG Group's (`http://www.ijg.org`) free JPEG software. This is the file delegate software discussed in Chapter 6. This software is free for use in both noncommercial and commercial applications. Please review the licensing information included here.

Description

From the Independent JPEG Group's Web site: This package contains C software to implement JPEG image compression and decompression. JPEG is a standardized compression method for full-color and gray-scale images. JPEG is intended for "real-world" scenes; cartoons and other non-realistic images are not its strong suit. JPEG is lossy, meaning that the output image is not identical to the input image. The user can trade off output image quality against compressed file size by adjusting a compression parameter.

The distributed programs provide conversion between JPEG "JFIF" format and image files in PBMPLUS PPM/PGM, GIF, BMP, and Targa file formats. The core compression and decompression library can easily be reused in other programs, such as image viewers. The package is highly portable C code; and has been tested on many machines ranging from PCs to Crays.

Licensing Information

From the Independent JPEG Group's Web site: We are releasing this software for both noncommercial and commercial use. Companies are welcome to use it as the basis for JPEG-related products. We do not ask a royalty, although we do ask for an acknowledgment in product literature (see the README file in the distribution for details). We hope to make this software industrial-quality — although, as with anything that's free, we offer no warranty and accept no liability. For more information about licensing terms, contact `jpeg-info@uunet.uu.net`.

B.5.3 TIFF

The CD-ROM includes the files necessary to build TIFF Software's free TIFF software (`http://www.libtiff.org`). This is the file delegate software discussed in Chapter 6. This software is free for use in both noncommercial and commercial applications. Please review the licensing information included here.

Description

From TIFF Software's Web site: This software provides support for the Tag Image File Format (TIFF), a widely used format for storing image data. The latest version of the TIFF specification is available on-line in several different formats, as are a number of Technical Notes (TTN's).

Included in this software distribution is a library, `libtiff`, for reading and writing TIFF, a small collection of tools for doing simple manipulations of TIFF images on UNIX systems, and documentation on the library and tools. A small assortment of TIFF-related software for UNIX that has been contributed by others is also included.

The library, along with associated tool programs, should handle most of your needs for reading and writing TIFF images on 32- and 64-bit machines. This software can also be used on older 16-bit systems though it may require some effort and you may need to leave out some of the compression support.

The software was originally authored and maintained by Sam Leffler. While he keeps a fatherly eye on the mailing list, he is no longer responsible for day to day maintenance.

Questions should be sent to the TIFF mailing list: `tiff@olympiakos.com`.

License Information

From TIFF Software's Web site:

Bibliography

[**Bulka99**] Bulka, D.; and D. Mayhew. *Efficient C++*. Reading, MA: Addison-Wesley, 1999. ISBN 0201379503.

[**Coplien92**] Coplien, J. *Advanced C++ Programming Styles and Idioms*. Reading, MA: Addison-Wesley, 1992. ISBN 0201548550.

[**Gamma95**] Gamma, E.; Helm, R.; Johnson, R.; and J.M. Vlissedes. *Design Patterns*. Reading, MA: Addison-Wesley, 1995. ISBN 0201633612.

[**Gonzalez02**] Gonzalez, R.C.; and R.E. Woods. *Digital Image Processing, Second Edition*. Boston: Addison-Wesley, 2002. ISBN 0201180758.

[**Lakos96**] Lakos, J. *Large Scale C++ Software Design*. Reading, MA: Addison-Wesley, 1996. ISBN 0201633620.

[**Langer00**] Langer, A.; and K. Kreft. *Standard C++ IO Streams and Locales*. Boston: Addison-Wesley, 2000. ISBN 0201183951.

[**Lunde99**] Lunde, K. *CJKV Information Processing*. Sebastopol, CA: O'Reilly, 1999. ISBN 1565922247.

[**Meyers96**] Meyers, S. *More Effective C++*. Reading, MA: Addison-Wesley, 1996. ISBN 020163371X.

[**Meyers98**] Meyers, S. *Effective C++, Second Edition*. Reading, MA: Addison-Wesley, 1998. ISBN 0201924889.

[**Meyers01**] Meyers, S. *Effective STL*. Boston: Addison-Wesley, 2001. ISBN 0201749629.

[**Nichols97**] Nichols, B.; Buttlar, D.; and J. Proulx Farrell. *Pthreads Programming*. Sebastopol, CA: O'Reilly, 1997. ISBN 1565921151.

[**Pratt01**] Pratt, W.K. *Digital Image Processing, Third Edition*. Indianapolis, IN: Wiley, 2001. ISBN 0471018880.

[**Siek02**] Siek, J.G.; L. Lie-Quan; and A. Lumsdaine. *The Boost Graph Library User Guide and Reference Manual*. Boston: Addison-Wesley, 2002. ISBN 0201729148.

[**Stroustrup00**] Stroustrup, B. *The C++ Programming Language, Special Edition*. Boston: Addison-Wesley, 2000. ISBN 0201700735.

[**Sutter00**] Sutter, H. *Exceptional C++*. Boston: Addison-Wesley, 2000. ISBN 0201615622.

[**Sutter02**] Sutter, H. *More Exceptional C++*. Boston: Addison-Wesley, 2002. ISBN 020170434X.

[**Vandevoorde03**] Vandevoorde, D.; and N.M. Josuttis. *C++ Templates*. Boston: Addison-Wesley, 2003. ISBN 0201734842.

Index

The C++ In-Depth Series
Bjarne Stroustrup, Series Editor

Modern C++ Design
Generic Programming and Design Patterns Applied
By Andrei Alexandrescu
0201704315
Paperback
352 pages
© 2001

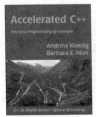

Accelerated C++
Practical Programming by Example
By Andrew Koenig and
Barbara E. Moo
020170353X
Paperback
352 pages
© 2000

Essential C++
By Stanley B. Lippman
0201485184
Paperback
304 pages
© 2000

C++ Network Programming, Volume 1
Mastering Complexity with ACE and Patterns
By Douglas C. Schmidt and
Stephen D. Huston
0201604647
Paperback
336 pages
© 2002

The Boost Graph Library
User Guide and Reference Manual
By Jeremy G. Siek, Lie-Quan Lee, and
Andrew Lumsdaine
0201729148
Paperback
352 pages
© 2002

Exceptional C++
47 Engineering Puzzles, Programming Problems, and Solutions
By Herb Sutter
0201615622
Paperback
224 pages
© 2000

More Exceptional C++
40 New Engineering Puzzles, Programming Problems, and Solutions
By Herb Sutter
020170434X
Paperback
304 pages
© 2002

C++ Network Programming, Volume 2
Systematic Reuse with ACE and Frameworks
By Douglas C. Schmidt and
Stephen D. Huston
0201795256
Paperback
368 pages
© 2003

Applied C++
Practical Techniques for Building Better Software
By Philip Romanik and Amy Muntz
0321108949
Paperback
336 pages
© 2003

Also Available

The C++ Programming Language, Special Edition
By Bjarne Stroustrup
0201700735
Hardcover
1,040 pages
© 2000

Written by the creator of C++, this is the most widely read and most trusted book on C++.

Register
Your Book

at www.awprofessional.com/register

You may be eligible to receive:

- Advance notice of forthcoming editions of the book
- Related book recommendations
- Chapter excerpts and supplements of forthcoming titles
- Information about special contests and promotions throughout the year
- Notices and reminders about author appearances, tradeshows, and online chats with special guests

Contact us

If you are interested in writing a book or reviewing manuscripts prior to publication, please write to us at:

Editorial Department
Addison-Wesley Professional
75 Arlington Street, Suite 300
Boston, MA 02116 USA
Email: AWPro@aw.com

Visit us on the Web: http://www.awprofessional.com

CD-ROM Warranty